THE
INDIAN
TRICOLOUR

THE
INDIAN
TRICOLOUR

Lt Cdr. KV Singh (Retd.)

Rupa & Co

in association with
FLAG FOUNDATION OF INDIA

Published in 2005 by
Rupa & Co
7/16, Ansari Road, Daryaganj,
New Delhi 110 002

Sales Centres:

Allahabad Bangalore Chandigarh Chennai
Hyderabad Jaipur Kathmandu
Kolkata Mumbai Pune

Typeset in 11 pts Nebraska by
Nikita Overseas Pvt Ltd,
1410 Chiranjiv Tower,
43 Nehru Place,
New Delhi 110 019

Printed in India by
Ajanta Offset & Packagings Limited
95-B, Wazirpur Industrial Area,
New Delhi-110 052

This book is dedicated to all those
who genuinely love India
and her flag, Tiranga

Contents

Foreword

It is surprising that India, with her rich and ancient heritage, did not have a single flag that she could call her own until 1947. For over four thousand years, India was ruled by a diverse assortment of kings, clans and dynasties, each with its own unique and independent flag. A glimpse into the past shows a vast array of flags adorning Indian history. Starting with the epic era of the *Ramayana* and *Mahabharata,* when the gods and goddesses each had their very own *dhvajas,* to the symbols and seals of the Indus Valley civilization, dating back to 2500 B.C., the golden period of the Maurya dynasty, Mughal rule (1526-1858), all the way through to British domination of the Indian subcontinent, flags of myriad hues fluttered across the Indian skies. The Indian populace humbly accepted the flags as a symbol of the authority of the king or the ruler. Ordinary citizens never had a flag that they could proudly call their own.

During the pre-independence era, there was no national flag anywhere in India. However, in 1906, the Bengal partition gave the nation its first Tiranga, or tricoloured flag, followed by the Charkha flag in 1921, which inspired the nation throughout the freedom movement until independence.

Independent India's national flag, the Tiranga, came into existence on July 22, 1947. Pandit Jawaharlal Nehru described it as 'a flag of freedom' while moving the resolution on the flag in the Constituent Assembly. And, for the first time in the long history of the nation, Indians could look up with pride and honour at their country's flag. However, to their utter dismay, ordinary citizens soon realized that they did not have the right to fly the Tiranga on all days of the year. The display of the national flag was the exclusive privilege of certain senior government dignitaries as mentioned in the Flag Code of India. The Tiranga was perceived as a flag of government authority and not as the ordinary citizen's tribute to nationhood.

I am glad that from January 26, 2002, after fifty-five years of independence, Indian citizens were permitted to fly their national flag throughout the year. This was the result of a long and protracted legal battle. And on January 23, 2004 in a historic judgment, the Honourable Supreme Court held that the right to fly the national flag freely, with respect and dignity, was a fundamental right.

The Tiranga has always been a great source of inspiration for me since my childhood. When we display the national flag, we rise above our religion, political affiliation and the region we belong to. In doing so, we don't merely show our love for our country — we concomitantly partake in our collective and individual pride in being Indian. The Tiranga also reminds us of our duties towards our country. When a company flies the national flag at its office or factory premises, it is indubitably a source of genuine inspiration for the workers and the staff, who feel that they are working not just for the company, but for the country as well. It is a symbolic way of placing national interest ahead of everything.

I feel strongly that since all of us now have the right to fly the Tiranga, we must display the national flag every day. The joy and happiness that it will bring to us is difficult to articulate, but it certainly will generate a powerful felt experience. The Tiranga fluttering across the Indian skies will, of needs, inculcate a deep feeling of patriotism and serve as a motivator for everyone, inspiring us to attain greater heights.

A liberal display of the national flag promotes patriotism. The Tiranga played a pivotal role in uniting people during India's freedom struggle. Holding the flag, flying it high above their heads, Indians all over the country braved the batons of the British, and when one flag bearer succumbed to the atrocities of the British, the flag was passed on to the other. The flag gave them the inner strength to fight the British.

The Tiranga, as a symbol of free India, reminds us that we are all equal, irrespective of our religion, caste, and creed. It evokes a spirit of brotherhood, a spirit of freedom, a spirit of nationalism, and a feeling of oneness. The Tiranga is not merely the strongest symbol of national unity; it is also a sacred symbol. All Indian citizens must be encouraged to own it, love it, respect it and display it.

It will be my endeavour to see that the national flag and the message it carries, both symbolically and literally, reaches all Indians. Mere display of the flag is not enough. We must live by its ideals, committing ourselves to the national spirit that it symbolizes. Reminding us of our commitment to our motherland, the Tiranga tells us to contribute our share towards the well being of the nation in a manner analogous to our predecessors. It tells us that our actions must do the nation proud. It also reminds us that we can take this great country forward. United, we can overcome all the difficulties and hardship that face the nation. The Tiranga inspires us to do any task that is assigned to us with honesty and integrity, and will inspire fellow citizens to lead a life of commitment, courage and virtue, both personally and in the work place.

The story of my crusade to liberate the flag would be incomplete if I didn't take this opportunity to mention those sources of my strength and inspiration that saw me through to victory. First, I would like to pay tribute to the glorious inspiration I got from my revered father, the late Om Prakash Jindal, a truly exceptional and remarkable man. Apart from his wisdom and encouragement, it was his own extraordinary life that mobilized me and accorded me the strength to pursue this dream.

I would like to thank my wife, Shallu Jindal, who genuinely comprehended the reasons driving my passion for the flag, and provided unwavering support in her own quiet way.

In my crusade to 'liberate' the flag, I was supported and guided by many people, including several legal luminaries. I express my sincere gratitude to all of them and would like to acknowledge their contribution to the cause. The names of Mr. Shanti Bhushan, senior advocate and former Minister for Law, Mr. Soli Sorabjee, former Attorney General of India, Mr. K.K. Venugopal, Mr. Harish Salve, Mr. Arun Jaitley, Mr. Abhishek Manu Singhvi, Mr. Jayant Bhusan, and Ms. Gauri Rasgotra deserve special mention.

The Tiranga belongs to over a thousand million Indians who live in India and abroad. It is a symbol of our freedom. It is every Indian's fundamental right to fly it with dignity and honour. If the national flag is flown by a larger number of Indians, it will revolutionize, significantly, the way we think and feel about India, making us a happier and prouder nation, while enhancing our sense of patriotism. Let us all work together towards popularizing the display of the Tiranga, our national flag, as a way of expressing our love for, and faith in, our nation.

JAI HIND!

Naveen Jindal
May 2005

From the Author

One hard fact of Indian history is that pre-independence India was never perceived as one nation. It had been a conglomeration of kingdoms, dynasties, clans, tribes and communities. Each had its own territory over which they ruled independently and hoisted their flags. During the freedom struggle, the country came together as a single entity. However, after India attained her freedom, the citizens gradually reverted to their basic psyche of being regional and religion-minded. Today, we are less Indian and more of a Punjabi, Gujarati, Marathi, Bengali and the like. Our religious identity as a Hindu, Muslim, Sikh or Christian has become more important. Even allotment of ministerial positions in the government, distribution of party tickets during elections, selection of players for our sports teams, admission to academic courses, appointment in government services are often based on region, religion, caste, colour or creed.

India has a history of being the world's spiritual leader. However, in the last five–and–a–half decades, our cultural values have been somewhat diluted. At an individual level, selfishness has become central, while nationalistic feelings have been rendered peripheral. Something that can re-kindle the true spirit of nationalism in our hearts is our National-flag, which stands for the whole nation and has no religion of its own, no belonging or love for any particular state or community. It is truly secular and 24-carat Indian, beyond the barriers of the three C's. It does not differentiate between men and women, between the rich and the poor. It belongs equally to all Indians.

During our freedom struggle, the Tiranga brought the whole nation together. Under its banner, the spirit of nationalism was at its peak. Our love for the country was our guiding force and we were proud of being called Indians. A large number bravely fought for independence. The Tiranga was the rallying point, the sight of which enthused even the most feeble-minded to act bravely. To uphold the honour of our flag, many of us laid down our lives holding the flag in our hands. Such was the magic of Tiranga. Its magic has not vanished. It still survives. We only need to revive our faith in it.

The first step is to educate ourselves and motivate our youth about this solemn symbol of the land. The Tiranga symbolises the whole nation, its pride, glory, ideals, dreams and aspirations. No wonder even the President of India salutes and respects it. There is a dire need to teach our youth to love and respect the National-flag. The Flag-code and flag etiquette should form part of their school curriculum. They should be brought up believing that an insult to the National-flag is an insult to themselves. Teaching these values would instil the spirit of nationalism in young minds and they would grow with a strong sense of Indianism.

As adults, we too, need to change our outlook. The Tiranga should help us visualise the whole of India, her past, present and the future. The philosophy 'self before the nation' must be banished from our hearts. Only then would India be able to carve out the place she deserves in the world. India is a vast land, with plentiful resources and wealth. If we all believe in the strength of unity and lift our sagging feelings of nationalism, no one can stop us from reaching the summit of the world.

Religion of an individual is something very personal. I, therefore, believe that there is little need for our sacred religious books to be exhibited in a court of law. Being Indian, we should take the oath in the name of Tiranga that stands for the whole nation, instead of the Srimad Bhagavad Gita, the Quran Sharif, the Guru Granth Sahib or the Holy Bible. And the same practice should be extended for our ministers and legislators, who, too, should take the oath of office and dedication in the name of our National-flag and the Constitution. As long as we continue to mentally divide and distinguish ourselves on the basis of regions and religions, we shall not grow into a mature nation.

The book is my tribute to the Tiranga. I am sure it would serve as a reliable reference guide on our National-flag and the other flags that have fluttered against the Indian skies.

I shall feel amply rewarded if, after reading this book, the readers get motivated to express their patriotic feeling and also realise the importance and significance of our National-flag.

Lt Cdr. KV Singh (Retd.)

Acknowledgments

In completing this book, several friends and a number of strangers lent their support to me. I am indebted to all of them. I record my sincere gratitude to Dr. Haridev Sharma, former Deputy Director, Nehru Memorial Museum and Library, for his inspiration, guidance and co-operation in providing me valuable reading material that helped me in shaping the book; the *Hindustan Times* for agreeing to go through its old files to authenticate certain historic events; Commodore S. K. Chatterjee (Retd.), who provided me with rare reading material on the flag of Sister Nivedita; the National Archives of India for permitting to publish the original confidential history sheet on Madame Bhikaiji R. Cama; the Director, Publications Division, for allowing me to publish excerpts from my earlier book brought out by them, the Directorate of Public Relations (Defence); Wing Cdr. Sanjay Thapar; Col. TPS Chowdhary; the Indian Mountaineering Institute; the National Museum of India, the National Gallery for Modern Art for supplying photographs for the book. My special thanks are due to Kanwar Vishvajit Prithvijit Singh of Kapurthala, who provided me valuable information about the flags of former princely States of India. My thanks are due to Ms Kavita Mittal, who wholeheartedly assisted me in arranging some rare photographs. For the uncommon pictures of the epic era, my thanks are due to the Gita Press Gorakhapur. I also express my sincere gratitude to Mr Frank Christopher, Joint Director, Lok Sabha Secretariat, for his warm co-operation in providing me a few historic photographs. I shall fail in my duty if I do not acknowledge the sincere and dedicated effort, editorial help and innovative ideas provided by Ms Swati Mehmi and Ms Deepthi Talwar. I am also greatly obliged to Ms Rajkumari, who immensely assisted me in typesetting the text, which duly helped in shaping the final layout of the book.

Finally, I thank Mr Naveen Jindal, who encouraged me to update the work, and for agreeing to write the foreword for this book.

The midnight session of the Constituent Assembly in progress
on
14-15 August 1947.

1

Dawn of Independence and the Tiranga

On July 22, 1947 the Adhoc – Committee on the Flag adopted, in the Constituent Assembly, 'Tiranga' as the National-flag for Independent India. The birth of the Flag was due to the sacrifices and blessings of all great souls, who brought freedom to India. On August 14, 1947, late in the evening at 10.45 p.m., the Central Hall of the Council House, now known as the Parliament House, was packed to its capacity. The galleries, too, were full of a cheerful crowd clad in *khadi*, while a surging colourful mass of humanity stood outside. At the appointed hour, the proceedings of the House commenced with the signing of *Vande Mataram* led by Mrs Sucheta Kripalani, the wife of the then Congress President, Acharya Kripalani. This was followed by a brief opening address by the Chairman of the Constituent Assembly, Dr Rajendra Prasad. Then followed Pandit Jawaharlal Nehru's famous speech *'Tryst with Destiny'*.

The first Governor-General of Independent India, Lord Mountbatten listening to the address of Dr Rajendra Prasad, on August 15, 1947, in the Central Hall of the Council House.

Finally, the resolution was moved to take the Oath of Dedication. The text of the oath ran "At this solemn moment when the people of India, by their suffering and sacrifice have secured freedom and become martyrs of their own destiny, I …. a member of the Constituent Assembly of India, do dedicate myself to the service of India and her people to the end that this ancient land attain its rightful and honoured place in the world and make its full and willing contribution to the promotion of world peace and welfare of mankind."

The oath was read by the Chairman, Dr Rajendra Prasad, first in Hindi and then in English. Accordingly, the oath was repeated by all the members, who took the oath standing. After the oath ceremony was over, Dr Rajendra Prasad moved a resolution from the chair that His Excellency, the Viceroy of India, Lord Louis Mountbatten, be intimated that the Constituent Assembly had assumed the power for the governance of India. The house approved the resolution amidst thunderous cheers, acclaimation and blowing of conch-shells. At that solemn moment, every stone of the Parliament House echoed with the roaring shouts of *Mahatma Gandhi ki jai* and *Vande Mataram.*

After the approval of the resolution, Mrs Hansa Mehta presented to the Chairman a Tiranga on behalf of the women of India, symbolising the birth of the Indian National-flag. While presenting the flag, Mrs Mehta said: "It is in the fitness of things that the first flag, that is to fly over this august House should be a gift from the women of India."

Mrs Hansa Mehta presented the first ever 'Tiranga` to Dr Rajendra Prasad, the Chairman of the Constituent Assembly, on the night of August 14-15, 1947, when the Constituent Assembly assumed sovereign power for governance of India. The same Tiranga was hoisted on the Central Dome of the Council House the next day, August 15, 1947.

Dr Rajendra Prasad warmly received the flag from Mrs Hansa Mehta and displayed it for all to see. After the flag-showing gesture of the Chairman, the proceedings of the historic day came to a close with the singing of *Sare Jahan Se Achchha Hindoostan Hamara,* and *Jana Gana Mana* (till then the song had not been adopted as the National–anthem of India).

August 15, 1947

The Independence Day dawned at 8.30 a.m. with the swearing-in-ceremony at the Viceregal Lodge (now the Rashtrapati Bhawan). The new Government was sworn-in in the Central Hall (now Durbar Hall). Two large-sized National-flags, along with Governor-General's flag in deep blue, hung majestically on the wall facing the distinguished gathering.

After the new Government took the oath, the Tiranga was proudly hoisted for the first time against a free sky of Independent India on the flagmast of the Council House at 10.30 a.m. It was the same Tiranga which was presented, the previous evening, to Dr Rajendra Prasad by Mrs Hansa Mehta.

As the Indian Tricolour moved up the flagmast, a thirty-one gun salute was accorded to the symbol of the newly born nation. Simultaneously, the four Union Jacks at the 'Great Place' (now known as Vijay Chowk), two each on the sentry towers of the North Block and South Block of the Central Secretariat were lowered. In their place four bright tricolours were hoisted. Since then, every morning, regardless of weather conditions, the four tricolours are hoisted by the CPWD staff at sunrise and lowered at sunset.

On the afternoon of August 15, 1947, the first public flag salutation ceremony was held at the War Memorial, Prince's Park, near India Gate. The ceremony was marked by a mysterious occurrence. As the first Prime Minister of India, Pandit Jawaharlal Nehru, unfurled the Tiranga against a

The Union Jack was lowered for the last time in India, at 10.30 a.m., on August 15, 1947 from the flagmast of the Council House, the present Parliament House. The lowering of the British National-flag, the last time on Indian soil, was done by emotionally stricken Lord Mountbatten himself. As the Union Jack was lowered, four Tirangas were hoisted two each on the North and South Blocks of the Central Secretariat as seen in the picture.

The first public flag hoisting ceremony was held at the War Memorial in Prince's Park, near India Gate, on the afternoon of August 15, 1947. Two Tirangas are seen flying atop the monument.

clear warm summer sky, a rainbow appeared on the horizon as though to bless the Tiranga. It was a phenomenal occurrence, which startled many in the audience, including Lord Mountbatten, who attended the function from a distance as his royal carriage could not reach the rostrum due to the thick and unmanageable crowd that had gathered there to witness the first public flag hoisting ceremony.

Lord Louis Mountbatten, as the first Governor-General of free-India, in his seventeenth Report dated August 16, 1947, which he forwarded to the Crown, made it a point to mention the mysterious and sudden appearance of the rainbow on the occasion of the flag hoisting ceremony. He wrote in his report that the three colours, saffron, white and green, in the flag of the new dominion resembled the hues of the rainbow. But, for the thousands of Indians present, the rainbow was interpreted as a salute of Lord Indra, the God of Rains, to the Tiranga.

Lord Mountbatten, the Governor-General of India,
saluting the Tiranga from his carriage as he could not reach the rostrum on
account of the thick and unmanageable crowd that gathered to
witness the ceremony at India Gate.

Flag hoisting ceremonies were held throughout the country. A number of erstwhile rajas and maharajas also hoisted the Tiranga at public gatherings expressing their allegiance to the solemn symbol of the nation.

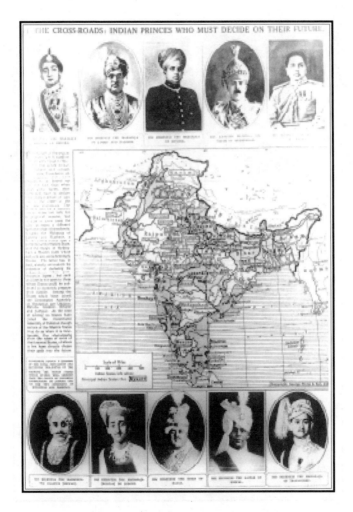

Some of the erstwhile rulers of Indian States, who merged their Kingdoms with Independent India, even hoisted the Tiranga in their republic States on August 15, 1947

Independence Day celebrations (August 15, 1947) inside the Darbar-e-Am of Bharatpur State. Tiranga displayed against the wall under the canopy is distinctly visible.

Independence Day banquet in the Vice Regal House on the eve of August 15, 1947. Tiranga is hung on the wall by the side of the Union Jack in the backdrop.

On the same day, the Tiranga was also hoisted abroad. In Karachi, the newly appointed Indian High Commissioner to Pakistan, Mr Prakasa, hoisted the Tiranga at his residence. Independent India's National-flag was specially flown to London and Sir P.P. Pillai, the special representative of the Government of India to the United Nations, carried it to Washington to give the Tiranga its rightful place amongst the flags of other free nations of the world.

A page from the National Herald, *dated August 16, 1947.*

THE TIMES OF INDIA
IN WASHINGTON

India's flag is raised in front of the Far Eastern Commission's headquarters in Washington. From left to right are Mr. Samuel S. Stratton, Acting Secretary-General of the Commission; Mr. Asaf Ali, India's Ambassador in the United States; and Col. B. N. Kaul, Military Attache to the Indian Embassy.

Horsemen carrying the Tiranga and the Union Jack in Fiji, celebrating India's Independence Day on August 15, 1947.

On August 15, 1947, India's Trade Commissioner, Mr M.R. Ahuja, in black suit, pulls the halyard unfolding the Tiranga in New York city. A three-year old girl holding the flag's front (Picture courtesy New York Times*).*

An illuminated 'Jai Hind` on the occasion of first Independence Day celebrations, 1947.

Tiranga fluttering on the ramparts of the Red Fort on the occasion of Independence Day.

The Tiranga on the ramparts of the Red Fort

The Tiranga was hoisted, for the first time, on the ramparts of the Red Fort at 8.30 a.m. on August 16, and not on August 15, 1947, as is commonly believed. The battalion in charge of the ceremony was 7 Sikh (L). The practice of hoisting the Tiranga on the ramparts of the Red Fort on every August 15 was initiated on August 15, 1948. Speaking on the historic occasion, Pandit Nehru mentioned Subhash Chandra Bose's dream of seeing the National-flag hoisted on the Red Fort and regretted that he was not there to witness the great day.

Surprisingly, the whereabouts of the Tiranga that was hoisted on the ramparts of the Red Fort on August 16, 1947 remained unknown for many decades. Following a media story in 2002, inquiring into its whereabouts, the valued flag was discovered in the Officer's Mess HQ Delhi Area, Delhi Cantt. Presumably, it must have been in the custody of the former Delhi and Rajasthan Sub-Area Mess all these past years.

The historic flag, made of bunting cloth, is 6 ft × 4 ft in size. The flag has recently been shifted to another Mess and is currently preserved in the Army Battle Honours Mess, New Delhi. It is hoped that this national relic will be well preserved for posterity.

2

A young crusader liberates the Tiranga

Throughout India's struggle for freedom, the Tiranga inspired and symbolized the resistance to British rule. No agitation, *satyagraha*, meeting, gathering, procession, *dharna* or march was held without the flag. Finally, on the threshold of independence, Pandit Nehru moved a motion on the adoption of the National-flag of India in the Constituent Assembly on July 22, 1947. He described the flag as the 'flag of freedom'. Other voices joined him. Sarojini Naidu said, "Under this flag there is no prince, no peasant, no rich, no poor." Freedom fighter Muniswami Pillai added that the flag did not belong to the rich or the wealthy, but to the depressed, oppressed and submerged classes. There were many more inspiring words hailing the flag on the occasion.

Ironically, as time passed, the use of this symbol of equality began to be restricted to a privileged few and to select dignitaries of the Indian Government. Only VVIPs, government offices and public sector undertakings were allowed the honour of displaying the flag on their premises. The common man was forgotten in free India. All those inspiring and lofty words about the flag were lost. That very flag, that leaders said belonged to the masses and the common man during the days of the freedom struggle, was placed beyond their reach in independent India.

It was the Flag Code, drawn in 1948-50, which laid down restrictions on its free display by common citizens. According to the Flag Code-India, the flag would fly only atop government buildings and official residences of certain government dignitaries. The rest of India could fly the Tricolour only on Independence Day, Republic Day, Mahatma Gandhi's birthday and a few other days in the year.

Somebody had to fight for the right of common citizens to fly the National-flag with all due respect on all days. Yet, in a country where millions had dedicated their lives to the flag during the freedom struggle, no one protested until 1994, when a young, spirited twenty-four year old, the dynamic Naveen Jindal, stood tall for the right of Indian citizens to freely fly the National Flag. He questioned the restrictions on the free display of the National-flag laid by the Flag Code-India.

Naveen reminisces that he had a fascination for the country's flag and its colours since childhood. However, his love for the flag grew stronger in 1990 while pursuing a Master's degree in Business Administration at the University of Texas, Dallas, in Dallas in the United States. One of the first things he noticed was how the American flag flew all over the country. The Americans even wore patterns of the U.S. flag on their clothes. The Americans' display of their national flag inspired Naveen to display his own National-flag in the U.S.

Naveen Jindal, the young industrialist who liberated the Tiranga from the restrictions of the Flag Code-India.

His passion for the flag was fuelled further during a casual visit to the residence of a Texas-based Indian businessman, who had been living in the U.S. for the last thirty years. Naveen noticed an ornately framed Tiranga in his host's living room — he had never seen this kind of display of the National-flag in any home he had visited in India.

Naveen's popularity soon saw him elected president of his university's Student Government. One of the perks of that position was his own office room in the Student Union building. He decided to display the National-flag in his office, to which neither the university or his American friends objected. In fact, within two days of his expressing this desire, an American student, Randy Miley, gifted him a huge Tricolour. "It was the first time I had held my country's flag,"

Naveen recollects. "It felt great holding the Tiranga." Naveen displayed it in his office in the Student Union building. The flag soon became a point of conversation as visitors began asking him about it, its colours and about Indian people. "I experienced great joy and happiness every time I saw the flag," Naveen says.

Naveen returned home in 1992 to take over as the Director of Jindal Strips Limited and was soon busy training under his father at their company's Raigarh plant in Madhya Pradesh.

The crusade begins

Then came the turning point. On Republic Day January 26, 1993, he hoisted the flag at his Raigarh factory. The next day the flag had disappeared. When questioned, the factory manager explained that the flag could not be displayed daily. Naveen was shocked and upset; he ordered the manager to hoist the flag and ensure that it was hoisted at sunrise and lowered at sunset every day, with the utmost respect and dignity.

"The flag looked so good," Naveen remembers. "It is a symbolic way of showing our love for our country. Psychologically too it was terrific. The workers felt they were working not only for a company but also for their country. One common thing that bound us together in our company was the flag."

During their official visits to the factory, the Raigarh Collector, superintendent of police and other senior government officials and people from the media would occasionally hint to the factory management that Naveen was not allowed to display the flag at the factory premises. However, none of them could counter his argument: "If I cannot fly my flag in my own country in a respectful manner with pride, then where else in the world can I fly it?"

The Raigarh factory from where the legal battle to liberate the National-flag for its free use by Indian citizens was started by Naveen Jindal in September 1994.

On September 6, 1994, the then Commissioner of Bilaspur, S.P. Dubey, when visiting the Raigarh factory, noticed the Tiranga fluttering in full glory. Angry inquiries elicited the information that the flag had been flying there every day for more than a year. Dubey ordered the superintendent of police to personally ensure that the flag was removed. Naveen, who was in New Delhi at that time, received a nervous call from factory officials. "I was very upset," he recalls. "How could they mistrust us like this in independent India, especially when we were flying the flag with the utmost respect." The unfortunate incident, however, strengthened his resolve and he decided to fight for his right to fly the National-flag.

To prepare himself for the legal battle, he first studied the Indian Constitution and the Flag Code, India, which prevented him from displaying the flag at his factory. He approached Shanti Bhushan, an eminent lawyer with a penchant for public interest issues. Naveen was told that there were two clear laws on the subject. The first, The Prevention of Insults to National Honour Act (1971), which stated that the National-flag should not be "mutilated, burnt, defaced, torn or trampled upon in public view". Offenders could be jailed for up to three years or fined. However, it did not prevent any one from flying the flag in a respectful manner!

The second law was related to the use of the National Flag: The Emblems and Names (Prevention of Improper Use) Act (1950). This Act stated that "the National-flag or the National-emblem could not be used for commercial purposes, nor could it be used as packaging". Armed with this knowledge, Naveen relaxed, as he had not violated any of the laws pertaining to the flag. On October 3, 1994, he drafted a letter to the Bilaspur Commissioner and the Ministry of Home Affairs stating that he was flying the flag in his factory premises out of patriotism and that the Tiranga inspired him to embrace greater heights. He asked why he was being prevented from flying the national flag on his company's premises, if there was no existing Indian law preventing him from doing so.

Naveen's senior company officials cautioned him against sending the letter. In their opinion, it was not prudent to annoy government officials. But Naveen remembered what his father, O.P. Jindal, had always maintained: "If you are in the right, God will be with you. No harm can come to anyone fighting for a noble cause."

Inspired by his father's advice, Naveen sent the letter. But there was no reply from the government. He shot off a reminder. The Bilaspur Commissioner finally replied saying, "The provisions regarding flying of the National-flag are contained in *Flag Code, India* published by the Government of India, Ministry of Home Affairs. A Section of the said Code

The letter from the Commissioner of Bilaspur restricting the display of the National-flag on all days in accordance with the Flag Code-India then in vogue.

restricts the displaying of the National-flag to certain occasions only. National-flag cannot be displayed on any day in whatsoever manner as you have mentioned in your letters. Sections of the Prevention of Insults to National Honour Act, 1971 contain the details of the punishments."

Naveen was appalled that "the government had turned the National-flag into a government flag". He once again sought legal advice from some of the best legal minds in the country. According to the legal advice given to Naveen, the Flag Code-India contained executive instructions and had not been passed by Parliament; as such, it had no legal sanctity especially when it infringed upon one's fundamental rights.

There were some who did not agree. A few people with whom Naveen discussed the subject had apprehensions about the fact that if everybody was allowed to fly the National-flag, then it might lose its sanctity and the chances of its misuse may increase.

"To me their apprehensions were ill-founded for two reasons," says Naveen. "Firstly, there is a law for prevention of any misuse and insult to the National-flag. Secondly, do we insist that idols and images of deities be kept only in places of worship for fear that they will be misused in homes?"

On February 2, 1995 Naveen filed a writ petition in the Delhi High Court requesting that all Indians and institutions be allowed to fly the flag in a respectful manner since the executive instructions contained in the Flag Code had no legal sanctity.

On September 22, 1995 the Delhi High Court allowed Naveen to fly the National-flag. In a landmark judgment, the Honourable High Court held that the government could not deprive citizens of their fundamental rights through an executive order. The court also held that the right to fly the National-flag was a part of the Fundamental Right of Freedom of Speech and Expression, and that right could only be restricted by Parliament as per Article 19(2) of the Indian Constitution. Since the restrictions imposed by the Flag Code, India, had not been authorized by any law framed by the

*The legal luminaries who were associated with the crusade (from Left)
Mr Shanti Bhushan, Mr Soli Sorabjee and Mr Abhishek Manu Singhvi with
Mr Naveen Jindal (second from right).*

*Senior lawyers who were also associated with the crusade, from left
Mr K.K. Venugopal, Mr Harish Salve,
Ms Gauri Rasgotra and Mr Jayant Bhushan.*

Indian parliament, these restrictions were not enforceable by law.

The historic judgment was hailed all over the country, and Naveen, along with thousands of Indians, started to display the flag every day. Naveen received thousands of letters and phone calls felicitating him.

However, in January 1996, the Government of India appealed against the Delhi High Court's judgment. In its special leave petition to the Supreme Court of India, the government advocated that the policy to restrict the use of the National-flag to the barest minimum was intended to ensure that the flag was not dishonoured. Mr Jindal, the petition said, had taken a questionable position by imagining that one of the ways of showing his patriotism and love for the country was to fly the flag.

The Supreme Court, on February 7, 1996, while admitting the special leave petition of the government, stayed the operation of the Delhi High Court judgment.

Full of despair, Naveen had to refrain from flying the National-flag. However, his senior counsel Mr Shanti Bhushan once again advised him that he could still continue flying the flag: it would not be a contempt of court since the Supreme Court judgment had only stayed the operation of the High Court judgment. There was still no law that prohibited the flying of the Tiranga in a respectful manner.

At this point, the factory workers at Raigarh met Naveen and told him that they too desired to see the National-flag flying at the factory premises. Naveen recalls telling them that he would do his utmost to ensure that the National-flag continued to fly at the factory premises and that he would fight for the right of all Indian citizens. A determined Naveen then asked his company's management to display the flag, and the flag was once again hoisted at the factory premises every day.

When the Collector of Raigarh noticed the flag atop the factory premises, he immediately sent a letter to the Ministry of Home Affairs. The Government of India filed a contempt of court petition against Naveen. When the contempt matter came up in Court, his Counsel explained that Naveen had the utmost respect for the country's judiciary and was not defying its order, nor did he mean any disrespect to it by hoisting the flag. He was doing so for the sake of his genuine love for the country.

Subsequently, the matter came up for hearing before the bench of the Supreme Court consisting of Justice V.N. Khare and Justice S.N. Variava. During the course of the hearing, the bench observed that prima facie they saw no reason why the citizens of the country could not express their patriotism by displaying the National-flag, and that the restriction of flying the National-flag only on certain days by private citizens seemed unsustainable.

In view of the Supreme Court's striking observations on the issue, the Government of India constituted an inter-ministerial committee on October 18, 2000 — headed by Dr P.D. Shenoy, Additional Secretary in the Ministry of Home Affairs — to consider the question of whether the people of the country should be allowed to freely fly the National-flag to express their feelings of patriotism and pride for the country. Naveen met the members of the committee and presented his viewpoint to them. He told them that although all the members of the committee were senior IAS Officers, they were not allowed to display the flag even on their office table. He further enquired from them that, if they were allowed to display the flag, would they disrespect or misuse it? They all responded in the negative. Naveen then asked them if they wanted to display the flag, to which they responded in the affirmative. Naveen then said to them:

"This is my whole point. If somebody wants to display the National-flag they should be allowed to do so." They all understood Naveen's viewpoint and seemed convinced by his line of thought. The Shenoy Committee submitted its report to the Minister of Home Affairs on April 12, 2001, recommending free use of the National-flag by all Indian citizens in a respectful manner on all days of the

Additional Secretary Dr P.D. Shenoy, who recommended in April 2001 to the Union Government, the free use of the National-flag by all Indian citizens.

year. In the mean while, from August 2000 to May 2001, the Government repeatedly sought adjournments before the Supreme Court. Not approving of such delaying tactics, on May 2, 2001, the Supreme Court permitted Naveen to fly the National-flag with respect, dignity and honour.

Finally, the Union Cabinet accepted the recommendations of the Dr Shenoy Committee and amended the Flag Code; a decision was taken on January 15, 2002, to allow common citizens to respectfully fly the Tiranga throughout the year with effect from January 26, 2002. After amending the Flag Code, the centre wanted to withdraw its appeal filed in the Supreme Court, but on Naveen's insistence, his legal counsel, Mr Abhishek Manu Singhvi, urged the Honourable court to make a definitive order on the pending issue. The court agreed to hear the case to decide on the constitutional aspect of the matter, i.e., whether the flying of the National-flag with respect and dignity is a Fundamental Right of citizens or not.

Finally, on January 23, 2004, in a historic judgment awarded by a bench of Honourable Judges of the Supreme Court comprised of the Chief Justice of India, Justice V.N. Khare, Justice S.B. Sinha and Justice Brijesh Kumar, it was held that:

1. The right to fly the National-flag freely with respect and dignity is a fundamental right of a citizen within the meaning of Article 19(1) (a) of the Constitution of India being an expression and manifestation of his allegiance and feelings and sentiments of pride for the nation.

2. The fundamental right to fly the National-flag is not an absolute right but a qualified one being subject to reasonable restrictions under clause 2 of Article 19 of the Constitution of India.

3. The Emblems and Names (Prevention of Improper Use) Act, 1950 and the Prevention of Insults to National Honour Act, 1971 regulate the use of the National-flag.

4. The Flag Code although not a law within the meaning of Article 13(3)(a) of the Constitution of India for the purpose of clause (2) of article 19 thereof, it would not restrictively regulate the free exercise of the right of flying the National-flag. However, the Flag Code to the extent it provides for preserving respect and dignity of the National Flag, the same deserves to be followed.

The appeal filed by the Union of India in January 1996 was dismissed by the Supreme Court. The contempt petition had been dismissed earlier, and the protracted legal battle finally came to an end. An elated Naveen, and millions like him, now fly the flag freely, and encourage other citizens of India to do likewise.

Shortly after Naveen's legal battle was over, his wife, Ms Shallu Jindal, joined him in his endeavour to promote the use and display of the Tiranga. She mounted an art exhibition in Delhi, 'Tiranga — Rights and Responsibilities'. The exhibition was later transformed into a travelling one, and has been taken to Mumbai and Jaipur. It will travel in the future to Hyderabad, Kolkata and other major Indian cities. Under the Flag Foundation of India, Ms

Ms Shallu Jindal, the chief patron of the Flag Foundation of India.

Jindal has brought out a coffee table book, *Tiranga: A Celebration of the Indian Flag*, with an aim to popularise the Indian National-flag.

Naveen feels that for the first time in the history of our great land, we have been allowed to own and display a flag that truly belongs to the people. He says, "Historically, we have always been governed by rulers — whether it was Ashoka, or Chandragupta — who had their own flags. Then came the Mughals, followed by the English; they too were monarchs and the flag belonged to the King and never to the people. Ironically, even when we became a Republic, the flag continued to be the flag of the government and the few in power. This is the first time that we have got the right to own, display and be inspired by our National-flag. We must therefore display the greatest symbol of our country with pride at our homes and workplaces. Most importantly, we must live by the ideals of the flag and work for the country." He strongly feels that when a person displays the National-flag he rises above his religion, caste, colour and political affiliations and reveals his love for his country and the pride he feels in being Indian.

SONIA GANDHI
LEADER OF OPPOSITION
(LOK SABHA)

D.O. No. 11n8 /LOP/LS/2002

44, PARLIAMENT HOUSE
NEW DELHI - 110 001
PHONE : 3016705, 3094946
FAX : 3017470

February 15, 2002

Dear Shri Jindal,

Thank you for your letter of February 2, 2002 and for sending a National Flag for my office. I commend you on your success in having the restrictions lifted on freely flying the Tricolour.

With good wishes.

Yours sincerely,

Shri Naveen Jindal
Jindal House
6, Prithvi Raj Road
New Delhi - 110011

15, JANPATH, NEW DELHI-110 011 TEL : 3012086, 3014481 FAX : 3018651

A letter from the Congress President
Ms Sonia Gandhi to Mr Naveen Jindal.

Naveen's passion for the flag did not wane with the winning of the legal battle. In fact, his conviction became stronger. In May 2004, he was elected as a Member of Parliament in the 14th Lok Sabha. One day, when he was in the august House wearing the National-flag in the form of a lapel pin, he was advised by Parliament staff not to wear it, as, in accordance with the Rules of Procedure and Conduct of Business in Lok Sabha, Members of Parliament are not allowed to do so. Naveen was shocked to learn about such a prohibition of the display of the National-flag in the form of a lapel pin. In Naveen's opinion, wearing of a badge of any political party, religion, institution, etc. may be disallowed in the august House; however, display of the National-flag as a lapel pin should not only be allowed, but rather be encouraged. He feels that when a Member of Parliament wears the flag-lapel pin, he rises above his religion, region and political affiliation.

With this conviction, he took up the matter with the Speaker of the Lok Sabha and also the other members of the Rules Committee of the Parliament for amending the restrictive clause of the Rules of Procedure and Conduct of Business in Lok Sabha, so that members of the House would be allowed to wear the National-flag in the form of a lapel pin. A considerable number of Members of Parliament have endorsed his view in the matter and have joined him in taking up the issue for amending the relevant rule.

At the time of this book going to the press, the matter was pending with the Honourable Speaker of the Lok Sabha.

A controversy on the use of the National-flag by members of the Indian cricket team started when an objection was raised to cricket superstar Sachin Tendulkar's wearing the National-flag along with the BCCI logo on his helmet. As a result, in February 2005, the Government of India issued instructions to the Indian Cricket Board to discontinue the practice of sporting the Tricolour on the clothing and equipment of the team. Naveen's views on the display of the National-flag by national sportspersons are also emphatic and supportive. He has taken up the matter of allowing sportspersons to wear the Tiranga on their clothes in a respectful manner. To fight for the cause, Naveen has raised this issue in the Parliamentary Standing Committee, Ministry of Home Affairs, Government of India, stating that the display of the National-flag on sports gear or T-shirts, enhances respect for the flag, and does not in any way disrespect it. He, therefore, strongly felt that the restrictive clause of the Prevention of Insults to National Honour Act, 1971 be amended. He further stated that the public in general and sportspersons in particular be allowed to display the Tricolour on headgear, vests, T-shirts, blazers in a respectful manner as is the practice in other countries. The members of the Standing Committee unanimously endorsed his views and the matter was referred to the Home Ministry for amending the said Act.

On July 5, 2005, the Union Cabinet decided to amend the clause of the Act which imposed a restriction on the use of the National-flag by the public as a part of any costume. However, the flag still cannot be used on any undergarment or used as an accessory on any dress or costume worn below the waist. The decision of the Union Cabinet will soon be implemented through another amendment to the prevention of Insults to the National Honour Act, 1971. The removal of the restrictive clause on the use of the National-flag is yet another feather in Naveen's cap.

I have no hesitation in stating that Naveen's name has become synonymous with the Tiranga and its cause.

3

The world of flags

The genesis

In the early days of civilisation, when man lived in small groups of families, clans and communities, life was closely enmeshed with nature, which provided food and shelter. Nature affected the life of the primitive man in almost every way and objects of nature that helped him in day-to-day life were held as sacred. Plants, trees, animals, etc., that aided him in his battle for survival, were immortalised through worship and reverence.

Subsequently, the primitive man even named his families, clans and tribes after such objects of nature which, with the passage of time, were adopted as totems. Each family, clan or tribe erected totem poles and pillars near their habitat as a mark of identification. Special rituals were performed at these totem altars. Anthological studies confirm that totemism, in one form or the other, was a significant part of the life of primitive man the world over. Evidence shows that among the American aborigines, the Dakota people inhabiting the Mississippi and Missouri river basins had societies named after animals and birds, such as the eagle, panther, tiger, buffalo, etc. Totemism was widely practised in Africa and India too. The Bachuana tribes of South Africa are still named after animals. The term *Bakatla* means 'they of the monkey', *Bakuona* 'they of the alligator', and so on.

One of the seals of Mohenjo-Daro depicts four men in a file, each carrying a standard. Of the two standards, clearly seen in the two impressions of the seal, one bears a figure of a unicorn and the other an incense burner. These impressions testify to the practice of totemism during the Harappan and Mohenjo-Daro Civilisations. There are references in the *Rig-Veda* to the existence of some sort of totemism in the Vedic period. The *vanara* tribe mentioned in the *Ramayana,* and the Nagas and the *garudas* in the

A seal from Mohenjo-Daro showing a standard with a unicorn.

The Vanara tribe of the Ramayana days, believed to be associated with some sort of totemism.

Mahabharata can be said to have been associated with some sort of totemism. The present day Santhals of Madhya Pradesh have over one hundred tribes named after animals and plants. The Bhils, too, have their clans named after the serpent, jackal, pumpkin, etc.

Primitive man looked upon these totems as protectors and sources of strength. They, therefore, worshipped them in their dwelling areas in times of peace, and carried them to the battlefield as divine protection. While it is evident that in their early stages totems were portable, in due course the form and size became huge, decorative and cumbersome. Subsequently, they were given a permanent place near the dwelling areas. When people migrated to other areas they carried only the replicas of their totems, leaving behind the massive and immovable ones.

The special requirements and conditions in a battle prompted men to think of better and convenient ways of carrying their totems. Perhaps for this reason, lighter material, such as hides and barks of trees, were chosen. And finally, totems were displayed on cloth, making for easy identification in battle or during a hunting expedition. That was the earliest form of flags.

The earliest flags

During ancient times, flags were in widespread use. It is, however, debatable as to where the earliest flags were first used. Most western vexillologists hold the view that the birthplace of flags was China. But, a wider and deeper study of recorded history provides ample evidence that the earliest flags belonged to India, and not

China. The history of flags in India is over five thousand years old. In the *Rig-Veda* (4000-3500 B.C.), widely regarded as the oldest book in the world, there is a clear and definite mention of the *Indra-dhvaja*, the flag of Lord Indra. In comparison, the first mention of flags in Chinese history is dated 1122 B.C., which is much later than the Rig-Vedic era. Also, some of the terracotta seals of the Indus Valley Civilisation irrefutably indicate that man carried flags, bearing the figures of a unicorn and an incense burner. The

A war scene in stone. The battle ensign in the vanguard of the troops can be distinctly seen. A relief panel from W. Bengal Charbengala Temple.

A 13th century chariot scene as drawn on the walls of Raichur Fort.

heroes of the two great Indian epics, the *Ramayana* and the *Mahabharata*, had their personal standards described in great detail in the two epics, and these were carried on their chariots and elephants.

The antiquity of the Chinese flags dates back to twelfth century B.C. when the founder of the Chau dynasty had a white flag carried before him. It is also well-known that in 660 A.D., a minor prince was punished for failing to lower his standard before his superior. According to the Chinese

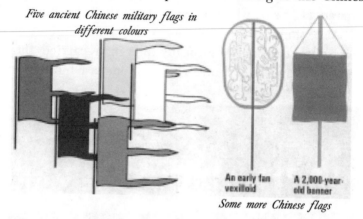

Five ancient Chinese military flags in different colours

An early fan vexilloid

A 2,000-year-old banner

Some more Chinese flags

custom, the royal flag had all the attributes of kingship, was identified with the ruler himself and treated with a similar respect. To even touch the royal flag-bearer was considered a crime. The fall of a flag in a battle meant defeat and for this reason kings rarely exposed their flag and their personal entourage together.

Even in India, flags were the first objects of attack in ancient times. In his *Raghuvansha*, Kalidasa mentions that while engaged in a duel with Lord Indra, Raghu, at one stage of the battle, shot an arrow fitted with peacock feathers which sliced off Lord Indra's flagstaff bearing his blue *dhvaja*. According to the *Manusmriti*, any damage to a dhvaja was considered sacrilegious and the offender had to repair the damage or pay a fine of five hundred *panas*[1]. Its fall would mean confusion, if not defeat, as was the case in China.

---

1. *Manusmriti*, IX. 285.

A special feature of ancient Indian flags was their triangular shape, in scarlet or green, with a figure embroidered in gold and a gold fringe around it. A figure similar to that displayed on the flag itself was often mounted on the flagstaffs. Besides the conventional use of identification, flags had also been used, both in China and India, for signalling and sending messages, a white flag being used in ancient times as a signal for truce. Flags also served as rallying points for organising armies and for identification of friend and foe during battles.

This practice, of carrying flags to battle and before kings and members of royalty during peacetime, was followed by almost all the early civilisations of the world, including the Egyptians, Assyrians, Greeks, Romans, Chinese, Indians and others. A study of history reveals that sacred emblems of special significance were carried before kings, and other similar insignia were borne by members of royalty, their military units and ships. An Assyrian statue, dating back to 671 B.C., shows a soldier with a standard of a military unit. Likewise, Egyptian ships of a later period are shown on pottery, bearing signs of harpoon, fish, etc., possibly to indicate their port of origin. This was another use of flags in ancient times.

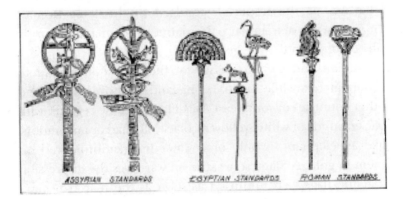

Old Assyrian, Egyptian and Roman standards.

The ancient standard consisted of a sacred object fixed on a bracket at the top of a pole, at times, with streamers attached to it. Different people used different objects or emblems on their flags. The Persians displayed a vulture on their flags, which were mounted on javelins. The Greeks chose an armour, while the Romans had an eagle or effigies of gods or figures of animals, such as wolves, horses and bears, on their standards. The Chinese standards usually bore figures of a dragon, a red bird, a white tiger, or a snake. They were carried on chariots and planted upon the walls of captured cities. An occasional variant in China was the display of the head of the vanquished. This might be the origin of the Greek custom of bearing a helmet or piece of armour on a spear point. The various Greek cities, however, had more distinctive signs, including a sphinx or a Pegasus.

The *vexillum*, the Roman cavalry flag, was the forerunner of the modern flag – as a square piece of cloth fastened to a bar placed crosswise on a spearhead. This description is confirmed by reference to Roman coins, medals and sculptures. It is still used in certain church ceremonies. The labarum, or the imperial standard of the later Roman emperors, was of a similar pattern, but larger, made of purple silk embroidered with gold.

Indian and Chinese usage of the flag soon spread to Myanmar (erstwhile Burma), Thailand (erstwhile Siam) and other countries in south-east Asia. Flags of these regions, with backgrounds of white, yellow or black silk, had animal motifs, like an elephant, a bull, or a water hen, embroidered on them in gold. A Siamese treatise on war gives the impression that the flags were unfurled as soon as the march began.

The Arabic word for flag is '*alam*', meaning signpost or flag. The terms '*liwa*' and '*raya*' are used for the flag banner or standard. In Persian, the word for banner is '*dirafsh*' and '*bayrak*' in Turkish. Prophet Muhammad, the founder of Islam, realised the need of a flag for his troops and adopted the 'Roman Eagle'[1]. His successors, the later Caliphs (Abbasids), however, adopted a black flag with the legend "Muhammad is the Apostle of God" (in Arabic) inscribed on it in white. Islam's prohibition of the use of any identifiable image as idolatrous obviously influenced the motifs and

Black and gold Islamic banners as illustrated in a
13th century manuscript.

1. James Douglas: *Bombay and Western India*, Vol. 1, p. 173.

designs on their flags. Islamic flags were simple, using plain black, white or red. Black, the colour of vengeance, was supposed to be the colour of Muhammad's banner. The Abbasids used a black flag in 746 A.D., whereas the Omayyads and Alids chose white by contrast and the Khawarij (Kharijites) chose red. Keeping the tradition, a plain red flag is retained by the modern Sultanate of Oman. Green was the colour of the Fatimid dynasty, which eventually became the colour of Islam. In adopting the crescent sign, however, in 1250 A.D., the Osmanian Turks were reverting to an Assyrian sacred symbol of the ninth century B.C. The crescent, with or without an additional star or stars, has since become the accepted symbol of Islam. In modern times, it has appeared mostly in white in the flags of Egypt, Turkey, Tunisia, Libya, Madagascar, Pakistan and some of the Malay states against a background of green, red or black.

In Europe, flags began with the Roman *vexillum* from which the term vexillology originated. The Saraccus probably transmitted the use of flags to Europe. European flags of various forms and purpose are known as colours, standards, banners, ensigns, pennants or pennons, guidions and burgees. Originally, they were used mainly in warfare. The standard was the largest and because of its size, intended to be stationary. It marked the position of an individual before a battle, during a siege, throughout a ceremony or at a tournament.

Interestingly, in the thirteenth and fourteenth centuries, many modern European nations adopted the Cross in their national flags and these flags are still being used. In 1864, at an international conference held at Geneva, representatives of twelve nations signed a treaty that allowed hospitals, ambulances and medical personnel of all armed forces the use of a red cross on white. This has since remained the symbol of the International Red Cross.

The modern flag

The English word 'flag' plausibly expresses the idea of something that flaps in the air. It seems to be of Teutonic German origin and, perhaps, came into use around the middle of the sixteenth century. The word evolved through different European languages, such as the Dutch 'vlag', the Scandinavian 'flagg', the Danish 'flag' and the German 'flagge', and signifies a piece of cloth, bunting or a similar material displaying the insignia of a king, an army, an office of authority, a community or an important individual. A flag, in the classical sense, is mostly oblong or square in shape, attached to a staff. In modern times, most frequently, a flag is rectangular, varying in size, colour and device. There are no definite rules about the size of a flag. The width is, however, usually greater than the breadth.

A flag is more than just a mere piece of cloth attached to a staff. The very sight of it arouses powerful emotions, patriotism and pride in any citizen. Indeed, there is something so compelling about the National-flag that people make even the supreme sacrifice of life for its sake. While any other flag stands as a symbol of faith in a family, a community or a clan, the National-flag stands for the whole nation, its ideals and aspirations, its hopes and achievements. It is a beacon of hope and courage, inspiring people to unite and defend the honour of their motherland. Rarely have flags been used to such a powerful propaganda effect as in the massive and impressive parades of the Swastika, seen in Nazi Germany during the 1930s.

Flags are a part of everyday life. They have become increasingly important and are used by countries, international bodies, organisations, companies, cities and provinces throughout the world as powerful and evocative symbols. The modern world is accustomed to seeing a newly born nation celebrate its independence by means of a grand flag–hoisting ceremony. In recent times, the political upheavals in the former Yugoslavia, the former USSR and South Africa led to redefining of their boundaries and national identities. Consequently, new states were born, and with them were born new flags.

The parts of a modern flag

When flags are hoisted, the flagpole is normally placed on the left side of the observer's view. The flag's side towards the viewer is referred to as the obverse, the other being the reverse. Flags are divided into four equal quarters, each of which is called a canton. The two cantons closest to the pole are known as the 'hoist' – the upper one known as upper-hoist and the lower as the lower-hoist. The other two cantons, that are furthest from the pole and float in the air, are called the upper-fly and the lower-fly.

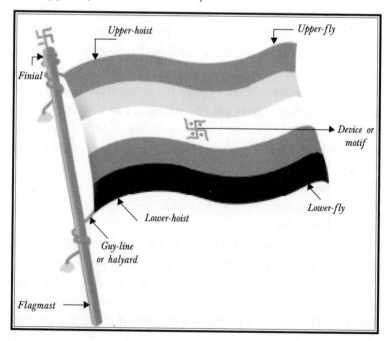

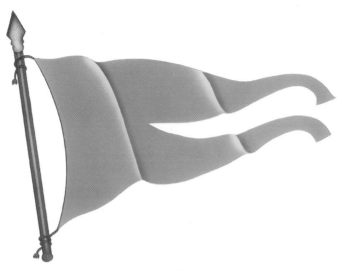

The Bhagwa-jhanda of Chhatrapati Shivaji.

Shivaji's Zari Pataka, which he adopted in addition to his father's flag, the Bhagwa-jhanda, after assuming the title of Chhatrapati.

The Hanuman banner of the Rani of Jhansi.

The revolt flag of Bahadur Shah Zafar used during the First War of Independence. According to another view, the flag had only the rising sun in the centre as the device.

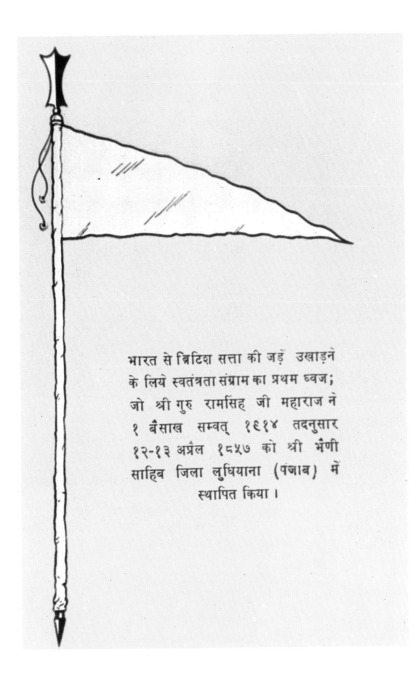

भारत से ब्रिटिश सत्ता की जड़ें उखाड़ने
के लिये स्वतंत्रता संग्राम का प्रथम ध्वज;
जो श्री गुरु रामसिंह जी महाराज ने
१ बैसाख सम्वत् १६१४ तदनुसार
१२-१३ अप्रैल १८५७ को श्री भैणी
साहिब जिला लुधियाना (पंजाब) में
स्थापित किया ।

*The Sikh banner of revolt as raised by Guru Ramsinghji Maharaj against the
British Rule on April 12-13, 1857 near Ludhiana, Punjab.*

The flag of Portuguese – India.

Flags, banners and standards are prominently seen as part of the royal procession of King George and his Queen Mary in Jaipur during the 1912 Durbar.

The flag of the Viceroy of India with the Jewel of India in the centre adorned by a royal crown on the top.

The flag of the Governor-General of India.

The flag of Sister Nivedita — 1905.

The Calcutta Flag that was hoisted for the first time on August 7, 1906 at the Parsi Bagan Square in Calcutta by Sir Surendranath Banerjea.

The flag of Madame Bhikhaiji Cama, which she raised on August 22, 1907 at Stuttgart, Germany.

The flag of the Home Rule League — 1916.

The first flag of the Indian Freedom Movement, as designed by Pingley Venkayya according to the wishes of Gandhiji. The Charkha in the flag was suggested by Raizada Hans Raj of Jullunder. The flag was known as the Swaraj-flag, Gandhi-flag and also the Charkha-flag.

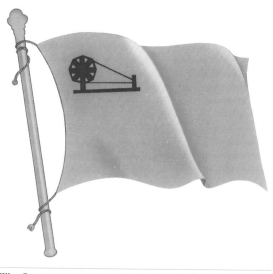

The flag as recommended by the Flag-Committee — 1931. However, it never came into use.

The officially adopted flag of the Indian National Congress — 1931.
In fact, this is the mother flag of our present National-flag.

The flag of the Indian Legion founded by Subhash Chandra Bose
in Germany in 1941.

The Spiritual Flag of India as conceived by Sri Aurobindo Ghosh.

The President of India's personal standard used between 1950 and 1971.
The President now uses the Tiranga as his flag.

Until August 15, 1971 the Governors of all the Indian states flew
a flag with the name of their respective states.

A portrait of Pandit Jawaharlal Nehru with the Tiranga in the background.

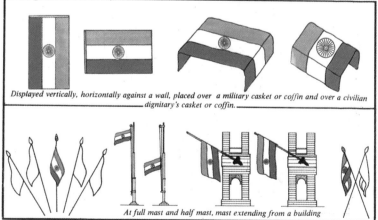

Displayed vertically, horizontally against a wall, placed over a military casket or coffin and over a civilian dignitary's casket or coffin.

At full mast and half mast, mast extending from a building

Displayed with a group of other flags of countries and states or societies (extreme left), and with another flag from crossed staffs (extreme right).

Proper display of the National-flag.

Tiranga in Indian postal stamps.

Squadron Leader Sanjay Thapar planting the Tiranga at the North Pole.

Tiranga is raised at Antarctica by a member of the Naval expedition team — 1982.

Tiranga cruised the world's waters on board Trishna under Col. TPS Chowdhary.

INS Mysore wearing the Tiranga, while alongside.

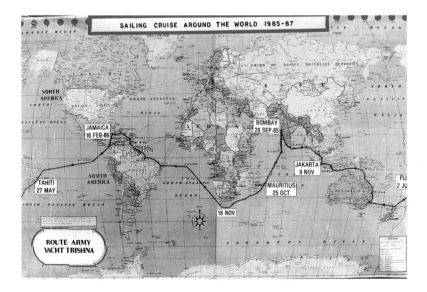

The cruise map of Trishna.

IAF helicopters carrying Tirangas during a flypast.

A motorcycle pyramid with Tiranga atop.

The flagmast is the pole on which a flag is hoisted or displayed. The terms flagmast, flagpole and flagstaff mean the same. The rope by which the flag is hoisted is known as the guy-line or the halyard. The part of the flag that houses the pole is called the sleeve. The motif or design on the flag is known as device and the background colour of a flag is referred to as the field of the flag.

Political flags

National-flags are political symbols as they stand for a nation's identity in the world. With the birth of more independent nation-states, flags have become an important political statement. Many newly-born states have chosen flags of the political parties that helped them gain independence. Most revolutionary or freedom movements create their own flags. However, in democratic countries, political parties vie with each other using distinctive flags for their party as symbols to rally support.

Political party flags can be of different types. While some may be simple in their profile, others are variations of their respective National-flags. One such example is the Italian Liberal Party which depicts the design of its National-flag with their initials inscribed on it. On the other hand, political party flags can also influence the design of National-flags, as is evident in some of the newly independent countries of Africa and Asia. A typical example is the Indian tricolour, which is a simple variant of the flag of the Indian Congress Party which helped secure independence for the country in 1947. The only difference is that the Indian Congress Party's flag incorporates the well-known spinning wheel or *charkha*, popularised by Gandhiji, whereas the Indian tricolour uses the Ashoka Chakra.

The flags of the communist world are more international in spirit and are often based on the traditional red flag with the five-pointed star and a combination of various implements of labour, such as the hammer, sickle and hoe.

Buddhist prayer flags on a stupa.

Religious flags

In ancient India, flags had religious connotations. A number of *Puranas* provide sufficient details to show that the Indian dhvaja enjoyed the status of a sacred object. The *dhvaja-dana,* or erecting a metal-cum-wooden flagpole in honour of a deity, was considered an act of merit. The *Puranas* describe in detail the various dhvajas sported by different Hindu gods and goddesses.

According to the *Adi-Purana,* the Jain kings used to offer dhvaja-dana at temples. The Buddhists, too, employed flags for propagation of their religion. Colourful flags can still be seen flying atop Jain temples and Buddhist *viharas.*

In Europe too, the standards carried by soldiers to the battlefield were regarded as sacred symbols personifying holy spirits. Egyptian, Greek and Roman armies believed that their standards radiated supernatural power and to concede one in battle was deemed disgraceful. Long ago, a similar belief existed in India when the loss of one's dhvaja on a battlefield was considered an act of great shame and dishonour. As such, a close relationship exists between the religious symbolism of the early standards and the spiritual totems created by various groups throughout the world. This is best illustrated by comparing a Roman standard with a totem pole carved by the Red Indians of northwest America.

The Romans, too, ascribed the same power to their first Christian standard, the labarum, of Emperor Constantine. The European armies of the medieval era firmly believed that the respective flags of their patron saints would protect them in battle and ensure victory. Curiously, the Union Jack of the United Kingdom is a combination of three crosses that represent three patron saints. Also, the likeness of Virgin Mary has been widely used on banners and standards in many Catholic countries.

Elsewhere in the world, other religious sects created their own flags. The Islamic black banners adopted ornate designs of fine calligraphy and the crescent that is still a universal symbol in the Islamic world.

Unicolour flags

Unicolour flags, such as white, red, green, yellow and black, have special significance. White is the colour of purity and peace, and in wartime, a white flag means surrender or truce. The Chinese, on the other hand, regard white as the colour of mourning.

The colour red often denotes danger and warning. On a shooting range, when firing is in progress, red flags are planted around the range as warning signs. Likewise, ships and army vehicles carrying explosives are required to display a red flag as a warning signal. According to road rules, vehicles carrying projecting loads, particularly sharp objects like iron bars, etc., are to display a red flag on the protruding load during day time and a red light at night (as a measure of caution). Contrary to common belief, the Chinese consider red as a colour of joy.

Traditionally, a green flag announces safety and the all-clear. A railway guard shows a green flag to start a train. On a swimming pool a green flag signifies that the pool is open for swimming. The colour green in contemporary National-flags symbolises a nation's forests and agriculture. Green was the favourite colour of Prophet Muhammad and for this reason most Islamic countries include green in their flags.

A yellow flag stands for sickness and unhygienic conditions and is known as a quarantine flag. For this reason, yellow flags are planted in and around areas affected with epidemics. As per practice, the toilet areas in large camps and gatherings are marked with yellow flags for convenient recognition.

Jolly Roger, the flag of the ancient sea pirates.

Black denotes death and mourning. A black flag is flown atop prisons after an execution. In ancient times, sea-pirates used a black flag bearing a white skull and two cross bones on their ships to intimidate the crew of other ships. This was also known as 'Jolly Roger'. In modern times, employees sport mini black-flags on their person to express their resentment against their management.

Tricolour flags

Most ancient flags were unicolour, but, during the medieval period, bi-colour and tri-colour flags came into being to denote alliances between like-minded people. A flag's field when divided horizontally, vertically or diagonally into three different colours is called a 'tricolour'. Which nation in the world was the first to have a tricolour as its National-flag is difficult to trace out; however, Austria is believed to have had a tricolour flag with horizontal stripes of red, white and red around the thirteenth century. The Dutch also used a flag of orange, white and blue in horizontal stripes of equal width in a revolution against Spain in 1574 A.D. Orange was gradually replaced by red in the seventeenth century, leaving the Dutch flag exactly as it is now.

The French Revolution began a new phase in flag designing. The neo-tricolour stood for revolution and the revolutionary French tricolour, intellectually and socially, invaded the rest of Europe in the late eighteenth century, and gradually spread to other parts of the world. The blue, white and red of France was revolutionary in intent, though it was not wholly novel in design, as Austria and Netherlands already had tricolours way back in the thirteenth and sixteenth centuries respectively.

The use of tricolour as the National-flag of a country is very common in the contemporary world. There are fifty-four countries that have a tricolour standard as their National-flag. Of these countries forty-one have horizontal, while thirteen have vertically arranged tricolour flags.

In fact, in the words of one of its chief designers, Sukumar Mitra, the Indian flag for freedom hoisted in Calcutta on August 7, 1906, was inspired by the French tricolour. It must be pointed out that the Indian tricolour, though popularly known as *Tiranga* (having three colours), in fact, has four colours. The blue of the *chakra* is commonly omitted and we fondly call it Tiranga instead of *chaturanga* (one having four colours).

The language of flags

Flags have a language of their own which they speak through their display. In earlier times, flags played an important role on the battlefield. During war, a flag called a guidion was used by the charging troops to locate their leader and the king. It also aided in finding direction of own troops. Another use of flags in the past was that they were rallying points on the battlefield.

Even in modern times, flags convey vital information and meaning. An interesting example is that when the Tiranga is not flying on the dome of the Rashtrapati Bhawan, the official home of the President of India, it conveys that the President is away and not at his official residence. As he enters the main gate, the National-flag would be hoisted on the building to mean that the President is back in residence.

During international summits, discussions and conferences between representatives of two countries, mini National-flags of both the countries are placed on the conference table to denote the nationality.

In car racing too, flags play a significant role. Through signalling flags, the race officials transmit information to the speeding car drivers. The participants watch for the flag signals to receive messages as they zoom past the pits because they cannot afford to stop. For instance, the black-and-white chequered flag pronounces the end of the race.

Flags play an important role on ships as well. As symbols, they have been used at sea since ancient times. Among the earliest flags were the unicorn motif flags of the Indus Valley Civilisation and the fish ensigns displayed with tassels on the prows of ships in the Aegean Sea over three thousand years ago. In the Middle Ages, ships flew flags for their identification from a distance. The nationality of ships was indicated by huge emblems painted on the sails and by the shields of knights on board along the gunwale, while the banner of the king or the noble in command of the ship would be hoisted at the masthead or stern. This tradition has continued in the modern times too, as the ensign (ship's flag) identifies the nationality of the ship.

Besides their ensign, ships also have signal flags. They were introduced in the eighteenth century and are still in use. These flags are known as alphabetical and numerical flags. For each alphabet (A to Z) and number (0 to 9) there is a separate flag. These are used to pass messages when both the sender and the receiver are within the sight of each other. Certain alphabetical flags have different meaning when flown on their own. The flag called 'papa' (for the letter 'P'), popularly known as Blue-Peter, when hoisted alone, means the ship is about to sail.

As symbols, different flags have different meanings when displayed. A flag when exhibited in a particular manner has a certain meaning. For example, a flag flown beneath a black ball at sea indicates that the vessel is in distress and needs immediate help.

Flag protocol, etiquette and custom

Over the years, a number of customs and ceremonies pertaining to flags have evolved. Everywhere flags are regarded as symbols of authority and, as such, accorded the respect due to them.

Most nations of the world have devised regulations, codes and customs to ensure that their National-flags are treated with dignity and respect. Strict rules have been drawn-up to prevent any disrespect to the National-flag. Care in the treatment of foreign National-flags is even more important. Appropriate protocol is essential not only in according equal status to flags of equal importance, but, also in following correct precedence when flying flags of different ranks. At times, diplomatic misgivings have taken place over some real or imagined disrespect to a national flag. Today, therefore, flag protocol is strictly and meticulously followed.

Ships flew flags for identification at a distance and many of the existing rules related to flag-use developed at sea. The traditions followed on ships are recognised internationally. As per an old custom when two ships pass each other, they dip their respective ensigns to salute and greet each other; with warships it's a norm the world over. On special occasions, while in port, ships are dressed with flags of the International Code of Signals. In a foreign port, ships fly the flag of the host country as a gesture of courtesy together with their own ensign.

On land, flags are often seen flying over private and government buildings on national occasions. Colours of the armed services are displayed in impressive military parades, while those no longer in use are ceremonially laid up for preservation, as per heraldic tradition.

National-flags are normally flown full-mast, but, in accordance with heraldic etiquettes and customs, they are flown at half-mast on the death of a national leader or a

Pandit Jawaharlal Nehru lying in state.

Tiranga at half-mast on Anand Bhawan, Allahabad, on the death of Pandit Jawaharlal Nehru on May 27, 1965.

person of great eminence. The flag is half-masted by first raising it briskly to the top of the mast and then lowering it slowly to the half-mast position. Half-mast implies hauling down the flag to one-half the distance between the top and the guy-line and in the absence of the guy-line, half of the flagmast. The half-mast position will depend on the size of the flag and the length of the flagpole. At half-mast, the flag should always be positioned on the flagpole more than its own depth or width. The belief is that the upper half space is left for Death's invisible flag, flying above the half-masted mourning flag.

Flags that created history:

Countless number of flags have existed in the past; most of them are now a part of history. However, a few of them created history by being adopted by succeeding generations and followers of the originators of such flags.

The garuda-dhvaja: In India, the *garuda-dhvaja* (eagle motif), the invincible flag of Lord Vishnu and Lord Krishna of the epic era, was a flag that was envied and much sought after. Garuda was a bird of great antiquity, an embodiment of keen far-sightedness and immense strength. Vishwakarma, the architect of gods, made the garuda-dhvaja. According to the legend, its *yasti* (flagpole) was gold-plated and studded with gems. On the staff's finial, the figure of resplendent garuda was placed. During the *Mahabharata* days, after the death of Lord Krishna, this dhvaja was carried away to *Vaikunth*, the abode of Lord Vishnu, by heavenly nymphs.

In the recorded history of India, the garuda-dhvaja was used by the Gupta kings during the sixth and seventh century A.D. The fourth century A.D. Iron Pillar near Qutb Minar, Delhi, according to an inscription, was originally erected for a Vishnu Dhvaja in memory of a mighty King Chandragupt

II Vikramditya at the Vishnupad temple in Vishnugiri near Gaya, Bihar. In ancient times, the Romans and Greeks also used an eagle-motif flag. Prophet Muhammad, too, chose the eagle for his standard. Even in modern times, the finial of the US President's flagpole can be seen mounted with the figure of an eagle, the modern version of the Garuda.

The dragon-flag: The dragon-flag was carried in numerous battles over thousands of years. Perhaps, no single flag has been more widely used than the dragon-flag. It varied slightly in form and use and has been used in countries like Persia (modern Iran) and Britain. Made of windsock construction, the light fabric of the dragon flowing from its gaping jaws snapped and twisted in the lightest breeze. The flag often contained a device that produced a shrill whistling sound. The dragon-flag was waved high above the heads of a charging cavalry with the intention of instilling fear in the ranks of the enemy as well as inspiring the soldiers who followed it.

The Labarum, the flag of Constantine: The Labarum first appeared in 312 A.D. when the Emperor Constantine defeated his rival, Maxentius at Saxa Rubra near Rome. The historian, Eusebius, records that the Emperor had seen a flaming Cross in the heavens and the writing 'In this sign you shall conquer'. Sensing the growing power of Christians in his empire and his army, the following year in Milan, Constantine ordered an end to the persecution of Christians. The flag bore the 'monogram of Christ' (composed of the Greek letters '*chi*' and '*rho*') and the united representations of Constantine and his children.

The standard of Genghis Khan: On unifying the divergent tribes of eastern Mongolia through his political sagacity and military prowess, the Mongol tribal leader, Temujin, announced his mission of conquering the world under a new name and banner, a nine-tailed white standard. Quoted from 'The secret history of the Mongols' it is stated "and so in the year of the Tiger (1206), having assembled at the head of the Onan River, and having planted a great white standard having nine feet, they then gave unto Jinghis Oahan the title 'Khan'. The nine 'feet' denoted the nine tribes. The feet were, in fact, flammules along the sides of the triangular banner, adopted from a century-old Chinese tradition. Each of the flammules was decorated with the tail of a yak signifying the importance of this domestic beast to the people of Central Asia. His guarding spirit, the gyrfalcon, was represented in the centre."

At the top of the flagpole bearing the great standard was a special gold finial resembling a flaming trident. Below the finial were attached four white horsetails, symbolising the power of the Khan over the four corners of the earth. Horsetails were chosen because the Mongols believed that the world could only be conquered on horseback. This special Mongol standard, which personified Genghis Khan, was always planted before his tent and mounted on his chariot during his lifetime. Even after the death of Genghis Khan, the tradition of his flag was preserved through oral tenets. The Kalmuck people continued its use upto the twentieth century.

The Oriflamme, the flag of Charlemagne: The flag of Charlemagne, the great European king of the eighth century A.D., was known as 'Oriflamme', presumably, because of its golden red colour. About the design of the flag nothing can be said with certainty. Its form appears to have been of the gonfalon type, a long flag with small tails. There were six gold discs or roses, each bordered in dark blue and red. The original mosaic from the Triclinium of St. John of the Lateran in Rome, showing Charlemagne receiving his banner has been lost forever.

The standard of Joan of Arc: The standard of Joan of Arc is perhaps best described in her own words, recorded on February 28, 1431, when she was under trial for heresy and sorcery, 'I had a banner of which the field was sprinkled with lilies; the world was painted there with an angel at each side, it was white of the white cloth called 'boccassin', there was written above it 'I believe JHESUS MARIA', and it was fringed with silk'. The flag was further described as having representations of God giving his blessings to a lily and two angels, and on the reverse the arms of France.

Joan of Arc's judges were interested in all the details of her flag design, and asked who made the flag. Joan of Arc replied that S.S. Catherine and Margaret had appeared to her in a vision, commanding her that she takes the standard in the name of the king of Heaven. On the battlefield she won honour for the French army by breaking the English siege at Orleans. The judges sharply questioned her on the role of her flag in the victory. She admitted good fortune followed those marching behind her standard, insisting that she loved her flag forty times better than her sword.

At the Coronation of Charles VII, her standard was carried into the Cathedral at Rheims because it had been present in the perils and that was reason enough for it to be honoured. Yet, through all her interrogation, Joan of Arc steadfastly maintained her innocence in the charges of her disloyalty to her land, her king or her religion.

Although, she did not live to see the day, Joan of Arc achieved honour among succeeding generations of French soldiers and statesmen. No vexillological history of France is complete without her flag. It was her influence that made white serve as the principal French national colour, from shortly after her death in 1431 till the French Revolution of 1789, almost 350 years later.

The flag of Columbus: The expeditionary flag of Christopher Columbus, like many other historical flags and banners, is known to us only through verbal descriptions. It is best described in a contemporary record as an ensign with two letters 'F' and 'Y'. Above each letter was a crown and between the two letters, the sign of the Cross. The original flag of Columbus, perhaps the first true flag seen  in the new world, however, was not considered to be of any importance at that time and has long since been lost.

Rear Admiral Peary's flag at the North Pole: On the afternoon of April 6, 1909, Rear Admiral Robert Peary and his party, consisting of his aide, Mathew A. Henson and four Eskimos, became the first men to reach the North Pole. In 1886, at the age of thirty, Peary made his maiden expedition to the North Pole. Since then, 'the lure of the North' ran through his blood and he made several unsuccessful attempts in the next eighteen years. Each time he returned wiser and more determined. In 1894, Mrs Peary made him a silk flag and at each of his farthest-north points on his unsuccessful journeys, he left inside a bottle a small piece of the flag for record.

In 1905, Peary set out again to the evasive North Pole, this time in the *Roosevelt*, a ship specially built for the arduous expedition, but hardships forced him to turn back about two hundred miles short of the Pole. In 1908, he made his eighth expedition, again on board the *Roosevelt*. This time, Lady

Luck smiled on him and Peary reached the North Pole on April 6, 1909. He flashed a message on the same day, but his signal did not get through to the world until September 6 of that year, when an unexpected message was flashed by telegraph and cable around the world:

'The Pole at last! The prize of three centuries, my dream and goal for twenty years, mine at last! I cannot bring myself to realize it! Stars and Stripes nailed to the North Pole.'

Admiral Peary and his group remained for thirty-six hours at the North Pole. Before leaving, Peary, Henson and the four Eskimos built a great cairn of ice cakes. At its summit they hoisted the American flag, which Mrs Peary had fondly made years before. When the party turned homeward, Admiral Peary deposited a glass bottle in the cairn with a strip of Old Glory and this note:

90.N. Latitude, North Pole, April 6, 1909

I have today hoisted the national emblem of the United States of America at this place, which my observations indicate to be the North Pole axis of the earth, and have formerly taken possession of the entire region, and adjacent, for, and in the name of the President of the United States of America.
I leave this record and the United States Flag in possession.

Robert E. Peary, U.S.N.

Flags of eminent world organisations

Certain eminent world organisations and bodies such as the U.N., International Red Cross Society, Olympic games, the Scouts, etc. have their own flags.

The United Nations flag shows a world map in the centre, encircled by two olive branches, the ancient symbol of peace, on a sky blue field. The flag was adopted on October 24, 1945, at the time of founding of the organisation.

The flag of the International Red Cross Society adopted in 1864 is unique for the reason that it has about four variances. No other flag in the world has as many variations. It is an organisation that helps people in distress, both during peace and war times, signifying neutrality and universal brotherhood. The Red Cross symbol was chosen to mark hospitals, medical vehicles, etc., and to accord them a special status so that they are not targetted during hostilities. In most countries, the Red Cross flag bears its traditional sign of the Red Cross on a white field, and personifies Saint George, the patron saint of England. In Islamic countries, for religious considerations, a Red Crescent was adopted in 1907 as the parallel symbol for the International Red Cross Society. Curiously, Iran used an altogether different symbol for the International Red Cross Society till the fall of the King Shah. The flag depicted a red lion wielding a sword, seen from behind the lion. There is yet another version of the flag, which is the Red Magen David in place of the Red Cross, adopted in Israel in 1948. The Red Cross flag, however, connotes neutrality in all its versions.

The flag of the Scouts shows three branches of the lily flower on a leaf green ground, symbolising the three promises a scout takes the day he joins the organisation.

The Olympic games flag displays five equal circles in red, green, blue, yellow and black on a white ground, representing the five inhabited continents. The coloured circles are linked together in a chain, the ancient symbol of unity. During the games, when a country wins a gold medal, his/ her national-flag is hoisted and the respective national anthem played as a mark of honour.

The flag of the Commonwealth depicts an outline of the world, surrounded by golden yellow rays, forming the letter 'C', on a blue field. Originally, there was to be a ray for each member state, but the practice proved impractical, and hence was abandoned.

The flag of the North Atlantic Treaty Organisation (NATO) is solid oceanic blue with a half blue and white compass depicting the God of the Atlantic Ocean. The four white cardinal lines denote the member states of the organisation on each side.

The European Union's flag has twelve five-pointed gold stars arranged in a circle in the centre of a blue field. The twelve stars are a notional number indicating completeness, and do not refer to the countries in the Union. The flag was originally adopted for the council of Europe in 1955.

The Arab League flag is plain green, the colour of Prophet Muhammad's daughter Fatima's flag. The traditional crescent emblem of Islam surrounds the Muslim creed. The chain encircling the crescent and the inscriptions imply the unity of the Arab states.

The green in the flag of the Organisation of the African Unity (OAU) represents the forest and grasslands and the orange stands for the African deserts. White in the centre signifies peace and co-operation. The map and the rings imply the unity of the states.

Some unique flags of the world

The tricolour is one single design that is widely used by about fifty-four countries in their national-flags, with or without a device. Different colour combinations have been used vertically, horizontally or diagonally. The most popular devices used are the crescent and star(s), followed by a single five-pointed star. The likeness of the sun has also been adopted as a motif on the national-flags of several countries. Interestingly, the colours red and blue are the most common colours used in world flags. Green is also a popular colour, particularly in the flags of the Muslim world.

The oldest national-flag in the modern world is the National-flag of Denmark. It was adopted in 1219 A.D., when King Waldemar, the Victorious is said to have seen a white cross against a red sky just before he won an important battle. Ever since, the likeness of that sign became the Danish National-flag and continues unchanged till date.

The present-day flag of Austria was born centuries ago on a battlefield. In 1191, Duke of Leopold V, of Austria, was badly wounded in a battle. As he removed his belt from his blood-soaked tunic, he noticed that a strip-like area remained white where his belt had been. The Duke got inspired by the self-evolved red and white design and decided to use a red flag with a white strip across its centre as his royal emblem. This age-old emblem was adopted as the Austrian National-flag in 1918 and continues. It is one of the oldest designs amongst the flags of the contemporary world.

Cyprus is the only country in the world that shows its map in ochre yellow on a white field on her flag. Under the map of the Cyprus island are two olive branches, the ancient sign of peace.

The flag of Nepal is the only National-flag that is not rectangular or square. It is the only double pennant in the modern world. Originally, two separate triangular pennants were flown one above the other, they were then joined together to form a single flag. On a crimson red field it has the figure of a crescent on top of which is a star in the upper pennant, while the lower pennant has the image of the sun in white. Its red is the colour of the rhododendron, the country's national flower. The red is also the sign of victory in war. The blue border of the pennant is the colour of peace. This version of the flag is dated 1962, when the two pennants were wedded together. The crescent and star stand for the Rana family, who once held the Prime Ministerial office and the control of the nation. The sun symbol embellishes the country's royal family.

The Union Jack of the United Kingdom is made up of three crosses representing three saints. The Red Cross in the centre on a blue field stands for St. George, the patron saint of England; the white diagonal cross stands for St. Andrew, the patron saint of Scotland; and the red diagonal cross personifies St. Patrick, the patron saint of Ireland. The present flag was adopted in 1801, when Ireland joined the Union and the cross of St. Patrick was added to the earlier form. Curiously, the Union Jack forms a part in the upper canton of twenty-five national and sub-national flags in the contemporary world, including Australia, Fiji, New Zealand, British Columbia and the Falkland Islands.

The French *tricolore* adopted in 1789 has been the most inspiring flag and stands for 'Liberty, Equality and Fraternity' and is used as the National-flag of five other countries, namely Reunion Islands, New Caledonia, Martinique, French Guiana and Guadeloupe.

The Swiss flag and the flag of the Vatican City are the only two flags that are completely square in shape, while most modern flags are rectangular. The Vatican City, created in 1929, is the smallest independent state in the world and lies within central Rome.

Fujairah, one of the seven emirates of the UAE, is the only sub-nation in the world to have a unicolour National-flag without any device on it. The flag has a solid red rectangular field.

The tallest flagmast in India.

The tallest flagmast in India

The tallest flagmast in India is at the Fort Saint George, Madras (now Chennai). It is 45.7 metres tall and is made of teakwood. In 1687, the then Governor of Madras presidency, Mr Yale, first hoisted the Union Jack on it. The flagstaff on which the Indian tricolour, Tiranga, now flutters was moved to its present position in the 1770s.

4

The ancient Indian dhvajas

The ancient Indian synonym for a flag is *dhvaja* and for a banner, Ketu. A dhvaja has been defined as a symbol of an army or of a king, carried on a staff. According to the *Ramayana*, a dhvaja was attached to a *yasti* and then fixed on the chariot. However, in the strict sense of the word, the term dhvaja implies three things, namely, the *pataka* (the piece of cloth or any other substance that floats in the air), the *ketu* (the crest or the emblem made on the pataka), and the yasti (the pole or staff that carries the pataka).

Most scholars, epigraphists and numismatists use the terms dhvaja and pataka as synonyms. However, there is a difference between the two, the most important being that the former invariably carries an insignia, whereas the latter does not. The dhvaja consisted of an adorned piece of cloth mounted on a pole or a staff bearing a crest. There is yet another difference. The dhvaja is rectangular in shape, while the pataka is triangular.[1] Patakas were made in various plain

---

1. त्रिकोणवै पताकास्तु चतुष्कोण ध्वजा स्म ता Vacaspatyam, p.42212.

colours such as red, yellow, white and black, and at times even bore figures of the sun, moon and the stars. In the great Indian epics of *Ramayana* and *Mahabharata*, the patakas are described as having been used by charioteers, elephant riders and the cavalry.

The Indian dhvaja was rectangular in shape, essentially with a ketu or motif on its field.

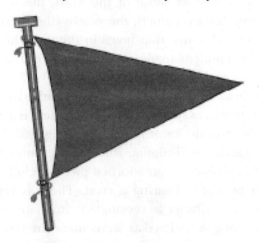

The Pataka was a triangular Indian ancient flag without any ketu or motif on its fields

An analytical study of ancient literature shows that a dhvaja essentially belonged to a kingdom or a dynasty, while a pataka to an individual warrior. A dhvaja was flown on forts and palaces, whereas a pataka was carried on chariots and elephants, etc. In most cases, especially during the epic era, a pataka was synonymous with its bearer. The demon king Ravana is said to have two flags, one bearing a *veena* as its device and the other a human skull. It looks as if the demon king had the veena on the dhvaja of his kingdom, Lanka, to denote his wisdom and wealth; and displayed the figure of a human skull on his personal standard to cause terror in the hearts of his opponents during a battle. Kautilya in his *Arthasastra* also treats the dhvaja and pataka as two different heraldic devices. In the works of Kalidasa, an army is referred to as *patakani*.

In Indian mythology, the planet Ketu, depicted as a headless human torso with a fish-body called the dragon's tail, is the ruler of flags and described as holding a flag of self-glory in one of his four hands, with '*om*' inscribed in the centre. In other words, a flag-bearer has always been held in high esteem and for this reason, all puranic heroes and warriors had their own flags.

In the *Vedas*, war banners of distinguished warriors were designated as ketus. The term ketu also means a crest or an insignia used on the dhvaja. In the *Mahabharata*, the term has been used in its true meaning such as the *vanara-ketu* for Arjuna, *sarpa-ketu* for Duryodhana and the *hastikashyamahar-ketu* for Karna. The *Atharva-Veda* describes the armies of the gods as *surya-ketu* (sun-bannered) and in the *Mahabharata*, an army is referred to as *dhvajani*.

In ancient days, a four-day festival called *dhvaja-mahotsava* or the *Indra-dhvaja-mahotsava,* named after Lord Indra, the Vedic God of War, was celebrated. During the celebrations, the *Indra-yasti* (a pole) was worshipped and the Indra-dhvaja was held aloft with a cord. It concluded with the lowering of the dhvaja (as is now done at the end of Olympics and Asiads). The celebration was performed at the end of a successful military campaign by kings. With the passage of time, the ceremony became more elaborate and ritualistic. In the *Ramayana* it is clearly stated that the Indra-dhvaja was held aloft on a pole with the help of a cord at the time of the *Mahotsava*. The ceremony lasted for four-five days commencing on *Duvadasi* and concluded on *Puranmasi* (full moon day).

Lord Indra riding his war elephant–Aravat.
A dhvajin is holding his blue banner behind him (Bharhut).

Lord Indra was the War God of the Aryans and it is believed that a symbol that served as their rallying point in their advances into India, later came to be known as the Indra-dhvaja. According to a description in the *Mahabharata*, the Indra-dhvaja was shiny dark blue[1] and beautiful like a blue lotus. The war standards of the subsequent periods of Indian history had their origin in the Indra-dhvaja. If a king desired to conquer his enemies and also wished to acquire fame he was advised to display the Indra-dhvaja on all important buildings of his kingdom. For this reason, the Indra-dhvaja later acquired another name – *Vaijanta* meaning the harbinger of victory.

A relief panel from Bharhut showing a female dhvajin holding a dhvaja while riding a horse.

---

1. Thapliyal, U.P.: *The Dhvaja*, p.19.

The Aryan practice of worshipping a dhvaja to seek divine blessing for victory before launching military expeditions led to the practice of erecting *dhvaja-stambhas* (pillars) in the temple premises. In the *Raghuvamsa*, there is a reference to the erection of *jaya-dhvaja* by King Raghu after the successful completion of his military expedition.

The term yasti or dhvaja-yasti refers to a pole or a staff to which a dhvaja or a pataka is attached. Originally, a yasti was made of perishable material like bamboo, sal-wood, etc. Later, when dhvaja worship became a permanent part of the temple rituals, yastis were covered with gold, silver, etc., which lent them durability as well as beauty. Yastis erected in temples were known as dhvaja-stambhas. These stambhas, in the later period were crowned with figures associated with the chief deity of the temple.

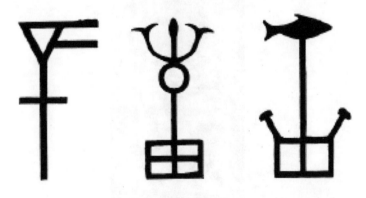

Dhvajas as punched on some of the Punch-marked coins of India.

Besides dhvaja-stambhas, the Vedic people erected wooden *sthunas* at their burial mounds as memorial columns. In the history of the later Vedic period there are references to *yupa-stambhas* (posts) erected by kings and their chiefs in commemoration of their having performed various Vedic sacrifices, such as the *ashwamedha-yagya*. These yupas were originally uncrowned monuments. Emperor Ashoka was perhaps the first person to crown yupa-stambhas with images of sacred objects, such as the *mahapasus* (like the elephant, bull and the horse). The later Brahmanical period saw the *garuda-stambhas*, *vrishbha-stambhas*, and the *makara-stambhas* representing the *vahanas* of Lord Vishnu, Lord Siva and the River Goddess Ganga.

Though sthunas, stambhas, yupas, etc., were closely associated with dhvaja ceremonies, they were at no stage of history deemed to be the dhvajas themselves. In the scheme of dhvajas, only the ketu held an important position and not the yasti or yupa.

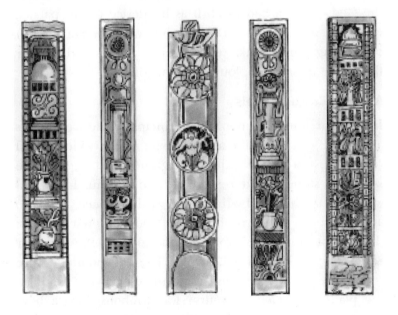

Dhvaja-stambhas as erected in ancient Indian temples.

The dhvajas were meticulously decorated with tassels, frills, tiny bells and garlands. Those of the reputed warriors were even embroidered with gold and studded with precious stones. The famous *kapi-dhvaja* of Arjuna was adorned with patakas of rainbow colours and studded with jewels.

Since dhvajas were closely linked with faith and religion of the people, the motifs or designs used on them invariably bore figures of religious objects. Because of their religious sanctity and people's faith in their protective power, dhvajas commanded great reverence. The very presence of a dhvaja indicated existence of a shrine. The dhvaja was a vital feature of an ancient temple complex.

According to the old Hindu scriptures, Lord Siva had Nandi (the humped bull) on his dhvaja, while Lord Vishnu bore the figure of garuda (the king of eagles). Kamadeva, the God of Love, had the fish as his device on his pataka, whereas Yama, the God of Death, exhibited *bhainsa* (a buffalo) on his flag. King Janaka, the father of Sita, is said to bear the figure of *seeta* (a plough) on his dhvaja.

Ancient dhvaja symbols

In ancient times, each of the principal Hindu gods was associated with a specific animal or an object, which would represent him symbolically. The garuda, *sesanaga* or the *salagrama* stone would represent Lord Vishnu. Lord Siva would be symbolised by the *vrasabha*, the *trishula*, the *naga* and so on. The consorts of the gods, too, had their symbols: the trident or the skull for Kali, the lotus or the swan for Saraswati, the Goddess of Learning. The sun and moon were represented by the disc and crescent respectively. Amongst the planets, *Buddha* (Mercury) was symbolised by a bow, *Mangala* (Mars) by a triangle, *Brahaspati* (Jupiter) by a lotus, *Sani* (Saturn) by scimitar, *Rahu* by a snake and Ketu by a fish.

People of the Vedic era made use of symbols to invoke their revered deities for success in life or in the battlefield. A brief review of the dhvaja motifs shows that they were related to the religion of the people. The dhvaja motifs can be classified into five heads, namely – animals and birds, plants and flowers, objects of nature, sacred objects, and weapons.

Animal and birds

Garuda (eagle): The concept of garuda seems to have evolved in the Vedic age. The mythical garuda is a bird of great antiquity and in the *Vedas* is generally associated with God Savitar on whose command he brought Soma from the moon. The might of the eagle has been mentioned in the *Upanisads*. The epics describe it as an embodiment of keen far-sightedness. According to the *Mahabharata,* once Lord Vishnu, pleased with the bravery and selflessness of the garuda, offered him a boon. The garuda asked for a high perch and Lord Vishnu gave him a place on his dhvaja. Lord Krishna, an incarnation of Lord Vishnu, too, carried an image of garuda on his standard and therefore, was called garuda-dhvaja.

Viswakarma, the architect of the gods, made the garuda-dhvaja. According to the legend, its yasti or staff was decorated with gems and precious metals. On the staff the resplendent garuda, the son of Vinata, was placed. The heavenly nymphs took this dhvaja away to Vaikunth when the chariot of Lord Krishna disintegrated immediately after the death of its master.

Kapi (monkey): Hanuman, the son of Pavana or wind, is a conspicuous figure in the *Ramayana* as well as the *Mahabharata*. The monkey standard was the most widely known dhvaja in ancient India. Arjuna, the greatest of all the warriors described in the *Mahabharata*, in fact, was known as kapi-dhvaja after his standard.

According to the *Mahabharata*, Prajapati Viswakarma created the kapi-dhvaja after a long penance. It was borne by King Soma during his successful encounters with the demons and was passed on from Soma to Varuna along with the chariot. Varuna gave it to Arjuna at Agni's request. It is significant that Agni, as a *parivara-devata*, is also described as bearing a kapi-dhvaja.

The staff of the *dhvaja* was made of gold. The divine Vanara, wearing a ferocious expression, was mounted on it. It was so high, yet it never got stuck in trees and hills. Some supernatural beings also inhabited it and were considered the harbingers of victory in war. It was adorned with divine images in small and big sizes, and despite its immense size, this extraordinary dhvaja neither increased the weight nor caused any hindrance to the smooth movement of a chariot. It was also adorned by rainbow-coloured banners.

The kapi-dhvaja was also called jaya-dhvaja, i.e., victory standard. The vanara-ketu made a positive contribution to the victory of Arjuna in the battlefield. The vanara made such a loud sound that it scared the enemies and shattered their morale so that Arjuna could easily kill them. At the end of the *Mahabharata*, when Arjuna's chariot disintegrated, the divine forces in the vanara-ketu also deserted it. Some South Indian dynasties appear to have used the vanara-ketu at a later date. In modern times, the Rani of Jhansi had the Hanuman/Vanara-dhvaja.

Varaha (boar): In the *Rig-Veda*, the term *varaha* is used for the boar to denote a sense of superiority and pre-eminence. In the Brahamana and Aranyaka literature, the boar is referred to as having retrieved the earth from the depth of the lower regions. The epic and the Puranic myths relate that Lord Vishnu in his incarnation as varaha rescued the earth by raising it above the waters of the cosmic deluge.

The Vrasabha-dhvaja of the Pallavas.

In the Hindu iconography, Sanishchra (Lord Saturn), the slow-moving planet, is described as bearing a varaha-dhvaja. Sidhuraja Jayadratha, the epic warrior, displayed varaha on his standard.

Vrasabha (humped bull): Vrasabha denotes superiority and power and was known to the Indus people and the Vedic Aryans. The Taurine zodiacal sign, symbolised by the bull, was the birth sign of Lord Buddha. In the epics and *Puranas*, vrasabha forms the dhvaja of Lord Siva. The deities associated with him such as Isana, Archraja, Patira, Maheswari and Virabhadra are also represented by the *vrasabha-dhvaja*. Krapacharya, the Kaurava general, also bore a vrasabha-dhvaja. In a seal from Bhita, dated around third century A.D., one Gautamiputra is described as vrasabha-dhvaja.

The Varaha-dhvaja of eastern Calukyas.

Hasti (elephant): In the *Rig-Veda*, the *hasti* has the connotation of bravery and uncontrollable vigour. In Indian mythology, it symbolises wisdom, self-sacrifice, strength and a majestic feel. It is associated with Lord Ganesha and Goddess Saraswati, the deities of Learning and Wisdom. It was the mount of Lord Indra and hence considered a symbol of glory and strength.

In the *Mahabharata*, King Bhoja, who fought on the side of the Kauravas, bore a vrasabha-dhvaja. Among the Saptamatrikas, Varahi and Indrani are described as bearing a *gaja-dhvaja*.

Simha (lion): In the *Rig-Veda*, *simha* denotes great strength and superiority. The mother goddess chose a simha for her vahana in her battle against the demons. In the *Ramayana*, the warrior Meghanaadh, also known as Indrajita, the son of Ravana, is described as *mirgaraja-ketu*. In the *Mahabharata* battle, the Pandava hero, Bhima carried a *simha-dhvaja*. In the *Matsya Purana*, the Sun and the Moon gods are said to have borne a golden lion as an emblem on their dhvajas. Among the parivara-devatas of Lord Vishnu, Varuna, Sri, Buddha, Durga, Agni and Kaumodaki are also said to have borne simha-dhvaja.

Hamsa (swan): In the *Rig-Veda*, the *hamsa* occurs as symbolic of the Asvins, the twin gods. At another place, the God Soma is compared to a swan. Subsequently, the supernatural power of discriminating the Soma and the water come to be associated with it. In the *Mahabharata*, Sahadeva, the youngest of the Pandava brothers, is described to display the *hamsa-dhvaja*. Among the parivara-devatas of Lord Vishnu, Sundari, Svaha, Samhladini, Raka, Sinivali, Apsarasa, Vipa and Brahmi are described as using the hamsa-dhvaja.

Sarabha (a mythical animal): In the *Atharva-Veda*, the *sarabha* appears as a frivolous animal with two heads, two wings of resplendent beauty, eight legs of a lion with sharp claws and a long tail. According to the *Puranas*, once Lord Siva assumed the form of sarabha to appease Lord Vishnu, who in the Narasimha avatara, could not control his anger. This symbol of immense power is widely represented in the Hindu iconography.

Nakula, a Pandava hero, carried a sarabha-dhvaja in war. Angaraka, the planet Mangala, is also depicted as holder of sarabha-dhvaja in iconography.

Naga (serpent): The snake is the very embodiment of strength. Yama, the God of Death, used a *byala-dhvaja*. The family deities of Lord Vishnu, viz. Vidhata, Javana, Balida, Rahu and Ketu, are described as bearing a *sarpa-dhvaja*. Again a deity named Turhana used an *ahi-dhvaja*. Duryodhana, the Kaurava king, also chose a snake as his dhvaja motif.

Mayura (peacock): The peacock has been widely used in Indian literature as a symbol of beauty and grace. The *Rig-Veda* appreciates it for the beauty of its plumes. It is represented on the dhvaja of Skanda, the army commander of the gods, who is called *mayura-dhvaja, sikhi-dhvaja* and *sikhi-ketu.* The coins of Kumaran Gupta, the Gupta king, bear the image of Skanda mounting a peacock. Virsasena, a king who fought for the Kauravas in the *Mahabharata* carried a mayura-dhvaja.

Makara (crocodile): The *makara* is identified as a dolphin or crocodile. According to a description, Kamadeva, the God of Love, chose it for his dhvaja. Among the deities of the Lord Vishnu, Parivara, Singhu, Taksaka and Madana bore a *makara-dhvaja.* Pradyumna, a son of Lord Krishna, also bore this dhvaja, and the shrine at Besnagar dedicated to him was marked by a makara-dhvaja as early as the second century B.C. The *Mahabharata* has also described him as bearing a makara-dhvaja.

Kukkuta (cock): The cock has been regarded as an embodiment of the fighting spirit. It was the vahana and dhvaja of Karttikeya, the Warlord of the gods.

Asva (horse): *Asva* is one that moves fast and was a popular and highly regarded animal among the Aryans. Great kings of India are known to have celebrated their supremacy over other rulers with the performance of horse sacrifice. Among the family deities of Lord Vishnu, Patanga, Prahlada and Surya bore the *asva-dhvaja.*

Gradha (vulture): *Gradha* means to covet or desire. In the *Rig-Veda*, the word is used in a derogatory sense. The term is generally applied to a vulture that is supposed to be very sharp eyed. In the *Mahabharata*, Ghatotakacha is said to have borne a *gradha-dhvaja.* The *Matsya Purana* describes that *rakshasas* as gradha-dhvaja, i.e., having a dhvaja with a vulture emblem.

Some animals of lesser importance also figure as dhvaja-ketus. In the *Matsya Purana,* the Yaksas are said to be *tamroluka-dhvaja,* i.e., having a standard with a red owl as emblem. The owl occurs in the *Rig-Veda* as a bird which can see better at night than during the day and thus symbolises the concept of darkness. *Srgala* (jackal) found a place in the standard of Alayudha, an epic warrior. *Mahisa* (buffalo) was represented in the dhvaja of Yama, the God of Death. Mahidhara and Vidyadhara, two minor deities, also bore it on their *dhvaja. Kurma* (tortoise) formed the dhvaja of Goddess Ganga. It was a symbol of perseverance and Lord Vishnu assumed the form of kurma in one of his incarnations. Goddess Yamuna's dhvaja displayed a *matsya* (fish). Jeystha, a benevolent deity, bore the *kaka-dhvaja* (crow). Two minor deities, Sura and Vatsarasa, bore *kapota* (pigeon) and *sasa* (rabbit) respectively on their dhvaja. Asura, a minor deity carried a *khara-dhvaja* (donkey). *Krkalasa* (lizard) formed the dhvaja of Nirruti, also a minor deity. *Mirga* (deer) was used in the dhvaja of Jambava and Aniruddha. God Soma used *kulira* (crab) on his dhvaja.

Plants and flowers

The plant world also provided for some of the dhvaja-ketus. Important motifs of this category include:

Tala (palm tree): *Tala* was a very popular tree in ancient India. It was also called *dhvaja-druma, taruraja, dirghapatra,* etc. The name suggests that it was held in high esteem. Its wood was considered sacred and was widely used to make the *dhvaja-danda.* The tala thus symbolised a sense of superiority and sanctity. Bhisma, the greatest of the Kaurava warriors, bore a *tala-dhvaja* and so did God Acyuta.

Kovidara (a tree): A beautiful tree with supernatural

qualities, the *kovidara* tree has also been referred to as *mandara* and *parijata* in literature. Bharata, who ruled over Ayodhya for fourteen years in the absence of his brother Lord Rama, displayed a *kovidara-dhvaja*. It was probably the dynastic dhvaja of the kings of Ayodhya. Dhrstadyumna, a great warrior, who joined the *Mahabharata* war on the side of Pandavas, also bore a kovidara-dhvaja.

Puspa (flower): Flowers were used in the worship of gods and hence were treated as sacred. Dhata, Pusparaksita and Halesa, among the family deities of Lord Vishnu, were known as *puspa-dhvaja*.

Kusa (grass): *Kusa* is widely used in Brahmanic rituals. Even in the Vedic age it was laid on the floor of the sacrificial chamber before the beginning of a ritual. Sanctity attached to kusa is also reflected in legend about Garuda's exploits. It is said that when he brought the pot of ambrosia from the heavens to his stepbrothers, the snakes, he placed it on a kusa mat. Sages like Vaikhanasa, Vamana, Brhaspati and Mudgala used it for their dhvaja. *Kurca,* probably the same as kusa, was used by sages such as Sanatana, Markendeya, Tapasa and Narada for their dhvaja.

Padma (lotus): *Padma* was considered sacred both by the Brahmins and the Buddhists. It symbolised purity, learning and fortune. Dhanada, the Lord of Wealth, bore a *padma-dhvaja*.

Nala (lotus stalk): The word *nala* is symbolic of softness and delicacy. The mythical land of the Kinnaras abounded in lotuses and this probably explains their association with *nala-dhvaja*.

Elements and objects of nature

Nature, too, provided inspiration for some dhvaja-ketus. They did not, however, become popular owing to the problem of actual representation associated with them. Some of these manifestations are:

Agni (fire): In the *Vedas*, *agni* is described as the God and Lord of Fire and Light, of heaven and earth, being the soul of all. Fire purifies and, therefore, symbolises purity.

Megha (cloud): The Yaksa chose it as their dhvaja motif. The association of the *megha* and the Yaksa is well brought out in Kalidasa's *Meghaduta*.

Chandra (crescent): In the *Rig-Veda*, Indu or Soma appears as a powerful god, capable of granting strength, glory and renown. "O Soma, set thou upon us the glory of a hundred men, the great renown of mighty chiefs." In the *Puranas* it is described as one of the preserves of Lord Siva obtained from *samudra-manthana*, i.e., churning of the ocean. Ravana, the demon king, had a sword named *Chandra haasa*, a broad-blade, crescent-shaped sword.

Sacred objects

Some objects associated with religious rituals were also used as dhvaja motifs. Some of the better known are described as follows:

Vedika (altar): The term *vedika* was applied to a raised platform built for the purpose of worship and sacrifice by the Vedic Aryans. The dhvaja of Dronacharya, the Kaurava warrior, bore the symbol of a vedika and a *kamandalu* with a bow.

Yupa (post): The yupa was a vital part of the vedika complex in the Vedic religion. It was a post set at a corner of the sacrificial altar, to which the victim was tied. Because of this association, the yupa acquired an aura of sanctity. In the epic war, Bhurisrava, a prominent warrior on the Kaurava side, carried a yupa-dhvaja.

Mridanga (drum): The *mridanga* was probably the same as the Vedic *dundubhi*. Its thunderous notes meant encouragement to friends and terror to foes. Yudhisthira, the eldest of the Pandava brothers, was represented by a pair of mridangas on the dhvaja, called *Nanda* and *Upananda*. These mridangas generated a melodious note without any human effort.

Kapala (skull): The *kapala*, generally speaking, is a symbol of Saivite significance. Lord Siva used it as a receptacle for his food and drink. Ravana, who was a devout worshipper of Shiva, adopted this motif on his dhvaja.

Sruva (ladle): *Sruva* was used for pouring oblations into the sacrificial fire. It was an important attribute of Lord Brahma. It was considered sacred and hence was used as a dhvaja motif. Mitra, Sukra, Atharva, Manika and Tumburu, among the parivara-devatas of Lord Vishnu, are mentioned as bearing *sruva-dhvaja*.

Juhu (wooden ladle): The *juhu* was a crescent-shaped wooden ladle used for pouring the sacrificial butter into the fire. Sage Atri chose to represent it on his dhvaja.

Kalasa (vessel): The overflowing vessel as a symbol of plenty and auspiciousness has a hoary antiquity. Lord Siva who generally used a vrasabha-dhvaja is associated with *kalasa-dhvaja* as a parivara-devata in a Vishnu temple. In the *Vamana Purana*, Lord Ganesa (i.e. Lord of the Ganas) is also referred to bearing the kalasa-dhvaja.

Samkha (conch): *Samkha* has always been treated as a sacred object in Brahmanic religion. In the *Mahabharata*, all the renowned warriors carried a samkha to serve as a trumpet in a war. Among the deities of the Lord Vishnu family, Varuna, Maruta and Vasu were always represented with a *samkha-dhvaja* in the temples.

Dhuma (smoke): *Dhuma* is symbolic of sacrificial fire and hence sacred. In the *Harrivamsa Purana*, Agni is described as bearing a *dhuma-ketu* on his chariot. The *Vishnu Purana* also describes him as mounted on a chariot bearing a *dhuma-dhvaja*.

Weapons

Weapons were again popular dhvaja motifs. *Cakra, dhanusa, khatvanga, bhindipala, sara* and *khanga* that were used as dhvaja motifs are described as follows:

Cakra (disc): In the *Rig-Veda*, the *cakra* (or the wheel) symbolises the sun and the concept of light. It is also identified with the supreme moral order in the form of *dharma-cakra*. In the Buddhist tradition, the cakra is symbolic of the Buddha and the preaching of the first sermon, i.e., Dharmachakra Pravartana. In art, *cakra-dhvaja* first appears in the third century B.C. with the use by Ashoka to represent the Buddhist concept of *Cakrawartin*, i.e., turning of the wheel of law by the Buddha.

Dhanusa (bow): The bow enjoys a high esteem in the Indian tradition. In the *Rig-Veda*, the bow was considered a symbol of victory. The Ceras, who ruled Kerala in the third century B.C., bore a *dhanusa-dhvaja*.

Khatvanga (club): The *khatvanga*, one of the principal weapons associated with Lord Siva, was a curious sort of club made up of the bone of the forearm or the leg, to the end of which a human skull was attached. The Pallavas of Kanct are stated to have used *khatvanga-dhvaja* in addition to their vrasabha-dhvaja.

Bhindipala (spear): *Bhindipala* was a weapon like a short javelin or an arrow thrown with the hand or shot through a tube. God Vivasvana carried *bhindipala-dhvaja.*

Sara (arrow): The *sara* was the most popular and sacred weapon of the Vedic Aryans. The Satavahana ruler, Gautamiputra Satakarni, displayed an arrow fitted on a bow on his coins as a sign of prowess. It is likely that he used it on his dhvaja also. The minor deities Kiskindha, Saranga and Tirtha bore a *sara-dhvaja*.

Khanga (sword): The sacrificial knife or sword was called a *khanga*. Gavistha, Kuhu, Anuimiti and Sunanda, the family deities of Vishnu temple, bore a *khanga-dhvaja*.

Vajra (thunderbolt): The *vajra* was the most celebrated weapon of Lord Indra. It was created out of the bones of Rishi Dadhichi to destroy the otherwise invincible demons. The vajra symbolised invincibility in war. In the *Kalika Uppurana*, Naranka, the ruler of Pragjoyotisa (modern Guwahati), is said to have a *vajra-dhvaja*. Naranka probably preferred this weapon for his dhvaja because it was associated with Lord Indra.

Seeta (tip of a plough), *viyadgati* (motion in air), *cuda* (tuft of hair), *bhuta* (spirit), *pisaca* (goblin) and *sukra* (Venus) are some other dhvaja types referred to in the *Vaikhanasa Agama*. It is not always easy to explain whether a particular dhvaja motif was associated with a god or not, but it is certain that some religious symbolism was attributed to each of them.

5

Flags of the Epic Era

The two great epics of India, the *Ramayana* and the *Mahabharata*, are not only the *itihas* or legends of the epic kings and princes, but, also a mirror of the social set-up of those times. A study of these epics reveals that flags were in great use and were given immense importance. The warriors performed elaborate flag ceremonies with a lot of rituals. It was an established custom for them to adopt personal flags according to their faith, lineage, military exploits, and qualifications. In due course, a particular flag became synonymous with its bearer. During battle, the presence of a warrior in the battlefield could easily be known by locating his flag.

Prince Bharata, the younger brother of Lord Rama, had adopted Kovidara (a beautiful supernatural tree) as a symbol for his flag. During the fourteen-year exile, along with Lord Rama and Sita, Lakshman sighted a huge army with the kovidara-dhvaja in the vanguard approaching their abode. He at once surmised that Bharata was coming[1]. Thinking that Bharata was approaching to attack them, Lakshman rushed to Lord Rama to seek his permission to destroy Bharata's kovidara-dhvaja, and thereby dishonour and disgrace him. Destruction or capture of a flag was considered a great dishonour and disgrace that one could inflict on the vanquished on a battlefield.

During the invasion of Lanka, Lord Rama fought against Ravana under the flag of his dynasty, the Raghuvamsa. According to the *Kurma* and *Skanda Puranas,* it had a motif showing three leaves of *shami-vraksha* (a large native tree) in the centre against a crimson field that looked like the flames of fire. Some scholars hold the view that it had the figure of Lord Surya, their *kula-devata* (family deity) on a crimson field. The flag of Ravana displayed the figure of a human skull (*kapala*)[2] and for this reason it was known as kapala-dhvaja. A kapala is also associated with Lord Siva, who is said to have used it as a receptacle for his food and drink. As Ravana was a devout *bhakta* of Lord Siva, he adopted kapala as an emblem for his personal pataka to invoke the Lord's blessings. Another reason for adopting such a symbol could be that a skull would intimidate his opponents and enemies. A severed skull was also symbolic of the Rakshasa cult, which Ravana had adopted. Some scholars believe that Ravana's flag carried the figure of a veena, since he was a good musician and a veena player. He had mastered all the *Vedas* and, therefore, to denote his wisdom and wealth he had adopted a veena as the emblem for his empire's flag. Ravana's son, Meghanaadh, however, adopted a simha (lion) for his

---

1. *Ramayana, Ayodhyakand,* p. 96.18.
2. ध्वज मनुष्य शीर्षम्, *Ramayana,* Yudha, 100.14.

flag and it was known as *mrigaraja-ketu*. A simha is also a saivite symbol, being the vahana (vehicle) of Goddess Durga, an incarnation of Parvati and the spouse of Lord Siva. The other warriors of Ravana, Prahasta and Kambhanan, had a snake and the sesanaga as symbols on their respective flags[1].

The details of the flags used by the Pandavas during the battle of Kurukshetra have been given by Sanjay in the *Bheeshmaparva* and those of the Kauravas in the *Dronaparva* of the *Mahabharata*. Yudhisthira, the eldest of the Pandavas, bore a pair of mridangas, called Nanda and Upnanda, on his standard[2]. The thunderous notes of these mridangas (drums) were said to have encouraged friends and terrorised foes. Likewise, the divine monkey on Arjuna's kapi-dhvaja terrified and demoralised the foes with his awe-inspiring chatter. It is likely that some of the chariots in those days were equipped with devices that produced notes or sounds of the ketu on the flag. Bheema, the second of the Pandavas, carried a simha-dhvaja. Nakula, the fourth Pandava, had the sarabha (a mythical animal) on his standard. Sahadeva, the youngest of the Pandavas, carried a hamsa-dhvaja (swan). The swan is a symbol of the twin *aswini-kumaras*. Abhimanyu, the son of Subhadra and Arjuna, chose a *saranga* (a bird) for his flag. The other warriors on the Pandava side also had their own flags. Dhristadyumna, the commander-in-chief of the Pandava forces, flew the kovidara-dhvaja, while Ghatotkacha, a rakshasa and the son of Bheema by Hidamba, carried a gradha-dhvaja (vulture). The *Matsya Purana* mentions that the rakshasa carried gradha-dhvaja, i.e., a dhvaja with a vulture emblem. He was also said to have had a chakra-dhvaja. The famous garuda-dhvaja belonged to the

---

1. *Ramayana*, Yudha, 57.26.
2. *Mahabharata*, Dronaparva, 23.84.

omnipotent Lord Krishna. His son, Pradyumna, had a makara-dhvaja (crocodile). And Balarama, the elder brother of Lord Krishna, had adopted a tala-dhvaja. The wood of the tala tree was considered sacred and was widely used to make the dhvaja-yasti (pole). Bheeshma, the greatest among the *Mahabharata* warriors, also had a tala-dhvaja. It had a figure of a tala tree with a cluster of five stars around it.

Duryodhana, the Kaurava king, hoisted a sarpa-dhvaja (serpent) on his chariot. According to the ancient scriptures, a snake is an embodiment of strength. Dronacharya, the preceptor of the Kauravas and Pandavas, adopted a vedika (altar) covered with the deerskin topped with a kamandalu and a dhanush (bow) as the ketu for his dhvaja. The great warrior had chosen these symbols very thoughtfully. He was a Brahmin by birth, hence he rightly chose a vedika covered with deerskin; since he pursued the *kshatriya-dharma* in life, he chose a bow, too. His brother-in-law, Kripacharya, had a vrasabha-dhvaja (humped bull). Vrasabha denotes endurance and strength. Dronacharya's son, Ashwathama, adopted *simha-lanchana*, a lion-tail, for his banner. Karna, the great but ill-fated archer, displayed a *hastikashyamahar-ketu* (elephant chain), on his dhvaja. According to some scriptures, the ketu for his dhvaja was the sun. Sindhuraja Jayadratha, the brother-in-law of Duryodhana, had a boar on his standard. Salya, the maternal uncle of the Pandavas, adopted an image of seeta, a plough, for his flag.

Certain customs and rituals were associated with flags. The warriors themselves mounted their dhvajas on their chariots before marching to the battlefield. Arjuna was very particular in observing these rituals. Before proceeding to a battle he circumambulated his chariot, Nandi Ghosh, and then with an armoured hand raised his kapi-dhvaja. Raising one's own flag before marching to a battlefield was an established custom. A number of references to codes for dhvajas are found in various ancient treatises such as *Kalpataru, Sutasamita* and *Kriyasar.*

In the epic era, the warriors are described to have been involved in destroying the flags of their adversaries. Arjuna, in his final encounter with Karna, first destroyed his dhvaja and then killed him. Similarly, Lord Rama is also said to have destroyed Ravana's dhvaja to disgrace him, before slaying the demon king.

Slicing of the dhvaja of an adversary.

A dhvaja bearing an inauspicious symbol was held in such contempt that even warriors of repute refused to fight its bearer. Bheeshma, the first commander of the Kaurava forces, declined to fight a great warrior Sikhandi on the Pandava's side because, besides being once a female, his dhvaja carried an inauspicious symbol[1].

The use of dhvaja as a decorative device during royal ceremonies was also a common practice. On festive occasions, warriors displayed their standards and flags. When Lord Krishna reached Indraprastha on the eve of the *Rajsuya Yajna,* conducted by the eldest Pandava Emperor Yudhisthir, the whole city bore a festive look with standards and flags flying high on city palaces and houses. The modern practice of hoisting of the National-flag on private houses on the occasion of Independence Day and Republic Day seems to be very much akin to this past practice. It must be pointed out that as per the amended Flag Code, Indian citizens can now fly the Indian tricolour, the Tiranga, on their houses and other premises on all days of the year.

---

1. *Mahabharata,* Bheeshmaparva, 103.78.

6

Flags of ancient, medieval and modern India

The seals, pottery and other evidences available on the Indus Valley Civilisation clearly indicate the use of flags by the people of that age. The people of Mohenjo-Daro held in high esteem certain objects and animals, especially a unicorn. Obviously, the flags used by them bore their figures. A seal from Mohenjo-Daro shows four men in a file, each carrying a standard. One is inclined to believe that these standards must have been the rallying point for the people both in war and in peacetime.

The *Puranas* and the *Agamas* provide convincing evidence to show that the flags in ancient India had religious significance. The act of hoisting a dhvaja in honour of a deity was called *dhvaja-dana* and it was deemed as an act of great merit. The details of dhvaja-dana to Goddess Durga have been given in the *Devi Purana*. Similarly, other *Puranas* throw light on the flags used by other gods and goddesses.

Specifications for standards or dhvajas meant for temples are given in the *Pancharatagama*. There is a temple of a Goddess Jhandewali in Delhi. The temple was visible from a distance in the past because of flags flapping in the air on trees around the temple complex. As per the legend, people used to offer triangular red flags to the Goddess when their wish was fulfilled and hence the name Jhandewali mata.

There is evidence to show that Buddhists, too, used flags to indicate their places of worship as also for propagation of their religion. Emperor Ashoka erected many dhvaja-stambhas at Buddhist holy places in order to spread the message of *dharma*. The *dharma-chakra* on our National-flag is taken from the icon capital of Sarnath built by him. Infact, dhvajas and dhvaja-stambhas were in the service of the Buddhists even before the time of Ashoka, as is evident from the art at Bharhut, Mathura and Amravati. They were used to spread the message of dharma.

A relief panel from Sanchi shows the Dharma-Chakra-dhvaja.

The Jains also hoisted dhvajas at their places of worship.

Lord Mahavira and the Jain-dhvaja.

In the *Adi Purana* of the Jains, there are many references to kings who made dhvaja-dana to temples. The *pali-dhvaja* is an integral part of a Jain shrine, according to this *Purana*. It has five stripes of saffron, *basanti* (a shade of yellow), white, green and black. One can notice such flags on any Jain shrine. There is a panel from cave number seventeen at Ajanta showing warriors with weapons, flags and buntings rejoicing in the capital of King Sibi.

The use of flags continued during the post-Gupta period, though certain changes were evident. In later Indian literature, the terms pataka and dhvaja lost their distinction and became almost synonymous around the tenth century A.D. However, the basic principles of the institution of dhvaja, as evolved in ancient India, remained unchanged in medieval times. Although, in the early thirteenth century A.D., the Turkish invasion had made inroads into India, the ancient influence in the use of flags continued.

The Rajput rulers held the dhvaja as a symbol of royalty. Bappa Rawal, the ancestor of the Ranas of Chittor, claimed descent from *Surya* (the sun) and hence carried a flag bearing a golden sun on the crimson field[1]. It was called *Changi*. The flag of the Ranas withstood many ups and downs. Rana Pratap fought the Battle of Haldighat under this flag. When, at one stage, he was thickly besieged by the Mughals, one of his chiefs, the Rana of Jhala, seized the Changi raised it over his own head and bore the brunt of the attack. Jhala's stratagem misled the Mughals and saved Rana Pratap in the battle.

The descendants of the medieval Rajput rulers continued to display their ancestral flags and state emblems till their political survival came to an end with the abolishing of the Privy Purses in 1971. The state flag of Bikaner had two colours, saffron and red, superimposed with the figure of a kite. In the seventeenth century, the motto *Jaya Jangla Dhara Badshaha* was added on the flag to commemorate the exploits of the then ruler of Bikaner, Maharaja Karansinghji, over the Mughal Emperor Aurangzeb in jungle warfare. The state standard of Jodhpur, known as Pancharanga, had five colours – salmon pink, white, red, yellow and green. It, too, like the flag of Bikaner, carried a figure of a kite in black. The bird is said to have represented the winged Goddess Durga.

The Bhonsle rulers of Nagpur carried two flags, viz., the *zari-pataka* and the *bhagwa-jhanda*. Shahji, the father of Shivaji, wielded the bhagwa-jhanda only. Shivaji, after his successful military exploits against the Mughals, adopted the zari-pataka

---

1. Tod. J: *Annals and Antiquities of Rajasthan*, Vol. 1., p. 196.
2. James Douglas: *Bombay and Western India*, Vol. 1, p. 173.

in addition to his bhagwa-jhanda as a symbol of royalty[2].

The Marathas observed the custom of rewarding their celebrated generals for acts of gallantry by bestowing on them the zari-patakas. In wars, a holder of the zari-pataka always led the infantry unit that formed the vanguard of the Maratha army. The Marathas seem to have adopted this custom from the Muslims, who already had the tradition when they came to India.

The rise of the crescent and star on the Indian political horizon and the interaction of indigenous and Islamic traditions gave birth to new customs and practices regarding the use of flags in war and peace.

The first Arab invasion on India took place in Sind, in 712 A.D. When the Muslim invaders came to India, they came flying their own flags and brought their own colours that

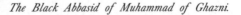

The Black Abbasid of Muhammad of Ghazni.

reflected Islamic traditions. Muhammad of Ghazni, during his invasions on India, carried the Black Abbasid with the crescent superimposed on it. His grandson, Ibrahim (eleventh century A.D.), however adopted the symbol of a lion for his flag. *Abbaids* were those Caliphs who ruled from Baghdad and had black flags.

Muhammad Ghori, in the two battles he fought with Prithviraj Chauhan in 1191 and 1192 A.D. at Tarain, carried his own flags and banners. Qutab-ud-din Aibak had a crescent and a lion on his standard. Ghiyas-ud-din Tughlak's flag had a motif of a fish. The Tughlak kings were rather fond of flags and hence had a separate state department called *Alam Khana* for the manufacture and upkeep of royal standards.

Presenting a standard to their war heroes was an old Muslim custom. However, it was perhaps during the Sultanate period that the custom of granting standards to Amirs, Khans and others started in India. The Mughals followed it up earnestly. But, for the Indians it was a new custom. The Marathas are believed to have adopted it from the Muslims. The modern practice of presentation of colours to the Armed Forces by the President of India in recognition of their distinguished services is very much akin to this old practice.

One thing common between the Hindus and the Muslims was that both of them derived strength and inspiration from the use of flags of their respective religions. In fact, such a tradition is universal the world over.

The principal royal standard of the Mughals was known as *Alam*. It was primarily moss green, though at times it was scarlet. Against a green field it displayed a rising sun, partially eclipsed by the body of a crouching lion facing the hoist of the flag. The Alam was supposed to be the flag of Hussain. Later, Taimur at Karbalah obtained it. As descendants of the great warrior, the Mughals adopted the Alam as their standard.

The royal Mughal standard was displayed to the right of the throne and also at the entrance of the Emperor's encampment, and in front of the Emperor during military marches. Most of the present flag regulations, as laid down in the Flag Code India, are similar to these medieval practices.

Mughal Standards as illustrated in Ain-e-Akbari.

Carrying flags, standards, banners, armours, etc., in

A procession of Emperor Jehangir. 'Alam ',
the Mughal standard, is seen carried on the back of an elephant.
(Padashahnama, courtesy Royal Library London).

processions was a common custom throughout the medieval period. Whenever the emperor went out, five flags were carried along with the *qur* (a collection of flags, insignias, arms, etc.) wrapped in scarlet cloth-bags. It carried the royal standards, too. The royal standards, flags, insignias and allied objects were displayed on days of military activities and festivities.

Advent of the Union Jack

The story of how the Union Jack came to India makes an interesting study. It all started in 1599 A.D. when the Dutch, who had been in exclusive control of the spice trade with India, increased their rate by five shillings per pound for European buyers. The increase looked rather unreasonable to the English traders. Consequently, twenty-four English traders joined hands and founded a company with a bare 125 shareholders and applied to the Crown for a licence to trade with India. It was granted in December 1599. Equipped with the licence, Captain Hawkins set sail for India in a ship named *Hector*. Flying the Union Jack, the ship anchored off the coast of Surat on August 24, 1600. From Surat, Hawkins marched

The structure in picture is the original 'Gateway of India', specially built to welcome King George V and Queen Mary in December 1911. The Union Jack is seen hoisted on a flagmast in foreground. The original structure was replaced by the present stone monument in 1924.

The obverse of a one rupee coin shows the Emblem of the English East India Company. The two lions facing each other are seen holding the Company's banner.

to Agra, the then Mughal capital, and reached the court of Emperor Jehangir to obtain the *shahi-ferman*. Thus, the Union Jack reached the soil of India to rule over the fate of her sons and daughters for the next three-and-a-half centuries.

With the advent of the English on the political scene of India, there appeared a new set of flags, banners, colours, standards, guidions, pennants, etc., representing European customs and traditions. Along with their traditions and culture came a new language, vocabulary, jargon, as well as rules and protocols with regard to the use of flags.

In the early phase of its rule, the East India Company had different flags for each of its armies in the Presidencies of Bengal, Madras and Bombay. With the transfer of power from the Company to the Crown, the flags used by the Presidency armies also underwent change. The most significant change was that the Royal Crown replaced the

Consecration ceremony before taking flags in use by the British Army.

Army men holding lance and pennants.

Scinde Horse, an old banner of the British Army.

crest of the East India Company, a Lion Passant Regardant holding a crown.

The Viceroy of India's standard was the Union Jack superimposed in the centre with the star of India. The star was a combination of a golden sunburst of twenty-six short and twenty-six long rays, a fine-pointed star, one point at the twelve o' clock position and a light blue garter, superimposed with the motto in capital letters 'HEAVENS LIGHT OUR GUIDE' starting at the seven o'clock point. A crown, probably the Tudor crown, was placed over the Star of India. It was also the official British-India flag for India, adopted in 1861 by Queen Victoria.

The Governor-General's flag had the royal crest in gold and a standing lion mounted on the Crown (the Tudor Crown) against a blue field. Beneath the motif was written 'India' in white with a semi-circular setting. Introduced in 1931, this design was uniform throughout the Commonwealth countries.

Bengal sanyasins wielding banners and swords in revolt against the British, 1770 A.D.

The British came to India as traders and turned into rulers. They impoverished and enslaved our country. Many efforts were made to put an end to their authority. The most notable among those was the revolt of the Bengal *sanyasins* in 1770 A.D., an uprising led by Rani Chennamma of Kittur in South India; the Santhal rebellion of 1855 and the great mutiny of 1857. However, all the valiant efforts on the part of the people failed and the Union Jack continued to rule over India till about the middle of the twentieth century.

The Flag of Portuguese-India

At the time of Independence, Goa, Daman and Diu were under the Portuguese Rule and remained so until December 16, 1961, when the Indian Army liberated these territories from the Portuguese. Notwithstanding the liberation of Goa, Daman and Diu, Portugal did not officially recognise the annexation until 1975.

During the Portuguese Rule between 1599 and 1961, the Portuguese-India's Flag was the National-flag of Portugal, with a shield in the lower fly quarter of the red field. The shield was divided into three areas, one with five bezants arranged in cross pattern and another with five waves in green. The remaining area had local emblems, which in case of the Portuguese-India flag, was a gold field with a watermill wheel in black and a tower in red. Similar designs were introduced throughout the overseas Portuguese territories, including India, by a decree on May 8, 1935.

7

Evolution of the Indian National-flag

One hard fact of our history is that we never had a National-flag for the whole of India. The stretch of land called India, in the true sense of the word, had never been one nation. There had been dynasties, clans, tribes, and communities. Each had its own territory, traditions, customs, and political set-ups. All these big and small kingdoms were ruled under their respective flags. There had, therefore, been dhvajas of the epic heroes, standards of monarchs, flags of the dynasties, banners of warriors, etc., but a National-flag for the entire length and breadth of the country never existed.

In early days, whenever a king extended his territory by defeating another king, he still allowed the vanquished to fly his flag. The garuda-banner of the Mauryas and the Guptas was more a dynastic coat-of-arms than a National-flag of India. Similarly, the Changi of Rana Pratap, the bhagwa-jhanda of Shivaji, the triangular Hanuman-banner of *Jhansi ki Rani* and the Alam of the Mughals were mere symbols of the Rajput, Maratha and Mughal pride. During the British rule, there were 565 princely states in India. They all had their own flags and royal emblems. Besides, the Viceroy and Governor-General of India, too, had their flags.

As people, we have never been true Indians in the strict sense. In our subconscious, we are regional and religion minded. We are either Punjabis, Sindhis, Kashmiris, Rajasthanis, Marathis, Gujaratis, Bengalis, Assamese or the like. We are also Hindus, Muslims, Sikhs, Christians, Jains, Parsis, etc. Such a fragmented political set-up of India suited the English who came to India as one nation and ruled over us under one flag, the Union Jack.

Indians awoke from their political stupor rather late. Ironically, it was the tyranny of the English rulers that sowed the seeds of oneness in us, which ultimately gave rise to the feeling of nationalism.

The Western political thought, especially the French Revolution and its slogan 'Liberty, Equality, Fraternity', inspired the Indians with the idea of nationalism. Raja Rammohun Roy, Ishwar Chandra Vidyasagar, Swami Vivekananda and Swami Dayananda Saraswati, to name a few, worked with a crusading spirit to instil in the people of India love for liberty and equality.

Raja Rammohun Roy was born in 1776. In the declining years of his life, he chose to visit England where he died at Bristol in 1833. His passion for liberty was irresistible. When he was sailing to England in January 1831, he limped his way from his ship to a French vessel that was berthed along side in the Cape Town harbour just to greet the French flag. For him the French tricolour was not a mere National-flag of a country, but, the very symbol of the French Revolution viz., 'Liberty, Equality, Fraternity'. Seeing the flag, he exclaimed: "Glory, Glory, Glory!" In the French tricolour, the great nationalist saw the dream of India's independence.

Raja Rammohun Roy, the father of Indian Renaissance, was greatly inspired by the French tri-colour that stood for Liberty, Equality and Fraternity.

But, truly speaking, our national consciousness was still not powerful enough to express itself into a National-flag of our own, though there had been an abortive attempt to adopt one during our First War of Independence. Bahadur Shah Zafar had adopted the lotus flower and *chapatis* on a green-and-gold field as the symbols of revolt on his standard[1]. According to another, the 'revolt flag' of 1857 was dark green with a rising sun in gold as its device.

A scene of mutineers assembled outside the Lahori Gate of Delhi Red Fort during the Mutiny of 1857.

In fact, Bahadur Shah Zafar had set May 31, 1857 as the day of 'revolt', to make a simultaneous attack on the British by the common people, the rajas, nawabs, and all freedom lovers. Alas, an impatient patriot, Mangal Pandey, could not wait for May 31 to dawn, and triggered the revolt on March

---

1. Kazim Rizvi: *Bahadur Shah Zafar* (India's Freedom Fighters by DAVP)

29 itself. It spread like wild fire throughout the country. From Meerut, a big contingent reached Delhi on May 10, raising the slogan "Death to the British, Victory to Bahadur Shah Zafar!" On arrival in Delhi, they accorded a thirty-one gun salute to Bahadur Shah Zafar, called him *Shahensha-e-Hindustan* and hoisted the green-and-gold flag on the Red Fort[1].

Meerut mutineers had accepted the green-and-gold flag as the banner of 'Revolt'. The Rani of Jhansi fought under her Hanuman-banner and we have reason to believe that most of the other martyrs also fought under their respective flags. No wonder, due to the lack of united efforts, the First War of Independence was waged and lost in just a year's time.

Nevertheless, the war of 1857 intensified the spirit of nationalism in the people of India. Though the war was fought under several flags, there was one common Flag- song and that speaks volumes for the growing sense of nationalism. Its words were:

"Hindu, Mussalman, Sikh hamara
Bhai-bhai pyara
Yeh hai jhanda azadi ka
Ise salaam hamara".

The language and text of the song make it obvious that it refers to the green-and-gold flag of Bahadur Shah Zafar. But for these four lines, no other details about this song are available.

Though the revolt was crushed, it made the people realise the need for a National-flag as a rallying symbol to drive out the English. According to one account, an initiative in this direction was taken in 1883 with the setting up of an organisation in Lahore, called the Indian National Society, founded by Sirish Chandra Basu, who authored a book,

---

1. Kazim Rizvi: *Bahadur Shah Zafar* (India's Freedom Fighters by DAVP)

Indian National Songs and Lyrics, published in 1883 by N.R. Nund, Manager, National Book Society, Lahore. On the cover page of the book, a flag bearing the figure of the Sun was printed with the caption 'Our National Standard'. The aim of the society was to foster amity between the Hindus and the Muslims. The members of this society took out a procession daily through the streets of Lahore singing a song and holding the flag in their hands.[1] However, our political aspirations at that time would not have gone beyond the demand for self-government. Hence, this flag could not have been designed as the flag of Independent India.

The idea of a National-flag for the whole of India did not take deep roots in Indian minds nor was there any all-India political organisation to educate the generally uneducated masses of India. The Indian National Congress came into being on December 28, 1885. It was an all-India organisation that fought for and won independence for India, but, it had neither a flag of its own nor a national song at the time of its inception, and until August 6, 1931. For a long time after its birth, the Indian National Congress continued to function under the Union Jack. The endeavours made by Burjori Nawrosji, the Editor of the *Hindi Pumch*, in suggesting designs for a National-flag in his ingenious cartoons on the Indian National Congress were futile.

Sister Nivedita's flag

At the beginning of the twentieth century, with the rise of the Swadeshi Movement, the quest for a National-flag assumed greater urgency.

Sister Nivedita, an Irish disciple of Swami Vivekananda, was one of the first to conceive the idea of a National-flag

1. Dr Bhupendranath Dutt: *Bharter Dwitiya Swadhinta Sangram* (Bengali), pp. 231-32.

Sister Nivedita, an Irish lady, who was the first person to conceive, design and make a National-flag for the whole of India in 1905.

for India. In 1904, while on a visit to Bodh Gaya, in the company of J.C. Bose and Rabindranath Tagore, she saw the *vajra-chinha* for the first time and was instantly inspired. As per the Buddhist belief, *vajra* (thunderbolt) is the symbol for Lord Buddha and is also connected with the Goddess Durga. Being the sign of strength, it is the celebrated weapon of Lord Indra.

Having been inspired by the vajra-chinha, Sister Nivedita designed a National-flag for India. In a letter dated February 5, 1905 to her sister, Miss Macleod, she wrote:

"We have chosen a design for a National-flag, the thunderbolt, and have already made one. Unfortunately, I took the Chinese war-flag as my ideal and made it black on red. This does not appeal to the people of India, so the next design is to be yellow on scarlet."[1]

She got another flag made by her pupils in scarlet and yellow. It was displayed at the exhibition organised by the Congress in its annual session at Calcutta, in December 1906.[2]

Sister Nivedita's flag was square in shape, with a crimson red field. It had a hundred and eight *jyotis* all along the borders and a vajra in yellow at the centre, with *Vande* on the left and *Mataram* on the right in Bengali script. The legend *Vande Mataram* was also in yellow.

Although, many eminent persons, including Sir J.C. Bose, recognised this flag, it failed to catch the imagination of the people. In an article 'Vajra as a National-flag' written in November 1909 in the *Modern Review*, Sister Nivedita suggested a design for a National-flag in which the vajra and a lotus were included to symbolise the spiritual heritage of India. She wrote that red implied struggle for freedom, yellow meant victory, and the white lotus denoted purity.

The Calcutta flag

Lord Curzon was the Viceroy of India from 1898 to 1905 and he antagonised the Indians by promulgating many unpopular laws. His decision to partition Bengal in the name of better administration, when the nation was groaning under the havoc caused by famine, earthquake and the plague, was most unfortunate.

The scheme of partition was to merge the eastern districts of Dacca, Shahi and Chittagong with Assam and form a new province of 'East Bengal and Assam'. The rest of Bengal was to be joined to Orissa and the new Province was to be called 'Bengal'. By doing so, the British Government wanted to set

---

1. 3 *Pravrajiha Atmaprana,* "Sister Nivedita of Ramakrishna Vivekananda."
2. Ibid.

the Hindus against the Muslims, disunite the country and thereby crush the upsurge of nationalism that was slowly taking root in Indian soil. The English had very skilfully tried to play the game of 'divide and rule'. Lord Curzon himself wrote in February 1905:

"Calcutta is the centre from which the Congress party has manipulated throughout the whole of Bengal and indeed the whole of India. Any measure in consequence that would divide the Bengali-speaking population; that would not permit independent centres of activity and influence to grow up; that would dethrone Calcutta from its place as the centre of successful intrigue..........is intensely and hotly resented by them."

Though, the Congress saw through the British Government's intentions, it somehow believed that the authorities would never disregard the popular sentiments of the people by taking such a step. The Government, however, did not care for the public sentiments and announced that partition of Bengal would take effect from October 16, 1905. Perforce, the anti- partition movement was initiated on August 7, 1905. On that day, a massive demonstration was organised in the Town Hall of Calcutta. From this meeting, delegates dispersed to spread the movement to the rest of the province. The leaders of the protest movement declared October 16 to be a day of national mourning throughout Bengal. At the break of day, groups of men and women marched down the streets of Calcutta singing Vande Mataram, which overnight became the theme song of Bengal. All sections of people, zamindars, merchants, lawyers, students, the rich and the poor and even women, rose in spontaneous opposition to the partition of their province. They pledged to do their utmost to maintain the unity of Bengal.

On April 14, 1906 at Varisaal, Bengal, the British bureaucracy played havoc. In protest, people marched down the township holding flags with the words Vande Mataram inscribed in English or Bengali. No further details of those flags are available.

The Bengal leaders felt that mere demonstrations, public meetings and resolutions were not likely to have much effect on the Government. They, therefore, launched the Swadeshi Movement and resorted to a boycott of foreign goods. Shops selling foreign goods were picketed. Mass meetings were held all over Bengal where a pledge to use only Indian goods and boycott foreign goods was taken.

On August 7, 1906, the first anniversary of the anti-partition movement, a huge rally was organised at Parsi Bagan Square (Greer Park), renamed Sadhana Sarkar Udyan, in Calcutta. For the first time a tricolour flag was unfurled there. The moving spirit behind the design of this flag was Sachindra Prasad Bose, a close follower of Sir Surendranath Banerjea and the son-in-law of the moderate Brahmo leader, Krishna Kumar Mitra.

Surendranath Ghosh, in his biography of Sachindra Prasad Bose, wrote: "In 1906, on the advice of his friend, Sukumar Mitra (son of Krishna Kumar Mitra), he (Sachindra Prasad) pleaded with Sir Surendranath Banerjea for a National-flag and a Swadeshi Movement. Sir Surendranath gladly accepted the proposal. He said: 'Design a flag and show it to me'."

The flag they designed had three stripes – green, yellow and red. It had eight half open lotuses on the top green stripe; Vande Mataram in blue on the middle yellow stripe and the sun and moon (crescent) in white on the bottom red stripe.

They presented the flag to Sir Surendranath, who called a meeting for its approval. According to Sukumar Mitra, the meeting was held at the Indian Association Hall, Calcutta, and was attended by Sir Asutosh Chowdhary, Sir Abdul Halim Ghaznavi and leaders from all the districts of Bengal. Some of the elders suggested that the eight lotuses, representing the then eight provinces of the country be placed according to their respective location on the map of India, instead of showing all the eight in a row on the top green band of the flag[1]. However, Sir Surendranath Banerjea preferred the original design. The meeting, too,

Sir Surendranath Banerjea was the first Indian to have hoisted the first Indian tricolour, the Calcutta-flag, on August 7, 1906 in Calcutta at Parsi Bagan Square.

1. Surendranath Ghosh: *Biography of Sachindra Prasad Bose*, pp. 32-33.

approved it unanimously.

On August 7, 1906, this flag was hoisted at the Parsi Bagan Square (Greer Park)[1] at 294/2, Acharya Prafulla Chandra Road, for the first time. The day was observed as Boycott Day to protest against the partition of Bengal. Narendranath Sen ceremonially consecrated the flag and sang a song. Bhupendranath Dutt (younger brother of Swami Vivekananda and the Editor of the *Yugantar*) handed it over to Sir Surendranath Banerjea, who hoisted it to the bursting of a hundred and one crackers[2].

The following day, the ceremony was widely reported in the newspapers, especially in the *Yugantar, Sanjivani,* and *Vande Mataram.* The *Yugantar* was the only newspaper to greet the new flag. Some people in the country decried the move for a National-flag. For moderates, like Surendranath Banerjea, Ghaznavi and Asutosh Chowdhary, the flag was a symbol of the country's aspirations for Home Rule, but, the young revolutionaries, such as Sukumar Mitra, Bhupendranath and Sudhir Banerjee, saw in it a dream of an Indian revolution. Later, the flag was hoisted on the rostrum of the 1906 session of the Indian National Congress held at Calcutta, on December 26, under the presidentship of Dadabhai Naoroji. The badges of more than 1,600 delegates who attended the session, too, had the same tricolour design.

The Lieutenant Governor of East Bengal, Mr Fuller, summoned the leaders and warned them that if they did not call off the agitation demanding the annulment of the partition, he would use the Gurkha troops to put it down. To add fuel to the fire, he banned the singing of Vande

---

1. The place has so far been described as Green Park instead of Greer Park.
2. Surendranath Ghosh: *Biography of Sachindra Prasad Bose,* pp. 32-33.

Mataram. These threats, instead of cooling the agitation, intensified it. The skies of Bengal resounded with the strains of Vande Mataram and the people boldly carried the flag aloft. The Government resorted to *lathis* and bullets, but to no avail. The song of freedom, *Vande Mataram*, could not be silenced, nor could the flag of independence be pulled down.

The movement soon transcended the boundaries of Bengal. The militant nationalists used it to arouse the people politically and gave the country a slogan of independence from foreign rule. The question of partition of Bengal became a secondary one and the question of India's freedom became the main theme of Indian politics. Krishna Kumar Mitra, a popular leader of Bengal, said: "Let us all, in the name of the motherland and for her good, take a pledge that whatever be the inconvenience, so long as swadeshi goods are available, we shall never buy foreign goods". The boycott of British goods became a passion of all ranks. Even young children joined the movement. And finally, the Government had to yield. In 1911-12, when King George V and Queen Mary visited India to attend the Delhi Durbar, the partition of Bengal was annulled.

Sukumar Mitra, one of the chief designers of the flag, died at the age of eighty-nine. Dr Bhupendranath Dutt, in his book *Bharter Dwitiya Swadhinta Sangram,* published in 1922, wrote: "When I went to him a few months before his death, he still had a clear memory of the flag. He said that those who had designed the flag had been inspired by the flag of the French Revolution and that is why they had made it a tricolour. The flag that he had made with his hands had eight lotuses. There was some confusion about the number of lotuses in the flag. Some people believe that there were only seven. The *Sanjivani*, however, confirms that there were eight lotuses on the top green stripe, as was stated by

Sukumar Mitra in his interview, representing the then eight Indian provinces, the yellow stripe in the middle had Vande Mataram in blue inscribed on it, and the red stripe at the bottom had the sun and the moon, as symbols of the Hindu and Muslim communities." The moon or the crescent had no star atop.

During the interview, Sukumar Mitra told Dr Bhupendarnath Dutt: "This flag gave strength to people during the Bengal agitation and was liberally carried in demonstrations through the streets of Calcutta till 1912. After the annulment of the partition of Bengal, the flag gradually receded into the pages of history as though it was born only to forge people during their fight for the reunion of Bengal."

However, the urge to have a National-flag had gripped the Indian mind, not only at home, but, elsewhere too. Some of the brilliant students studying in Europe felt humiliated when asked by their fellow students about their National-flag. A few of them intently thought of designing one. Veer Savarkar was one of them. He is said to have even designed a flag in which he had used saffron, white and green colours.

8

Madame Cama and the National-flag

In the history of India's National-flag, the name of Madame Bhikhaiji Rustom Cama is inscribed in gold. She was one of those soldiers in our fight for freedom who strengthened the movement from abroad. She was the first Indian to have raised an Indian flag on foreign soil and announced to the world about our political fight with the British for the country's Independence.

According to a secret history sheet on Madame Bhikhaiji Rustom K. R. Cama,[1] maintained by the Criminal Intelligence Office of the British Government (the original report is in the National Archives of India, New Delhi), on August 22, 1907, in the presence of a thousand delegates from different countries who had gathered at Stuttgart, Germany, for the Second International Socialist Congress, a lovely, fair skinned lady, with large dark eyes, dressed in a sari with an exquisite

---

1. Appendix 1.

border of delicate embroidery, made a fiery, eloquent speech that kept her audience spellbound. At the close of her emotion-laden speech, she unfurled a tricolour in green, gold and red, with a dramatic gesture. Waving the flag, she passionately declaimed:

> "This is the flag of Indian Independence. Behold, it is born. It is already sanctioned by the blood of martyred Indian youths. I call upon you gentlemen, to rise and salute this flag of Indian Independence. In the name of this flag, I appeal to lovers of freedom, all over the world, to cooperate with this flag in freeing one-fifth of the human race."[1]

Madame Cama was the first person to unfurl India's flag at an international forum. The flag that she unfurled on August 22, 1907 had three broad bands. The top one was green, the colour of the Muslims; the middle was a golden saffron, the colour close to the heart of both the Buddhists and Sikhs; and the bottom band was in red, the sacred colour of the Hindus. There were eight lotuses in a line representing the eight provinces of British India. On the middle golden band, Vande Mataram was inscribed in *Devnagari* script. However, it was spelt differently as वन्देमातरं. From a photograph showing Madame Cama displaying her flag, it appears that the lotuses were perhaps embroidered. Maybe Madame Cama herself did the embroidery since Parsi ladies are believed to be good at embroidery. On the bottom red stripe, there was a figure of the sun towards the fly and a crescent towards the hoist of the flag.[2] There was no star atop the crescent on the flag and drawings of her flag with a star above the crescent are incorrect.

---

1. Published by the Secretariat of Bureau of the Socialist International, Brussels.
2. Emily Brown: Har Dayal, p.68.

Madame Cama, the first Indian lady to have raised an Indian National-flag on foreign soil at Stuttgart, Germany, on August 22, 1907.

Madame Cama's flag was carefully conceived and, in all probability, was jointly designed by her and her close associates, Veer Savarkar and Shyamji Krishna Varma. The flag was made by Hem Chandra Das (Kanungo), a young revolutionary from

Bengal, who was later convicted and jailed in the Andamans. He was a good photographer, singer, hunter, mechanic, chemist and an able artist in Western style. He was born in a village of District Midnapur and received his revolutionary training from Aurobindo. He sold his land and property and went to Paris to join and teach the art of bomb making.

This fact is corroborated by the leaflet titled, *A Message to the People of India* (*The Vande Mataram*, 1908), in which Madame Cama had stated:

> "This flag of Vande Mataram, which I wave before you was made for me by a noble, selfless, young patriot, who is standing at the bar of the so-called court of justice in our country."

Hem Chandra Das Kanungo in his book, *Banglay Biplab Pracheshta*, also confirms that he had made the flag in Paris for Madame Cama and gave it to her when she was leaving Paris to attend the Stuttgart Congress.

The study of the British Intelligence Report on Madame Cama suggests that she used several flags in her lifetime with different legends, emblems, and devices. But whatever be the form and size of her flags, she had made it a practice after unfurling the Stuttgart flag in August 1907, to address an audience only after displaying her flag on the wall behind her or on the rostrum. She also had a picture of her flag on the cover of her journal *The Talwar*.

Eight to ten weeks after her triumph at Stuttgart, Madame Cama went on a tour of America to create awareness of India's plight and to provide impetus to the Indian National Movement in that country. She toured the whole country and wherever she went, her flag went with her.

On November 24, 1908, while making a speech at a Sunday meeting at India House, London, she displayed a flag woven in silk and gold with the inscription, "In memory of the martyrs of 1908". On December 19, 1908, she attended a lecture on "Indian Nationalism" delivered by B.C. Pal. At the conclusion of his speech, she stood up and waved two flags in the air and demanded a hearing.[1]

Madame Cama's passion for the National-flag and the variations she made in the original Stuttgart flag to suit the occasion are evident from the report of the other meetings she attended.

On December 29, 1908, a historic meeting was held at the Caxton Hall, Westminster, to celebrate the birth anniversary of Guru Gobind Singh. It was attended by V.D. Savarkar, Lala Lajpat Rai, B.C. Pal and other revolutionaries. Savarkar spoke of Guru Gobind Singh's bold resistance to alien domination. There is a monumental souvenir and a precious record of the occasion in the form of a group photograph taken on the *Guru Parva*. This photograph is currently preserved in the British Museum Newspaper Library. It shows, among others, Bipin Chandra Pal in the centre, Madame Cama to his left, and Lala Lajpat Rai to her left. What deserves special attention is that in the background there is a big banner with the legend 'Indian Freedom' with eight stars (not lotuses) on the top green stripe denoting the then eight Indian provinces, and the sun for the Hindus and the crescent for the Muslims in the lower stripe, seen fluttering on either side of the dais. (It is possible that this particular flag was made and displayed by the organisers of the Guru Parva, who, instead of lotuses, mistakenly showed stars on the flag).

At the meeting of the London Indian Society held on February 20, 1909 at Essex Hall, Strand, Madame Cama also

---

1. Appendix 1

spoke and before commencing her speech, she displayed a silk flag on which were inscribed the words Swadeshi and Vande Mataram[1].

Madame Cama was in contact, through correspondence, with the famous Russian writer Maxim Gorky. Besides writing to him, she sent him some Indian Revolutionary literature. The letters Madame Cama wrote to Gorky are preserved in the archives of the great Russian writer along with her photograph which shows her next to an unfurled Indian flag.

Our tribute to Madame Cama, in the evolution of the Indian National-flag, would be incomplete without tracing the subsequent history of the original flag unfurled by Madame Cama at Stuttgart. According to the facts available, Madame Cama, before finally returning to India in December 1935, had an attack of paralysis. As a result, she had become physically very weak. Even her eyesight was fading. She knew her end was coming near. But, the flag had to be kept flying. The struggle had to continue. She called one of her associates, Madhav Rao, to her bedside, in Paris, and handed over her precious flag to him. In December 1935, she returned to India after thirty-three years of exile and, on August 16, 1936, she died quietly in Bombay, unwept and unsung.

According to Dr Minocher K. Contractor, the flag which Madame Cama handed over to Madhav Rao before leaving Paris for Bombay, was smuggled into India along with other records of the revolutionary patriots, by the well-known Gujarati Socialist leader, Indulal Yajnik, and kept in a secret place in Bombay. When he was in Yervada Jail, Poona, in 1937, he took the opportunity to invite G.V. Ketkar, the

---

1. Sethna K.A. *Madame B.R. Cama*, p. 80.

Veer Savarkar hoisting a flag on the Vande-Mataram Day, on October 26, 1937.

grandson of Lokmanya Tilak and former Editor of *Kesari*, and gave him a scrap of paper. With the help of that paper, Mr Ketkar could obtain a bundle of important papers and documents, together with records of the revolutionaries. The bundle also contained Madame Cama's original flag. Veer Savarkar publicly unveiled it in Poona on October 26, 1937. The day was observed as Vande-Mataram Day. It was later neatly mounted on an ornamental frame and taken out in a procession in Poona. Today, this flag, duly framed in a silver frame, is hung in the library hall of the Kesari-Mahratta Trust in Pune.[1]

There is a close similarity between the Calcutta flag and Madame Cama's flag. Is such a striking similarity a rare coincidence or is it due to certain lesser-known facts, which hitherto had not surfaced?

An in-depth analysis of the facts indicates that Madame Cama was inspired by the Calcutta flag, which was hoisted on August 7, 1906, more than a year before she unfurled her flag at Stuttgart on August 22, 1907. Both had eight lotuses in white on the top green band. Both had Vande Mataram in the centre on the middle yellow or saffron band. However, the Calcutta flag had the words in dark blue, whereas Madame Cama's flag had the same in white. Another difference between the two flags is the difference in the spelling of the word Vande Mataram. On the Calcutta flag it is inscribed as (वन्देमातरम्), whereas in Madame Cama's flag it is spelt as (वन्देमातरं). The bottom band on both flags bears figures of the sun and the moon. The variance in spelling of the words Vande Mataram seems to be because of the fact that Madame Cama's flag was designed by Hem Chandra Das Kanungo, a

---

1. Sethna K.A., *Madame B.R. Cama*, p. 73.

Bengali revolutionary and the Bengali influence is evident in the spelling. Instead of writing the words as रम् he has written them as रं.

Madame Cama's speeches, at Stuttgart and after, bear ample evidence that she was influenced by the Calcutta flag in conceiving and designing her flag. In a speech on August 22, 1907, after unfurling her flag at Stuttgart, she observed:

> "This flag is of Indian Independence. Behold, it is born. It is already sanctioned by the blood of martyred Indian youths".

In 1907, the Bengal agitation was in full swing and Indian youths were in the forefront of the movement. So her reference to the martyred Indian youths obviously refers to the Bengal youths. In one of her other speeches, she said: "this is the flag for which Khudiram and Prafulla Chaki died".

With this hypothesis, another question springs to mind, 'if she did not independently design her flag, how did she lay her hands on the Calcutta flag?' Dr. Bhupendranath Dutt in his Bengali book, *Bharter Dwitiya Swadhinta Sangram* (p. 155), writes:

> "Khasi Rao, the revolutionary brother of Madhav Rao, a General in the army of Baroda State, had gone to Switzerland for military training. He had carried with him a small replica of the Calcutta flag. In Geneva he met the Bengali revolutionary, Hem Chandra Kanungo".

This meeting explains how the Calcutta flag reached Madame Cama through Hem Chandra and how she designed her own flag in consultation with her associates, in particular Shyamji Krishna Varma.

The Berlin Committee flag

The story of the development of the Indian National-flag on foreign soil does not end with Madame Cama. Soon after the outbreak of World War I, the Indian Independence Committee, set up by the Indian revolutionaries in Berlin (better known as the Berlin Committee), adopted Madame Cama's tricolour as their flag with some modifications. Dr Bhupendranath Dutt, in his *Bharter Dwitiya Swadhinta Sangram,* writes:

"After travelling in disguise through many countries, I (the author) reached Berlin in the summer of 1915. There I saw a flag in the office of the Berlin Committee. It was a plain tricolour with the same colour scheme as that of Madame Cama's flag minus the legend and the motifs. I asked Virendranath Chattopadhyay, a member of the Committee, 'Why have the sun and the moon, and the legend been renounced?' Virendranath replied, 'Well, those objects were the creations of Madame Cama, and we have simply dispensed with them'."

This flag, however, was not freely used in public, in Germany, at that time. But, it was openly used in Mesopotamia by the volunteer force, organised by the Berlin Committee with the help of Indian prisoners and deserters from the British Indian Army and some Ghader revolutionaries.

In 1948, Kartaramji, a former member of the Berlin Committee, told a journalist in Jamshedpur that he still had the Berlin Committee flag with him. Though he is no longer alive, the flag might still be lying uncared for with any of his relatives or may have been destroyed with time.

The Ghader Party flag

The Ghader Party, formed in the U.S.A., also adopted the tricolour as the National-flag. The top stripe was green, followed by yellow and red, and had an emblem of crossed swords at the centre. In the early years of the freedom struggle, the tricolour was widely used by Indian revolutionaries in the U.S.A., Germany and Mesopotamia.

The Spiritual flag of India

Before turning spiritual, Aurobindo was an active revolutionary during the Indian freedom struggle. A young Aurobindo Ghosh wielded the Swaraj flag while fighting the British Raj, but later, on becoming Sri Aurobindo, he developed a new flag called the Spiritual flag of United India. The flag is still in use by the Sri Aurobindo Society at Pondicherry and its branches across the country. Its square form, colour and other details of design have a symbolic meaning. It was first hoisted in Pondicherry on August 15, 1947 and re-hoisted there in a befitting ceremony on November 1, 1954, when Pondicherry was united with the Indian Union.

The flag represents the symbol of a full-blown, golden lotus at the centre of a silver-blue square. The petals are arranged in two rows – four petals on the inside and twelve outside. The blue represents the spirit, the gold is the colour of the Supreme Mother, and the red, surrounding the flag, signifies physical consciousness.

9

First Flag of the Freedom Movement

While Great Britain was engaged in the First World War, Indian leaders like Tilak and Annie Besant decided to give impetus to the National Movement – Swaraj. The Englishmen did not relish the word Swaraj and considered its utterance as 'seditious and dangerous'. Tilak, to avoid resistance from the government, decided to use Home Rule, in place of Swaraj, as the goal of the movement. On April 28, 1916 the Indian Home Rule League was set up under the leadership of Tilak with its headquarters at Pune. And a similar Home Rule League was founded by Mrs Annie Besant on September 15, 1916 with its headquarters at Adyar, near Madras.

After the annulment of the partition of Bengal by King George V at the Delhi Durbar in 1912, the Calcutta flag had gradually gone into disuse. The political arena at home was now without a flag. When political activities once again gathered momentum during World War I, the need for a flag symbolising the new political ideology and aspirations was felt. In 1917, some Congressmen tried hard to get the Congress to take up the question of a National-flag[1], but the response was lukewarm.

However, the Central Committee of the Home Rule League, under Mrs Annie Besant, appointed a committee of experts, including Rabindranath Tagore, to design a flag which would symbolise the then prevailing political aspirations of the people. The deliberations of the Committee were, however, abortive[2].

Mrs Annie Besant, who hoisted and saluted the Home Rule League`s Flag at Ollcott Cottage, Coimbatore, in July 1917.

---

1. The Bombay Chronicle, July 9, 1923.
2. Ibid.

The Home Rule flag

From 1917 onwards, the struggle for India's freedom made considerable headway. The Home Rule League became popular and broke fresh ground even in small towns that hitherto had little or no political consciousness. Bal Gangadhar Tilak and Mrs Annie Besant, the two pivots of the movement, designed a new flag. It comprised five red and four green horizontal stripes arranged alternately, with seven stars denoting the *saptarishi* configuration. On the left upper quadrant, towards the hoist, it had the Union Jack, and on the upper right quadrant, towards the flag's fly, there was a crescent and a star[1]. The red colour in the flag denoted the Hindus and the green, the Muslims. It is believed that the flag was conceived by Dvijendranath Thakur and was hoisted for the first time at the 1917 Congress session held in Calcutta, under the presidentship of Mrs Annie Besant[2].

The Home Rule Flag became quite popular amongst the extremists. The British Government strongly disapproved of it because it served as a rallying point for political workers, whom the Government considered seditious and anti-British. Lokmanya Tilak and Mrs Annie Besant were branded as arch-enemies of the Government.

During her internment, in July 1917, in Ollcott Cottage in Coimbatore, Mrs Annie Besant had hoisted the red and green flag on a forty-eight foot high pole and saluted it as the symbol of India's freedom. The Madras Government warned her and asked her to bring it down. However, the Government of India took a liberal view of the situation and, in pursuance of an outwardly tolerant policy, asked the Madras

---

1. *Our Flag*, Publications Division, Ministry of Information and Broadcasting, Government of India, pp. 1-2.
2. *Flag and Freedom* (Documentary Film), Films Division, Ministry of Information and Broadcasting, Governmnt of India.

Government either to postpone or quash the court proceedings against the Home Rule Flag.

During 1917-18, the Home Rule flag was hoisted at a number of places. At Gaya, Durga Prasad, the Honorary Secretary of the Local Home Rule League, flew the flag on his house continuously for three months and even carried it in a procession in the city. The Government of India went into the Gaya incident thoroughly and concluded that, since public feelings did not appear to have been influenced by the flag, it would be better not to take any action against Durga Prasad. The Government feared that taking cognisance of the incident would make an obscure mofussil lawyer a 'national hero'.

The inclusion of the Union Jack in the flag expressed political compromise, as it meant self-government within the British empire and acceptance of the Montague-Chelmsford reforms. This made the flag unacceptable to the masses. The goal of the Home Rule Movement was dominion status only. It did not agitate for complete independence. Because of its limited goals, the movement did not become widely popular. Gradually it died out and the flag became a part of history.

The political situation in the country called for a new leader and brought Mohandas Karamchand Gandhi to the forefront of the Indian National Movement. And with him, a new era dawned on the political horizon of India.

The First Flag of the Freedom Movement

In about 1916, Pingley Venkayya, an Andhra youth from Masulipatnam, was in his own humble way trying to devise a common National-flag for the whole of India. His efforts got fresh impetus when Umar Sobani and S.B. Bomanji, of Bombay, in collaboration with him started the Indian National-flag Mission, with branches in many parts of the country[1].

---

1. "Sri Pingley Venkayya" by P. Rajeshwara Rao in Triveni, Vol. XXXVIII, No. 3 P.94.

Pingley Venkayya, who was greatly enthused about designing a flag for the whole of India. Finally, he designed the first ever Charkha-Jhanda in white, green and red as per the instructions of Gandhiji in 1921.

Pingley Venkayya's passion for a National-flag encouraged him to write a book, titled *A National-flag for India*, which was published with a foreword by Sir B.N. Sharma, a member of the Indian Legislative Council. The expenses for printing and publishing the book were borne by Sir C.P. Ramaswami Aiyar[1]. Venkayya offered several designs for an Indian National-flag and placed them at every session of the Congress for four consecutive years before 1921.

When Gandhiji came to be the accepted leader of the national movement, Venkayya tried to get him interested in his mission. He even suggested a flag design for India, after researching into about thirty kinds of flags from all over the world, but, it did not appeal to Gandhiji. The latter was not indifferent to the need of a National-flag, but, he saw little in Venkayya's design that could stir the entire nation to its depths. The flags designed and exhibited before 1921 generally did not catch the fancy of the Indian masses and soon went into disuse. Once, during a discussion with Gandhiji, Lala Hans Raj, Raizada, of Jullundur, suggested that the charkha should find a place on the Indian National-flag symbolising progress, self-reliance[2] and the common man. The originality of the idea fascinated Gandhiji. He saw in the charkha an embodiment of India and redemption of all its ills. Gandhiji summoned Venkayya to the meeting of the All India Congress Committee at Bezwada (now Vijayawada) on April 01, 1921, and asked him to give a design for a National-flag with a charkha on red (denoting Hindus) and green (for Muslims) background.

Within three hours, Venkayya, prepared a flag and placed it in the hands of Gandhiji. It had two equal bands of red

---

1 "Sri Pingley Venkayya" by P. Rajeshwara Rao in Triveni, Vol. XXXVIII, No. 3 P.94.
2. "The National Flag" by M.K. Gandhi, *Young India*, April 13, 1921.

Raizada Hans Raj of Jullundur, Punjab, who suggested in 1921 the inclusion of the Charkha on the Congress-flag to represent the common man of India. Gandhi decided on the colours – white, green and red – and the order in which they would appear.

and green, with a large charkha covering both the bands. However, it could not be presented to the Congress Committee for approval as Gandhiji received it a little late. In a way, the delay was a blessing in disguise. A bi-colour flag would have created its own problems, as it would not have represented the minorities in its design.

On mature consideration, Gandhiji realised that the National-flag should have three colours, representing the

Hindus, Muslims and other religions. Left to him, he would have preferred a uni-colour flag, symbolising unity of the nation, but, he was swayed by the contingencies of the then prevailing political conditions of the country. The three colours he conceived for the National-flag of India were white, green and red, in that order.

Having evolved the philosophy behind the flag of India and having made up his mind about its design, Gandhiji summoned Venkayya again and advised him to add a band of white to the earlier flag. He also instructed him to place the white band on the top, the green band in the middle and red at the bottom with a charkha in the centre covering all the bands. Venkayya made the flag according to the wishes of Gandhiji. Thus was born the first flag of the All India Congress, nay, the flag of the freedom movement, nay, the flag of India. This flag was later referred to by several names including the Swaraj flag, the Gandhi flag, the Charkha flag and the Congress flag.

By giving colour representation to various religious groups in the National-flag, Gandhiji was not creating a division amongst them. In fact, he wished to bridge the gulf that had existed between them for centuries. He had recognised the separate identity of each community without impairing the fundamental unity of the country. For the first time in its long history, India had a flag for which a Hindu, Sikh, Muslim, Christian and Parsi would be willing to lay down his life. To quote Gandhiji's words:

"On maturer consideration, I saw that the background should represent the other religions also. Hindu-Muslim unity is not an exclusive term; it is an inclusive term, symbolic of the unity of all faiths domiciled in India. If Hindus and Muslims can tolerate each other, they are together bound to tolerate all other faiths.

The unity is not a menace to the other faiths represented in India or to the world. So I suggest that the background should be white, green and red."[1]

The arrangement of the colours was also meaningful. According to Gandhiji:

"The weakest numerically occupy the first place, the Islamic colour (green) comes next, the Hindu colour (red) comes last, the idea being that the strongest should act as a shield to the weakest"[2].

Each colour was given an equal size. Its significance was "to represent the equality of the least of us with the best, an equal part is assigned to all the three colours in the design."[3]

The National-flag was to have a full size charkha on it. The charkha spoke for itself; its disappearance had brought poverty, misery and unhappiness to India, and it was hoped that it would bring back her lost happiness and affluence. Gandhiji said:

"But India as a nation can live and die only for the spinning wheel..... No industrial development schemes can solve the problem of the growing poverty of the peasantry of India ..... India is not a small island, it is a big continent which cannot be converted, like England, into an industrial country. And we must resolutely set our face against any scheme of exploitation of the world. Our only hope must centre upon utilising the wasted hours of the nation, for adding to the wealth of the country, by converting cotton into cloth in our cottages.... It follows that the

---

1. "The National-Flag" by M.K. Gandhi, *Young India*, April 13, 1921.
2. Ibid.
3. Ibid.

flag must be made of khaddar, for it is through coarse cloth alone that we can make India independent of foreign markets for the cloth."[1]

The *Deshabhimani* of Guntur explained the significance of the charkha in an article as follows:

"Mr Gandhi has given in *'Young India'* what shape the Indian National-flag should take. On the flag there will appear the picture of a spinning wheel. In the war of peace, the spinning wheel serves the purpose of *Sudarshana-chakra* (Lord Vishnu's weapon) to destroy the wicked. The guns throw shells and destroy men. They commit horrible deeds and are a source of sin. The weapon of the spinning wheel attacks the English who are thousands of miles off and will put out their pride, arrogance and greed. In short, it will destroy their bad qualities and will teach them to depend on self-help. Now being accustomed to appropriate money from India, they have ceased to depend on themselves, and are eager to plunder India. If we establish spinning wheels and stop the annual flow to them of 60 crores of rupees, their pride will be put down and they will prostrate themselves. This confirms that the spinning wheel is the best means to secure for India economic independence and complete Swaraj."[2]

Although, Gandhiji's flag had not been accepted by a formal resolution of the All India Congress Committee, its

1. "The National-Flag" by M.K. Gandhi, *Young India*, April 13, 1921.
2. Venkatarangaiya, Prof. M: *The Freedom Struggle in Andhra Pradesh*, Vol. III (1921-1931) and A History of the *Freedom Struggle in Andhra Pradesh*, pp. 170-71.

approval by Gandhiji made it acceptable to all and was hoisted at all functions of the Congress. With frequent usage and passage of time, it became synonymous with the Congress and was referred to as the National-flag.

In 1921, this large sized charkha flag was hoisted, for the first time, at the annual session of the All India Congress Committee held at Ahmedabad. Thereafter, it became on its own strength, without any official sanction of a resolution, the National-flag of India. This was the flag that was unfurled on the midnight of December 31, 1929, on the banks of the Ravi at the Lahore session of the Congress. This session had declared *Purna Swaraj* as the goal of the Congress. On January 26, 1930, this was the flag under whose shadow, thousands of Indians took a solemn pledge that it was a crime against man and God to submit to the British rule, and this ultimately found expression in the famous Dandi March. The breaking of salt laws at Dandi shook the British Government and, to stall the movement, it arrested all the prominent Congress leaders.

With the Non-Cooperation Movement, the charkha flag gradually gained popularity. People all over the country fondly carried it in processions and proudly displayed it over Party buildings. It gave Indians the strength to withstand British oppression. With its help, the national movement reached the remotest corner of India. The Indian people lost their sense of fear. The brute force of British power in India no longer frightened them. The growing popularity of the flag began to cause concern to the authorities and they tried to prohibit its use and even forcibly pull it down on several occasions. Two instances are worth mentioning here. Once, when the flag was flying over the Congress office at Pagoda Street in Cocanada (present Kakinada in Andhra Pradesh), the District Magistrate, G.T. Bracker, who passed by that way with some Europeans noticed it. He stopped and asked the

From under the Charkha-flag, Gandhiji issued a call for nationwide protest against the Rowlatt Bill.

Congress workers present there to bring the flag down, failing which he threatened to use force. Mosala Kanti Thirumal Rao, a local Congress worker, refused to obey the order since the flag had been hoisted under the Party's instructions. The District Magistrate then called the Deputy Superintendent of Police and ordered him to forcibly pull down the flag.

In February 1923, a similar instance took place at Bhagalpur in Bihar. At an industrial exhibition held there, one of the stalls had hoisted the tricolour. Mr B.C. Sen, the Divisional Commissioner of Bhagalpur, objected to it. The non-cooperators took a firm stand and refused to pull it down. To avoid an untoward situation, a compromise was arrived at between the organisers of the exhibition and the non-cooperators. It was agreed to fly the Union Jack and the tricolour side by side and the former a little higher.

The Government of Bihar did not appreciate the idea. The Superintendent of Police of Bhagalpur, who was an

Englishman, wrote in his confidential diary: "The whole business had been a most disagreeable one, and the European community strongly resent the compromise".

Mr B.C. Sen, the Divisional Commissioner, was severely reprimanded by the Governor of Bihar for coming to terms with the Congressmen. The former had to tender an apology. The matter did not end there. It went up to the Secretary of State for India, in London, as the issue was raised in the British Parliament. The British Government in London accepted the apology of the Bihar and Orissa Government in this regard, but issued a warning. "They desire to make it clear that in no circumstances should the swaraj or Gandhi flag be flown in conjunction with, or even below, the Union Jack".

In fact, after 1921, the Government had become more hostile towards the use of the National-flag, but could not openly object to it. However, they objected to its use on grounds of 'public peace and public order' and looked upon the charkha flag as a 'revolutionary symbol'. In its popularity, they foresaw a danger to their imperialist interests.

10

The Jhanda Andolan, 1923

The year 1923 is very significant in the history of our National-flag. That year, an incident took place that stirred the entire nation. It had its beginning at the Lucknow session of the A.I.C.C., in June 1922, with the appointment of a Civil Disobedience Enquiry Committee, comprising Hakim Ajmal Khan, Motilal Nehru, Vithalbhai Patel, Dr M.A. Ansari, C. Rajagopalachari, Jamnalal Bajaj and Seth Chhotani, to enquire into the prospects of launching a nationwide Civil Disobedience Movement. Hakim Ajmal Khan was its President and the Committee toured the whole country.

On July 10, 1922, during the course of their tour, the Committee reached Jabalpur and was accorded a civic reception. The swaraj flag was hoisted on the Town Hall on the occasion[1]. Hoisting of the flag on a public building and presenting a civic address to a Committee of the A.I.C.C. caused consternation in England. Raising the issue in the

---

1. "Rashtriya Jhanda Andolan" by Mukut Bihari Verma, *Prabha*, August 1923, p. 126.

House of Commons, Col. Yate asked: "The Jabalpur Municipality hoisted a 'Revolutionary Flag'. What action had been taken by the Government of India in this regard?" In reply, Col. Yate was assured that such incidents would not be allowed to recur[1].

The Civil Disobedience Enquiry Committee submitted its report in October 1922. It recommended that the country was not ready to embark upon a general mass civil disobedience and that the Congress should seek election to the Councils to obstruct their functioning from within. Motilal Nehru, Hakim Ajmal Khan and Vithalbhai Patel accepted the recommendations of the Enquiry Committee but the other members opposed them. On the recommendations of the committee, in December 1922, the Indian National Congress split up into two factions, viz., the 'No-Changers' and the 'Pro-Changers' at Gaya. The 'Pro-Changers', led by C.R. Das and Motilal Nehru, had no faith in Gandhiji's programme of non-cooperation and insisted on a change in the Congress strategy. They also wanted to contest the Legislative Council elections and non-cooperate from within. On the other hand, the 'No-Changers', headed by C. Rajagopalachari, did not approve of any change in the Gandhian policy of non-cooperation and were opposed to contesting the elections. The 'Pro-Changers' lost by 1,970 to 894 votes[2]. Consequently, on January 1, 1923, C.R. Das resigned from the Presidentship and formed the Swaraj Party.

The Congress remained in the hands of the 'No-Changers'. At this meeting, it was decided to collect twenty-five lakh rupees and enrol fifty thousand volunteers by April

1. "Rashtriya Jhanda Andolan" by Mukut Bihari Verma, *Prabha*, August 1923, p. 126.
2. Rajendra Prasad: Autobiography (Bombay, Asia publishing House, 1957.), p. 189.

30, 1923. For this purpose, a deputation comprising Rajaji, Dr Rajendra Prasad, Seth Jamnalal Bajaj and Devdas Gandhi toured the country. It was to reach Jabalpur on March 11, 1923. The members of the Jabalpur Municipal Committee sought the Deputy Commissioner's permission to hoist the National-flag on the Municipal building (now Gandhi Bhawan) in honour of the deputation. The permission was refused. The refusal became a prestige issue for the Municipal Councillors and, in due course of time, rocked the country for the next five months up to August 18, 1923. The elected members of the Municipal Committee resigned in protest and decided to fight the Government on the issue of the National-flag.

The Deputy Commissioner cordoned off the Town Hall on March 11 in order to make it impossible for the Municipal Councillors to hold the civic function. To avoid a nasty situation, the Congress held the reception at Tilak Bhoomi. Rajaji and Dr Rajendra Prasad in their addresses exhorted the people to safeguard the honour of the National-flag and to prepare themselves for a prolonged satyagraha. Pandit Sunderlal, President of the Central Provinces (Hindi) Congress Committee, assured the delegation that Jabalpur and the Central Provinces were ready to make any sacrifice to redeem the honour of the National-flag. He publicly announced his decision to fast till Jabalpur enrolled two thousand satyagrahis and collected five thousand rupees in accordance with the decision taken during the Gaya Session in December 1922. The vow of Pandit Sunderlal alarmed the local Congressmen and immediate efforts were made to fulfil his pledge. The whole of Jabalpur was stirred up and this was the beginning of the flag satyagraha.

On March 18, 1922, Gandhiji was sentenced to six-years' imprisonment for seditious writing in *Young India.* On the first anniversary of his conviction, the members hoisted the swaraj-flag at the Town Hall. The flag was hoisted by Subhadra Kumari Chauhan and the city Congress took out a big flag procession from Tilak Bhoomi to the Civil Lines via Omati Bridge. At the Omati Bridge Clock Tower, the Assistant Superintendent of Police stopped the procession from entering the Civil Lines and served the following order on Sunderlal, Nathuram Modi and the other organisers:

> "Whereas it has been brought to my notice that a procession is being taken to the Civil Lines and Cantonment by you, Messers Nathuram Modi, Sunderlal and others, I hereby direct, under Section 30 of the Police Act, that no procession shall be taken to the Civil lines and the Cantonment without obtaining a licence".

Sunderlal and Nathuram offered to take the licence on 'terms commensurate with the dignity and honour of the citizens and of the National-flag'. They also gave an assurance that they would commit no breach of public peace. But it was of no avail. According to an eyewitness, the following conversation took place between Sunderlal, the leader of the procession, and the Assistant Superintendent of Police.

> A.S.P.: *I can give you the licence, but a procession of ten thousand of people will disturb the peace of the inhabitants of the Civil Lines.*
> Sunderlal: *Only ten persons will go in procession.*
> A.S.P.: *But ten persons can also disturb the peace.*
> Sunderlal: *All the ten will go with cloth tied on their mouths.*
> A.S.P.: *But they will go with the tricolour flag.*
> Sunderlal: *Surely, they will go with the tricolour flag.*
> A.S.P.: *Listen, we may plainly tell you that we have no*

objection even if you take these thousands of people shouting slogans, but in no case permission would be given to carry the flag in the procession.

Sunderlal: *Then listen, we also want to tell you plainly that only one man would go with cloth tied on his mouth, but he would have the flag in his hand.*

And that ended the matter. After the failure of the talks, Sunderlal made the following endorsement on the police order:

"I have read this order and appealed to the Assistant Superintendent of Police concerned to issue a licence for the National-flag procession. On no condition whatsoever is he prepared to issue a licence for the flag procession. I, therefore, reserve to myself the right of action dictated by my conscience and in conformity with the honour of the National-flag which, as I have explained to him, is a flag not of revolt but of peace and love."

Nathuram Modi endorsed his remarks in these words: "I fully endorse the remarks of Pandit Sunderlal."

The Congress leaders decided to disobey the police order. The procession with about ten thousand people was asked to continue the march in a peaceful manner, and make Jabalpur the centre of Civil Disobedience and freedom. They halted near the Clock Tower, where Pandit Sunderlal called for ten volunteers to initiate the Civil Disobedience against the police order. A number of volunteers came forward. In fact, the whole congregation was willing to stand by the National-flag. But the ten selected to form the first batch of satyagrahis were Sunderlal, Nathuram Modi, Sheoprasad Varma, Abdul Sahed, Bishembar Nath Pandey, Makhanlal Chaturvedi, Gopal Prasad, Devi Prasad Shukla, Todarlal and

Volunteers carrying the Swaraj-flag during the Jhanda Andolan-1923.

Subhadra Kumari Chauhan. The rest of the procession was given instructions to return to Tilak Bhoomi. The first batch marched to the Civil Lines with the National-flag aloft in their hands and singing patriotic songs. They were stopped at the outskirts of the Civil Lines by the Magistrate and ordered to return to the city. On their refusal to comply with the order, the Magistrate declared them as an unlawful assembly and issued an order for their arrest. The assembly of more than ten thousand people at Tilak Bhoomi, unprecedented in the history of Jabalpur, received the news of the arrest of the first batch of volunteers with joy. More and more people came forward to enrol themselves as volunteers and, despite the fact that it was past midnight, they waved the National-flag in defiance of the police order. The next day, i.e., on March 19, the volunteers were released. Their unconditional release was hailed by the satyagrahis as a victory for the Congress. Enthusiasm mounted and, with that, the number of satyagrahis also went up.

Soon after their release from the police lock-up, Sunderlal and others wrote to the Government asking for the return of the flag that was confiscated by the police. But the District Magistrate refused to do so. In a public meeting called soon after the receipt of the communication from the District Magistrate, the people reaffirmed their determination to avenge the dishonour to the National-flag. The Jabalpur Municipal Committee adopted a resolution which condemned the Deputy Commissioner for his high-handed behaviour in preventing the hoisting of the Congress flag on the Municipal building. The die was cast. Of the sixteen members of the Municipal Committee, fourteen resigned. The City Congress became active. Separate batches of women and old people were organised; Jabalpur seemed ready to launch an unprecedented satyagraha to save the honour of the

Police atrocities against women volunteers. An English policeman is seen forcefully pulling out the flag from a woman volunteer's hands.

National-flag.

Meanwhile, the news of the flag procession in Jabalpur, on the first anniversary of Gandhiji's conviction, reached England. Col. Yate again raised the issue in the House of Commons and observed: "This was a repetition of the previous hoisting of the Gandhi flag as a defiance of British authority by the Municipal Committee. Why disciplinary action, by withdrawal of Government grants to the Municipality, was not taken by the Governor of the Central Provinces instead of merely repeating his previous warning which had been proved to be ineffective?"

The Under Secretary of State for India, Mr Earl Winterton, assured the Colonel that "the action taken by the Deputy Commissioner in the latest case was effective, as the flag was not allowed to be flown on the building of the Municipal Committee". With that assurance in the British Parliament, the attitude of the British Government towards the Indian National Movement and the National-flag became more hostile. Orders were issued prohibiting the use of the charkha flag on public buildings, especially Municipal Committee, and to deal with any such situation with a firm hand.

Despite the prohibitory order, batches of volunteers carried the flag to the prohibited area and courted arrests. Pandit Sunderlal was arrested for the second time on April 6 and was charge-sheeted for making inflammatory speeches. On April 16, he was sentenced to 6 months' imprisonment.

At the time of his arrest, Pandit Sunderlal nominated Bhagwandin as his successor. The latter shifted the agitation to Nagpur as that was his political field and where he had set up the Asahayog Ashram. Moreover, Nagpur was centrally located and the capital of the then Central Provinces and Berar. It was, therefore, strategically an ideal place for carrying on the agitation.

On April 13, the last day of the national week and the anniversary of the Jallianwala Bagh massacre, the Nagpur City Congress Committee organised a flag procession through the city under the leadership of Mr M.R. Atwari, a Parsi gentleman. All the volunteers joining the procession were required to take an oath of non-violence. Everything was peaceful till the procession reached the Secretariat, where it was stopped by the Superintendent of Police, Manchershah Atwari, on the orders of the District Magistrate, Mr Hyde Gowan. The leader of the local volunteers called upon all volunteers, who were prepared to court arrest, and asked them to come forward in batches of ten to defy the order of the Superintendent of Police. The first batch of satyagrahis included Manchershah Atwari, Kalicharan Sharma, Narayan Rao Badhe, Tulsiram Lodhi, K.N.Ramrao, Waman Devidas Patki, Pandarinath Ambulkar, Laman Prasad Dubey, Abdul Rafiq and Abdul Karim. As they stood in a row of twos, the police snatched flags from their hands, assaulted them brutally and arrested them. The next day they were produced before the Magistrate who fined them sixty rupees each. The satyagrahis refused to pay the fine and so they were sentenced to two months' simple imprisonment.

To the citizens of Nagpur this was both a provocation and a challenge. They were in no mood to take the police action on the satyagrahis and the insult to the National-flag lying down. A deputation of volunteers met Seth Jamnalal Bajaj, narrated to him the political events and apprised him of the mood of the people. Seth Jamnalal Bajaj accepted the challenge and agreed to organise the flag satyagraha in a big way. At a meeting of the Wardha Town Congress Committee held on April 22, he announced the launching of satyagraha in Nagpur from May 1, 1923 to defend the honour of the

*Women Members of the Cotton Committee holding
the Swaraj-flag in Nagpur.*

National-flag.

On May 1, the first batch of ten satyagrahis accompanied by Seth Jamnalal Bajaj took out a flag procession from Asahayog Ashram. To the Government, this was a wanton display of defiance almost amounting to subversion. It, therefore, imposed a prohibitory order in the Civil Lines, under section 144 of the Criminal Procedure Code, which forbade all processions and meetings of more than five persons. However, no arrests were made on the first day. The District Magistrate, Mr Hyde Gowan tried in vain to persuade Seth Jamnalal Bajaj to change the route of the procession.

The following day when the volunteers reached the prohibited area, the police swung into action. There was a *lathi* charge on the flag-carrying satyagrahis. After a severe beating, they were arrested, under Section 127 of the Criminal Procedure Code, for forming an unlawful assembly. When one batch was removed, another appeared on the scene, and this went on for days. To fill in the place of the arrested volunteers, new volunteers came from the neighbouring districts. The satyagraha was now no longer a local affair. It had assumed an all-India status.

The All India Congress Committee took it over from the Nagpur city and entrusted the responsibility of directing it to Sardar Patel. It was also decided by Dr Ansari, the Congress President, to issue an appeal 'Nagpur *chalo*' and to observe June 18 as the Flag-day all over India. He also instructed all the provinces to send six volunteers each to Nagpur to take part in the flag satyagraha. Volunteers from all over India assembled in Nagpur. The British authorities were alarmed at the popularity of the movement. Even the Secretary of State for India called for daily reports of the flag hoisting ceremonies.

The British Government tried her best to abort the June 18 procession by arresting many leaders before hand. On the eve of June 18, the Central Provinces Government arrested Seth Jamnalal Bajaj, Mahatma Bhagwandin, Baba Saheb Deshmukh, Dr N.S. Hardikar, Vinoba Bhave and 275 other volunteers under sections 55 (a) and 109 (b) of the Criminal Procedure Code. Nothing could be more humiliating than the application of these sections to satyagrahis, which were applied to those who had no ostensible means of livelihood and were suspected of being vagrants. Seth Jamnalal Bajaj was sentenced to eighteen months' rigorous imprisonment and fined three thousand rupees. On his refusal to pay the fine, his car was put to auction but no one in Nagpur participated in the bidding. It was later taken to Kathiawad and sold to one of the princely states.

Pandit Makhanlal Chaturvedi succeeded Mahatma Bhagwandin as the new leader. On June 18, more arrests

Makhanlal Chaturvedi, one of the heroes of the Jhanda Andolan, 1923.

were made. The Nagpur jails were full to capacity and the new batches of prisoners were sent to Akola. In a letter to his brother, Pandit Makhanlal Chaturvedi wrote that the whole city of Nagpur was under strict surveillance. The houses and property of those who did not pay the fines were auctioned off. All those who were found with white caps and tricolour flags were arrested[1]. Far from demoralising the people, the flag satyagraha received increasing public response. In order

---

1. Appendix 4.

to boost the morale of the satyagrahis, a statement was issued under the signature of Jawaharlal Nehru, Purushottamdas Tandon, V.G. Joshi, George Joseph and Arjunlal Sethi[1]. On hearing about the arrest of Seth Jamnalal, Sardar Patel arrived in Nagpur to take charge of the struggle. He was a past master in conducting satyagrahas. The Nagpur city railway station became the centre of his activities. To suppress the movement, the administration arrested many incoming volunteers at the Nagpur railway station. Even passengers who were causally dressed in khadi were harassed. When this high-handedness was questioned in the Legislative Council, the Government replied: "Persons unable to give satisfactory account of themselves were arrested under the Criminal Procedure Code". As many as 219 people were arrested at the Nagpur railway station, including a satyagrahi from Nepal.

Subhadra Kumari Chauhan of Jabalpur also courted arrest. Rajagopalachari commended her bravery in these words: "This brave act of Subhadra Devi will be heard and felt in every home in India". Another lady, whose three sons had gone to prison, came with her twelve-year old daughter and insisted on sending her with a flag as a satyagrahi. Hearing of such enthusiasm amongst the females, Kasturba herself came to Nagpur from Wardha and asked Vallabhbhai Patel to include ladies among volunteers, but Patel, knowing the ways of the police, did not agree.

Mention must be made here about the patriotism of two fourteen-year old boys, Mohan and Abhimanyu. Mohan, when dissuaded by C. Rajagopalachari and others from joining the satyagraha as a volunteer, beseeched them with tears to allow him to be included. He was roughed up by the police but

---

1. Appendix 5.

not arrested because of his age. Abhimanyu was badly hurt and had to be taken to the hospital. The moment he recovered, he again reported for satyagraha. This time he was not included among the satyagrahis, but was given office work along with Mohan. The two worked diligently every day from 6 a.m. to midnight.

The magnitude of the satyagraha and the mood of the people compelled the Government to relent. The Governor of Central Provinces and Berar, Sir Frank Sly, invited Sardar Vallabhbhai Patel and Vithalbhai Patel for a closed-door meeting. As a result, Section 144 was lifted on August 14 and permission was given for the flag procession to pass through the prohibited areas.

On August 18, the Jhanda Andolan, however, came to an end, when a hundred satyagrahis sporting white caps and holding the National-flag, led by Makhanlal Chaturvedi, Vallabhbhai Patel and Babu Rajendra Prasad, marched through the prohibited areas. The police did not use force against the satyagrahis who were shouting slogans such as "Mahatma Gandhi *ki jai*", "Rashtriya *jhande ki jai*". When the procession reached the Church at Civil Lines, the DSP on duty requested them to observe silence. Accordingly, all the flags were collected, placed in a tonga and carried to the city office. Addressing a public meeting, Sardar Patel said: "The honour of our flag and our right to hold public processions in a peaceful and orderly manner has been fully vindicated. I regard this as a triumph of truth, non-violence and our ability to suffer for things we cherish most."[1]

Thus, precisely after five months, the flag satyagraha was successfully concluded. All the detainees were released and

---

1. Tahmanekar, D.V.: *Sardar Patel*, p. 71.

the prohibitory orders on the use of the National-flag withdrawn. The whole city was jubilant.

The management of the satyagraha needs special mention. During the satyagraha, the Nagpur City Congress Committee had delegated responsibilities to its members. Ganpatrao Tikekar was in charge of the office, Baba Saheb Deshmukh looked after publications, while the finances were being controlled by Seth Jamnalal Bajaj. There was no shortage of funds, the money came in from many sources. The volunteers were enrolled by Dandekar and Vinoba Bhave, who also looked after the kitchen. For collecting food, a cart would go to the city for collection of provisions. People freely gave ghee, wheat, rice, vegetables, etc. When the cart was full, it returned to the satyagraha office. The satyagrahis never had to buy any food. Everything was donated by the people.

On September 15, a special session of the Congress was called to congratulate the sayagrahis for their dedication and sacrifices.

It is interesting to note that the Jhanda Andolan of 1923, that popularised the flag throughout the length and breadth of India, was staged on the soil of Madhya Pradesh, and coincidentally, the crusade to liberate the Flag from the shackles of restrictions of Flag Code-India was also fought on the soil of Madhya Pradesh.

11

Between the years
1924 and 1930

The most significant achievement of the Jhanda Andolan was that it gave us a flag for which every Indian, irrespective of his caste, creed or religion, was willing to lay down his life. It evoked emotions which found expression in patriotic parades and songs. In 1924, at the time of the Belgaum Congress, some workers of the Seva Dal devised a flag ceremony, or dhvaja-vandan, to accord the tricolour due courtesy and respect.[1] It soon became a part of all the Congress functions. The procedure of dhvaja-vandan is given in Appendix VI.

In the same year, Shyamlal Parshad, the famous freedom-fighter from U.P., composed *Vijayi Vishwa Tiranga Pyara, Jhanda Uncha Rahe Hamara*, which was sung by the workers of the Congress Seva Dal for the first time at the Kanpur session of the Congress in 1924[2]. Later, the song became very

---

1. *Congress Varanika*, January, 1987, p. 22.
2. Ibid.

Volunteers and Swayam Sewaks learning the procedure for Dhvaja–Vandan, the flag salutation ceremony, 1924.

popular and was subsequently made a part of the dhvaja-vandan as *dhvaja-geet.* The full text of the song is given in Appendix VII.

The years following the flag satyagraha were crucial in our freedom struggle. Many important events took place under the umbrella of the tricolour for which the entire nation, and especially the people of Nagpur, staked their lives.

In February 1924, Gandhiji, who had been sentenced to six years imprisonment in March 1922, was prematurely released owing to his illness which necessitated surgical treatment. To his dismay, he found that, following the withdrawal of the non-cooperation movement, disorganisation and disintegration had set into the Congress. Apart from splitting into the 'No-Changers' and the 'Pro-Changers' and both groups failing to stem the spreading rot, the country seemed less responsive to his message than it had been in

1920-21. The Hindu-Muslim unity forged during the non-cooperation movement seemed to be in danger under the shocks of frequent communal riots. Many Muslims, prominent among them, M.A. Jinnah and Mohamed Ali and Shaukat Ali (popularly known as the Ali brothers), had left the Congress. Gandhiji, who had repeatedly asserted that the 'Hindu-Muslim unity must be our creed for all time and under all circumstances', tried to intervene and improve the situation. In September 1924, he fasted for twenty-one days in Delhi, to do penance for the inhumanity revealed in the communal riots. But his efforts were of little avail.

The situation in the country appeared to be dismal indeed. But, behind the scenes, forces of national upsurge had also been growing. The Tiranga aroused them out of their despondency. With the appointment of the Simon Commission, in November 1927, to look into the question of Constitutional reforms, India again emerged out of darkness and entered into a new era of political struggle. As the Commission had no Indian member, the announcement was greeted by a chorus of protests. The British action was seen as a violation of the principle of self-determination and deliberate insult to the self-respect of Indians. The Commission's arrival in India led to a powerful protest movement in which nationalist enthusiasm and unity reached new heights. Wherever the Commission went, the people rallied under the tricolour flag and greeted him with *hartals,* black flag demonstrations and slogans of 'Simon go back'. The Government used batons and bullets to break the popular movement. Many suffered blows, beatings, arrests and torture, but kept the tricolour flying. Consequently, Simon had to go back to England empty-handed. The country was once again in a mood to struggle.

The Congress, too, reflected this new mood. Gandhiji came back to active politics and attended the Calcutta session

Anti-Simon demonstrations at Madras. Black banners silently protested against the Commission.

in December 1928, presided over by Pandit Motilal Nehru. He now began to consolidate the nationalist ranks. Pandit Jawaharlal Nehru and Subhash Chandra Bose refused to accept the all-party constitution prepared under the chairmanship of Pandit Motilal Nehru, as it had provided for dominion status. They were not prepared to accept anything short of Purna Swaraj. Gandhiji suggested a compromise, which was, that if the British Government did not accept the Draft Constitution within one year, the Congress would agitate for complete independence. The year 1929 remained a year of waiting only.

On December 29, 1929, the Congress met on the banks of the Ravi, at Lahore, under the presidentship of Jawaharlal Nehru. The session gave voice to the new militant spirit of the people and passed a resolution declaring Purna Swaraj as the goal of the Congress. On December 31, 1929, Jawaharlal Nehru hoisted the tricolour on the banks of the Ravi and

The Swaraj-flag unfurled by Pandit Nehru at midnight on December 31, 1929, on the banks of the Ravi at the Lahore Session where "Purna-Swaraj" was declared as the goal of the freedom movement.

gave a call for Purna Swaraj. He asked the people, all over India, to observe January 26, 1930 as the first Independence Day by taking a pledge that "it was a crime against man and God to submit any longer to the British rule." From then on, this day was observed every year. This session of the Congress also announced the launching of the Civil Disobedience Movement and Gandhiji was given a free hand to draw up the programme.

On March 12, 1930, Gandhiji launched a second Civil Disobedience Movement. Together with his seventy-eight chosen followers he set out on foot from Sabarmati to Dandi, a village on the Gujarat sea-coast, to violate the salt laws. In the morning, when the march began, a large crowd lined up on both sides of the road holding tricolour flags and flowers. The party reached Dandi on April 5, 1930, covering a distance of two hundred miles in twenty-five days. On April 6, Gandhiji and his followers made salt in violation of the salt laws. The next step was to raid the Government salt godowns at Dharasana (Gujarat). But, before he could do that, he was arrested. The Government, once again, resorted to violence and all over the country people were arrested and beaten up.

After Gandhiji, the leadership passed on to Abbas Tyabji and on his arrest to Sarojini Naidu. With a tricolour in her hand and accompanied by volunteers, she raided the Dharasana salt godown on May 15 and courted arrest. The same evening, another batch of 220 volunteers, with flags in their hands, courted arrest. Despite the brutality of the police the number of satyagrahis did not wane.

Over ninety thousand satyagrahis were arrested. The Congress was declared illegal. Meanwhile, in 1930, the British Government summoned the First Round Table Conference of Indian leaders and the spokesmen of the British Government in India at London to discuss the Simon Commission Report. The Congress boycotted the conference and, therefore, its proceedings proved abortive.

The movement now spread rapidly. Everywhere in the country people observed hartals, joined demonstrations and picketing of shops selling foreign goods. A notable feature of the movement was the participation of women. Thousands of them left their homes to offer satyagraha. They took active part in picketing shops selling foreign goods. Thirteen-year old Rani Gaidiliu of Nagaland led a rebellion of her people against the British. In 1932, she was captured and sentenced to life imprisonment. She was finally released in 1947 by the Government of India. A brochure published by the National Archives of India gives numerous incidents of women being punished by the British authorities for participating in flag processions or attending flag salutation ceremonies.

12

Flag Committee: 1931

By 1930, the Swaraj-flag had become very popular and was accepted by nationalists all over India. Some people were, however, not happy with the communal interpretation given to the three colours at the time of its approval and adoption by Gandhiji. In 1924, the All India Sanskrit Congress, which met at Calcutta, suggested inclusion of saffron or ochre colour and the *gada* of Lord Vishnu in the flag as a Hindu symbol. In the same year, on the eve of the Belgaum session of the Congress, Dvijendranath Tagore and C.F. Andrews suggested inclusion of *geru* or ochre colour in the flag, as it typified the spirit of renunciation and was also the colour which was acceptable to the Hindu *yogis* and *sanyasis* as well as the Muslim *faqirs* and *darveshes*[1]. In 1929, the Sikhs had brought the issue to a head and their deputation met Gandhiji at Lahore and demanded that either the Sikh colour, a shade of yellow, be added to the National-flag or it be divested of communal

---

1. Dr Suniti Kumar Chatterjee, *The National-Flag and Other Essays*, pp. 3-4.

representation. The Sikhs had raised a similar demand earlier in 1921, when Venkayya's flag was first approved by Gandhiji.

In view of these developments, the Congress Working Committee, at its Karachi meeting on April 2, 1931, appointed a seven member Flag Committee comprising Dr B. Pattabhi Sitaramayya (Convener), Pandit Jawaharlal Nehru, Sardar Vallabhbhai Patel, Maulana Abul Kalam Azad, Master Tara Singh, Dr N.S. Hardikar and D.B. Kalelkar. The Working Committee appointed the Flag Committee and passed a resolution noting, "Objection has been taken to the three colours in the flag on the ground that they are conceived on a communal basis." The terms of reference for the Committee were to examine the objections raised about the flag and to recommend a new design and report by July 31, 1931.

Dr Pattabhi Sitaramayya drafted a questionnaire and sent it to Jawaharlal Nehru for his views on the subject. The reply he received was

```
                                    April  12,  1931
Dear  Pattabhi,


I  have  your  letter.  I  agree  with  you  that  the
questionnaire  suggested  by  you  should  be  sent
to  the  provincial  Congress  Committees  and  to  the
Press.  I  am  very  much  interested  in  the  flag
question,  but  I  may  be  away  for  the  next  few
weeks.  I  am,  therefore,  giving  you  below  some
very  rough  ideas  of  mine  of  the  subject.

1. Ordinarily,  I  would  be  greatly  averse  to
   changing  the  present  flag,  which  has  become
   very  popular,  but  having  regard  to  the
   circumstances,  perhaps  some  change  is  necessary.
   This  change,  however,  should  not  interfere  too
   much  with  the  present  flag.
```

2. We should make it perfectly clear that our flag is not based on communal considerations.
3. The present arrangements with the white at the top are bad, as the white does not show unless there is a colour background. Therefore, in any event the white should either be put in the centre or should give place to another colour.
4. The present flag is, I believe, identical with the Bulgarian flag, which is undesirable.
5. I am inclined to think that the colour white should give place to basanti colour or light saffron. My reason for this is not that the Sikhs desire it as their colour, but because this colour is an old Indian colour and is associated with sacrifice in our past history. Further, this colour has been adopted by the women of India and it would be a graceful and deserving tribute to the women to order this colour. The exact shade of the colour must be carefully considered. The place of the colour in the flag must also be considered from the aesthetic point of view. Thus, it may be either at the top or at the centre.
6. I would like to retain both red and green as they are beautiful colours.
7. The final design chosen should be that which satisfies the aesthetic sense and should be in accordance with the heraldic principles.

These are some suggestions made on the spur of the moment just to give you some idea of what I have in mind.

Yours sincerely,

J. N.

Dr Pattabhi Sitaramayya.

Later, Dr Pattabhi Sitaramayya sent the questionnaire to all the provincial Congress Committees, eminent personalities and well-known social organisations for eliciting their views. The letter containing the questionnaire read:

Masulipatnam
23-4-1931

Dear Sir,

Permit me to bring to your notice that the following resolution regarding the National-flag was passed by the Working Committee at its meeting held on April 2, 1931.

Text of the Resolution: 'Whereas the National-flag now in vogue has gained in popularity by usage and convention and whereas objection has been taken to the three colours in the flag on the ground that they are conceived on a communal basis, the Working Committee hereby appoints a committee for the purpose of examining the objections and recommending a flag for acceptance by the Congress. The Committee shall have the authority to take such evidence as it may consider necessary and to send its report and recommendations to the Working Committee on or before July 31, 1931' .

May I request you to answer the following questions in particular, and send up your suggestions in the matter.

1. Is there any feeling amongst any group of people or community in your province, in regard to the design of the National-flag, which in your opinion should be taken into consideration by this Committee?
2. Have you any specific suggestions for making the flag more popular?
3. Is there any defect or drawback in the design now in vogue, which you consider demands attention?

Note: Let me submit that in sending up your suggestions, you will be greatly adding to their weight if you take the trouble of accompanying them with a flag preferably in cloth so as to illustrate your ideas.

Further, I would suggest that these replies might be sent up by the PCCs and the public by the end of May. If the Committee considers it necessary, it will ask you to tender oral evidence later.

Yours sincerely,

(Dr Pattabhi Sitaramayya)
Convener, Flag Committee

The Committee received suggestions from eight Provincial Congress Committees and fifty individual suggestions in response to the questionnaire. The Central Sikh League also sent up a memoranda. Some scribbled in their suggestions on a postcard. Others sent in lengthy typewritten essays complete with drawings. Some anxiously followed up their first communication with one or more copies to ensure against loss in transit. One person sought to advocate his suggestions by orchestrating a spate of supportive telegrams to the committee. A few others sought to lobby their suggestions by writing letters and articles for major newspapers. Dr Suniti Kumar Chatterjee, a professor at Calcutta University, was against giving any communal representation to colours. He said if any particular community finds a secret pleasure in thinking of a certain colour or symbol which has been adopted to be their own, they may be left to think so. Prof. Chatterjee objected to the white, green and red colour scheme of the flag then in use saying Bulgaria has an identical arrangement of colours. This view was also echoed by Pandit Nehru in his letter dated April 12, 1931 to Dr Pattabhi Sitaramayya.

Dr Suniti Kumar suggested a four-colour flag for India comprising scarlet red, green, white and ochre with a wheel, instead of the charkha in the centre. He alternately suggested a tricolour of green, ochre and red. Sir C.V. Raman, Prof. Ramananda Chatterjee and Dr Radhakrishnan favoured Dr Suniti Kumar's tricolour flag. Some of the other suggestions made by various eminent respondents were:

R.D. Tiwari: A triangular white flag with the charkha for cultural unity as well as purity, simplicity and peace.

Charkha symbolised the economic ideal of cottage industries. The triangular shape, oriental in concept, typified the meeting of cultures.

Sir Mirza Ismail: Red or yellow oblong flag with *tarazu* (a balance) in the centre symbolising justice and fair play to all the communities.

Saul Johnson Orai (UP): A tricolour with white for purity, blue for tolerance, equality and fairplay and red for sacrifice.

T. Benjamin Shah: A tricolour, with different coloured stars for different communities, on the pattern of the star and stripes of the American flag.

Sardar Sardul Singh Caveeshar: A tricolour with blue, gold, and green with a bunch of cotton flowers surrounded by rice and wheat corns in the centre.

Dr Benod Bihari Banerjee: A red flag with fifteen five-pointed white stars representing the fifteen Indian provinces. White stars indicated dawn of freedom and the red field symbolised firm determination of the people to attain complete independence. A small Union Jack to be added near the flagstaff if the Government granted Dominion Status willingly.

T. Ramaswami (Bezwada): A flag named *pranava-pataka* with an outer ring of black, a central ring of red and an inner spot of white representing *tamas, rajas* and *satvik* qualities respectively.

However, a number of other respondents opted for the existing flag with minor changes. In fact, Mr N.S. Hardikar, one of the members of the Committee, signed the final report rather reluctantly being of the view that the original flag should stand and should arouse no objection from any quarters if the Congress repudiated all communal interpretations of the colours in the flag. Even Pandit Jawaharlal Nehru was averse to changing the existing flag as was evident from his letter to the Convener of the Committee.

Sardar Vallabhbhai Patel, another member of the Committee, however, was all for a saffron coloured National-flag in keeping with the Indian traditions.

The Flag Committee had two meetings on 8th and 9th July. After much deliberation and examining the various replies received it came to a unanimous decision that the new flag must be distinctive, artistic, rectangular and non-communal. The Committee finally went on to note, "Opinion has been unanimous that our National-flag should be of a single colour except for the colour of the device. If there is one colour that is more acceptable to India as a whole, even as it is more distinctive than another one that is associated with this ancient country by long tradition, it is the kesari or saffron colour. Accordingly, it is felt that the flag should be of kesari colour except for the colour of the device. That the device should be the charkha (in blue) is unanimously agreed to". The charkha suggested by the Committee was of a small size to be placed on the flag on its upper left quadrant.

The Congress Working Committee, however, rejected the suggested design when it met in the first week of August at Bombay. Consequently, the saffron flag with the mini blue charkha never came into existence and remained a mere part of the report of the Flag Committee-1931.

In this rare setting, Jesus Christ, holding the banner of victory, emerges from his tomb and stands triumphant over death. A painting by the 15th century Italian artist Piero della Francesca.

The standard of Joan of Arc.

The standard of Genghis Khan displays his personal emblem, a gyrfalcon. The nine flammules denoted the nine tribes he ruled over. The triangular banner was adopted from an old Chinese tradition.

Pirates in the old days used a black flag exhibiting a white skull and two crossed bones to intimidate their victims.

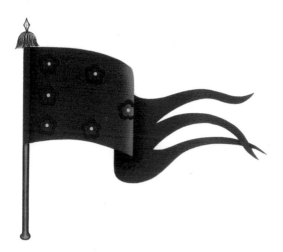

The Oriflamme, the orange and red flag of Charlemagne.
Its shape was that of the gonfanon.

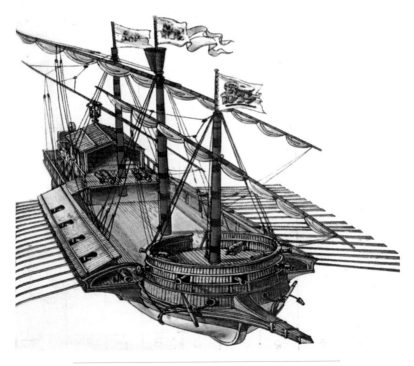

A type of 16ᵗʰ century oared frigate armed with cannons.
Her ensigns are flapping on sail masts.

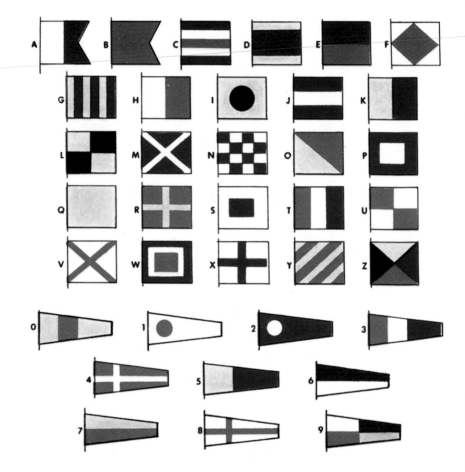

The alphabetical and numerical flags, collectively known as Signal flags, used to send and receive messages at sea when within visual distance.

Display and carrying of standards and banners as part of any royal procession was an established Mughal tradition. Picture above from Padshahnama shows the gift offering ceremony during Prince Dara Shikho's marriage. Courtesy, The Royal Library, London.

The flag of the Kundalini-Shakti, the serpent power that lies coiled up at the base of the human vertebrate.

The Goddess Rati wielding a sugarcane bow mounted with a five-flowered arrow. Her banner flies behind her on the elephant.

The planet 'Ketu', portrayed as a headless torso with a fish as his lower body is the ruler of flags. He holds a flag of self-glory in one of his four hands with 'OM' inscribed on its field.

The Kapala-dhvaja, the battle banner of demon king Ravana.

Ravana abducting Sita in his Pushpak viman.
Jatayu, a giant bird, preventing him.

The Imperial ensign of the demon king Ravana displays a veena denoting the prosperity and wealth he enjoyed.

A scene from Lanka Dahan. The Imperial flag is seen torched.

The Tala-dhvaja of grandiose Bheeshma.

The duel between Bheeshma and his guru Parushram. The woman on the battlefield is Princess Amba whom Bheeshma refused to marry. Respective flags of both the warriors are seen on their chariots. A rare illustration of the episode.

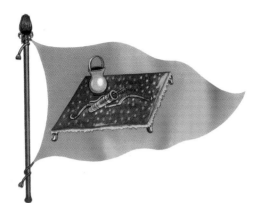

The personal standard of guru Dronacharya, the warfare teacher of the Kauravas and the Pandavas.

The Kaurava king Duryodhana (right) deliberates war strategy with his guru Dronacharya (left). The personal standard of Dronacharya is seen against the sky, mounted on his chariot.

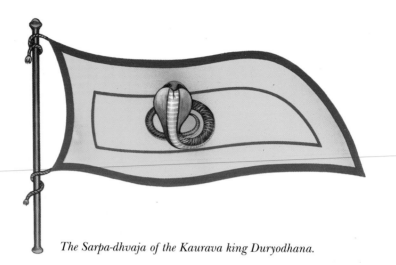

The Sarpa-dhvaja of the Kaurava king Duryodhana.

The Sarpa-dhvaja on the Kaurava king Duryodhana's chariot at the battlefield of Kurukshetra.

The Garuda-dhvaja of Lord Vishnu.

Lord Krishna armed as a warrior. A very rare picture of Krishna. He adopted the Garuda-dhvaja as his personal banner.

Lord Shiva's standard, the Vrasabha-dhvaja.

Shiva (with his Vrasabha-dhvaja) and Yama Raj against each other over the issue of young Markande's life.

The Vanara-dhvaja fluttering atop Arjuna's chariot, the Nandi Ghosh.

Lord Indra riding his war elephant Aravat with his blue banner.

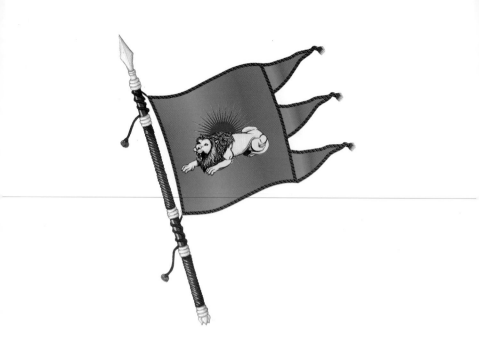

'Alam', the royal standard of the Mughals. The Alam was believed to be the flag of Hussain. Taimur obtained it at Karbalah and the Mughals later adopted it as their standard.

'Changi', the flag of Maharana Pratap. The Ranas of Chittor claimed descent from the Surya Dynasty, hence their flag bore the figure of a golden sun on its field.

13

The Official Flag of the Indian National Congress

The Flag Committee recommended a plain *kesari* unicolour flag with a small charkha in blue near the upper hoist. On August 5-6, 1931, the report and design of the flag submitted by the Flag Committee was discussed at a meeting of the Congress Working Committee, which met at Bombay. It was presided by Sardar Patel and attended by Mahatma Gandhi, Sarojini Naidu, Pandit Jawaharlal Nehru, Dr Ansari, Dr Syed Mohammed, Sardul Singh Caveeshar, J.M. Sen Gupta and M.S. Aney, Jairamdas Daulatram, Maulana Abul Kalam Azad, Pandit Madan Mohan Malaviya, Dr Pattabhi Sitaramayya, T.A.K. Sherwani and Purushottam Das Tandon.

The Working Committee did not approve the new design recommended by the Flag Committee for the reason that it was totally different from the existing flag. The committee felt that the flag in vogue had been associated with the national struggle for the past several years, and many had laid down their lives to save its honour. Therefore, it would be unwise to change its design drastically and it was resolved:

> "Having considered the report of the Flag Committee, the Working Committee appreciates its labours and endorses its view that the National-flag should not bear any communal significance and that it should be distinctive and not capable of being mistaken for the flag of any other country. The Working Committee, however, feels that it would be desirable to have as little change as possible in the existing flag." The Committee, therefore, recommends, to the A.I.C.C. for its adoption, the following change:
> "The 'National-flag' shall be three coloured, horizontally arranged, as before, but the colours shall be saffron, white and green in the order stated here from top to bottom, with the spinning wheel in dark blue in the centre on the white stripe, it being understood that the colours have no communal significance, but that saffron shall represent courage and sacrifice, white peace and truth, green faith and chivalry, and the charkha, the spinning wheel, shall represent the hope of the masses. The proportions of the flag should be from fly to hoist, as three to two."[1]

The resolution was carried by an overwhelming majority. And thus, for the first time, the Indian National Congress had an official flag of its own. It had a new colour arrangement. Saffron on the top, white in the centre and green at the bottom with a mini charkha in dark blue on the centre white band. It was free from all communal interpretation. Gandhiji welcomed the flag saying: "It is a matter of great joy that the

---

1. *The Times of India*, August 6, 1931, p. 10.

spinning wheel has been retained as the hope of the masses. …No doubt it will be defended with our lives, but the true defence will consist in assimilating the qualities represented by the colours and giving the spinning-wheel a place in every home. Then we shall need no picketing of foreign cloth. If we will die for the flag, let us learn to live for the flag".

The Working Committee then adopted another resolution calling upon all the Congress organisations, throughout India, to celebrate August 30, 1931 as a Flag-day by hoisting the new flag.[1]

The A.I.C.C. entrusted the responsibility of manufacturing the new flags to Dr N.S. Hardikar. The original design of the flag had the spindle of the charkha near the pole. But it was later observed that the flag looked much better with the wheel near the pole and not the spindle. Accordingly, the position of the charkha was altered. The samples of the new flag were prepared expeditiously and sent to all the Provincial Congress Committees. The Flag-day was observed with great zeal throughout the country.

Soon the new flag was pitted against the Union Jack, when it was only four months old. After the boycott of the First Round Table Conference by the Congress and its subsequent failure, Lord Irwin negotiated an agreement with the Congress in March 1931. It is commonly known as the Gandhi-Irwin Pact. As a result of the agreement, the Government released all those political prisoners who had remained non-violent during the Civil Disobedience Movement. In return the Congress suspended the Movement and agreed to attend the Second Round Table Conference. The younger generation of the Congress was opposed to the Gandhi-Irwin Pact as the Government had not accepted any

---

1. *The Indian Annual Register,* 1931, Vol. II, July-December, p. 76.

of the major demands of the Congress. Even the death sentence of Bhagat Singh and his two associates was not commuted to life imprisonment.

In September 1931, Gandhiji went to England to attend the Second Round Table Conference. Nothing came out of it. The British Government refused to concede to the demand of immediate grant of Dominion Status. Immediately after the failure of the Conference, the British Government in India promulgated an emergency in UP, NWFP and Bengal and arrested all the prominent Congress leaders. The Congress was declared illegal. Its funds, property and premises were confiscated. As soon as Gandhiji landed in Bombay, on January 4, 1932, he too, was arrested. By April 1932, about 1,20,000 people were arrested. The Government's repressive measures succeeded in the end and helped in widening differences among Indian leaders on communal and other issues. The Congress officially suspended the movement in May 1933 and withdrew it in May 1943. Gandhiji once again retired from active politics. But the lull was only for a short time.

Under the Government of India Act, 1935, autonomy was provided to the provinces. But that was only in name. The Governors were given special powers to veto legislations and legislate on their own. The Congress decided to contest the elections with the aim of showing how unpopular the Act was. In 1937, in seven out of eleven provinces, the Congress Ministries were formed. Though they could not change the basic imperialistic character of the British administration, they did try to improve the condition of the people within the narrow limits of the powers given to them. In 1938, the 51st session of the Indian National Congress was held at Haripura in Gujarat. To symbolise the occasion, fifty-one bullock carts were bedecked with the National-flag and paraded through the town.

In September 1939, World War II broke out. The Government of India sent Indian troops to the war for the defence of the British Empire without consulting the Congress. In protest, the seven Congress Ministries resigned. The Congress stand was that India would assist the British Government in the war effort only as a free and equal partner, which the latter was not prepared to concede. From that time there was no looking back. Many incidents of revolt against British rule took place under the umbrella of the tricolour and many of our compatriots courted arrests and underwent torture to defend its honour. Each incident, each movement was epoch-making. In 1940, Gandhiji launched a limited satyagraha with a select few. Following the spectacular success of Japan in 1942, Winston Churchill sent Sir Stafford Cripps, a member of the War Cabinet, to India with some constitutional proposals. Those were not acceptable to the Congress. The failure of the Cripps-Congress talks prompted Gandhiji to adopt a sterner policy. On August 8, 1942, he gave the historic call to the British to 'Quit India' and exhorted the people 'to do or die' for the flag and freedom of the country.

In the early hours of August 9, all the members of the Working Committee and other prominent Congress leaders were arrested. This motivated the people to show that although the leaders could be imprisoned, the flag would still fly. Aruna Asaf Ali, a young lady came forward and hoisted the tricolour with full honours at the Govalia Tank Maidan, now known as 'August Kranti Maidan' (exactly forty-five years later, during the fortieth year of India's independence on August 9, 1987, Aruna Asaf Ali re-enacted the flag hoisting ceremony at the same maidan). The police lathi charged the crowd and fired bullets, but the satyagrahis kept the flag flying. The British Government made hoisting of the flag a crime, liable to two years imprisonment. But the people defied the orders and some of the martyrs to the cause included the brave young mill-hand Kumaran of Tiruppur, in Tamil Naidu, who defied the British till he was shot dead in a labour resistance carrying the Tiranga in his hand. In Patna, seven students were shot dead while attempting to hoist the tricolour atop the Council Hall. In Assam, Kanak Lata was killed while hoisting the National-flag on the Collectorate. In Midnapur, Matangini Hazra died of a bullet in her head, but she had the flag firmly held in her hands. The list is endless.

INA and the Congress Tricolour

In early 1941, Subhash Chandra Bose secretly fled to Berlin. There he formed the Indian Legion with the three thousand Indian prisoners of war captured in North Africa and Europe. It adopted a tricolour red, white and green with a leaping tiger in the centre white stripe. Subhash Chandra Bose had planned to reach India with the help of the Axis-powers to liberate her. But, with the defeat of Germany at Stalingrad and El Alamein in Africa, he changed his plans and went to Singapore. In the eastern sector, circumstances were more favourable. Japan had occupied the Andaman and Nicobar Islands and was knocking at the frontiers of India. Capt. Mohan Singh (later Major), had organised the prisoners of war into the Indian National Army

A rare picture of Subhash Chandra Bose disguised as Maulvi Ziauddin while escaping to Germany in 1941.

(INA). In August 1943, Subhash Chandra Bose officially took charge of INA as its Supreme Commander and, on October 21, 1943, formed the Provisional Government of free-India (*Arzi-Hakumat-e-Azad Hind*). He adopted the tricolour of the Indian National Congress as the flag of his provisional government. Addressing the soldiers of the INA, he said: "Let us continue to fight till the National-flag flies over the Viceroy's House in New Delhi and Azad Hind Fauj holds its victory parade inside the ancient Red Fort of the Indian metropolis."[1]

Tiranga hoisted by Subhash Chandra Bose on the naval flagmast at the Government House at Andaman, December 1943.

In December 1943, Japan handed over the Islands of Andaman and Nicobar to Subhash Chandra Bose. He renamed the two islands as 'Shahid' and 'Swaraj'[2] and hoisted

---

1. Colonel Naranjan Singh Gill: Story of the I.N.A., pp. 48 (Publications Division).
2. Ibid. p. 50.

In December 1943, Japan handed over the Andaman and Nicobar Islands to Subhash Chandra Bose. He re-named them 'Shahid` and 'Swaraj` and hoisted the National-flag on the Cellular Jail.

the National-flag on the Cellular Jail and the naval mast in front of the Government House. While hoisting the Indian tricolour Subhash Chandra Bose roared Jai Hind. Maybe, it was for the first time that the vibrations of Jai Hind physically echoed on the soil of India. Earlier, Subhash Chandra Bose used to conclude his talks on radio in Singapore roaring Jai Hind, meaning 'victory to India'. Col. S.A. Malik of the Azad Hind Fauj hoisted the tricolour at Moirang (now in Manipur) after its capture. His troops entered India roaring Jai Hind.

In February 1946, some Royal Indian Naval Ratings mutinied.
Holding the National-flag, the Ratings paraded
through the streets of Bombay.

It was Subhash Chandra Bose, who had coined the slogan in 1943 as a battle-cry for his army, Azad Hind Fauj (INA), raised in Singapore. Pandit Jawaharlal Nehru, however, immortalised the slogan when he echoed it thrice after his first ever speech from the ramparts of the Red Fort on August 16, 1947. Ever since the roar of Jai Hind has become an integral concluding part of the Independence Day speech by all Prime Ministers.

The Quit India Movement and the emergence of the Azad Hind Fauj made the situation in the country very explosive. In February 1946, some Royal Indian Naval Ratings mutinied and refused to take orders from their British officers. The mutineers hoisted the National-flag over the naval barracks and buildings. Holding the National-flag, the Ratings paraded through the streets of Bombay. The National-flag with a photograph of Subhash Chandra Bose was also flown above one of the Royal Indian Navy's Ensigns.

14

India adopts her National-flag

By 1947, the British had fully realised that the time had come for them to leave India when they saw the writing on the wall. An overwhelming majority voted to end the British rule in the sub-continent by June 1948. The Prime Minister, Mr Clement Attlee, appointed Louis Francis Albert Victor Nicholas Mountbatten as the new Viceroy of India, who became the last Englishman to govern India.

British soldiers leaving India. A silver model of Gateway of India and a folded Tiranga placed on a frame are seen being taken away as mementos.

British troops boarding a ship that would take them home after Independence.
The Royal Naval Ensign and Tiranga are hung on board.

On March 24, 1947, Lord Mountbatten took charge from the outgoing Viceroy, Lord Wavell, and made the historic announcement about the decision of the British Government to free India. With this announcement, the national leaders instantly became alive to the need of having a National-flag that would be acceptable to all the political parties. The Constituent Assembly, therefore, established an adhoc Flag Committee headed by its Chairman, Dr Rajendra Prasad, to design the flag for free India. The

Pandit Jawaharlal Nehru presenting a sample of Tiranga to the Constituent Assembly on July 22, 1947, to be adopted as the National-flag of Independent India.

Committee, besides the Chairman, consisted of Abul Kalam Azad, K.M. Panikar, Sarojini Naidu, C. Rajagopalachari, K.M. Munshi and Dr B.R. Ambedkar.

The Flag Committee was constituted on June 23, 1947. It held several meetings and studied the question in depth. On July 14, 1947, after detailed deliberations it arrived at the following decisions:

1. The flag of the Indian National Congress should be adopted as the National-flag of India with suitable amendments, to make it acceptable to all parties and communities in India.

2. The flag should be tri-coloured, with three bands horizontally arranged.

3. The colours should be in the following order: saffron on top, white in the middle and dark green at the bottom.

4. The emblem of the flag should be an exact reproduction of the wheel on the capital of Ashoka's Sarnath Pillar, superimposed in the middle of the central white band.

5. The colour of the emblem should be dark blue.

Having arrived at these decisions, the Committee immediately arranged to prepare samples of the new flag. The Committee met again on July 17 to examine the samples that had been prepared. After critically examining all the samples, the Committee finally approved the sample prepared by Mrs. Badruddin Tyabji, whose husband was an ICS officer of the 1934 batch and Deputy Secretary in the Constuent Assembly. Both were artists and great art connoisseurs, and therefore considered suitable by Pandit Nehru and Dr. Rajendra Prasad for the task of helping design the National-flag and the National-emblem of free India.On July 18, the

Committee finalised its recommendations and decided that Pandit Jawaharlal Nehru would place the recommendations before the House on July 22, 1947. Accordingly, Pandit Nehru tabled the resolution on the due date.

Players of the Partition.

While moving the resolution, Jawaharlal Nehru observed:

I am sure that many in this House will feel the glow and warmth which I feel at the present moment for, behind this Resolution and the Flag, which I have the honour to present to this House for adoption, lies history, the concentrated history of a short span in a nation's existence. Sometimes, in a brief period we pass through the tract of centuries ... I remember the ups and downs of the great struggle for freedom of our great nation. I remember, and many in this House will remember, how we looked up to this Flag not only with pride and enthusiasm, but with a tingling in our veins and also how, when we were sometimes down and out, the sight of this Flag gave us courage to go on. Many who are not present here today, many of our comrades who have passed away, held on to this Flag, a few of them even unto death, and handed it over, as they sank, to others to hold it aloft. Therefore, behind these simple words of the Resolution there is the struggle of the people for freedom with all its ups and downs, and trials and disasters, and a certain triumph – which, I feel, in moving this Resolution – in the conclusion of that struggle.

This Resolution defines the flag, which I trust you will adopt. In a sense this flag was adopted, not by a formal resolution, but, by popular acclaim and usage, adopted much more by the sacrifice that surrounded it in the past few decades.

It is a flag which has been variously described. We thought of a flag which, in its combination and in its separate parts, would represent the spirit of the nation, the tradition of synthesis, which has characterised us for thousands of years.

Now Sir, may I say a few words about this particular Flag. It will be seen that there is a slight variation from the one many of us have used during these past years. The colours are the same, a deep saffron, a white and a dark green. In the white, previously there was the charkha, which symbolised the common man in India, which symbolised their industry, and which came to us from the message which Mahatma Gandhi delivered. Now, this particular charkha symbol has been slightly varied in this flag. Why has it been varied? Normally speaking, the symbol on one side of the flag should be exactly the same as on the other side. Otherwise, there is a difficulty which goes against the conventions. Now, the charkha as it appeared previously on this flag had the wheel on one side and the spindle on the other. If you see the other side of the Flag, the spindle comes the other way and the wheel comes this way. There was this practical difficulty. Therefore, after considerable thought, we were convinced that this great symbol which enthused the people should continue, that it should continue in a slightly different form, that the wheel should be there and not the rest of the charkha, i.e., the spindle and the string which created this confusion. The essential part of the charkha should be there, that is, the wheel. So the old tradition continues in regard to the charkha and the wheel.

But what type of wheel should we have? Our minds went back to many wheels, but, notably to one famous wheel which had appeared in many places and which all of us have seen, the one at the top of the capital of the Ashoka column and in many other places. That wheel is a symbol of India's ancient culture, it is a symbol of the many things that India has stood for through the ages. We, therefore, thought that this wheel, this charkha emblem, should appear on our flag. For my part, I am exceedingly happy that we have associated with our flag not only this emblem but, in a sense, the name of Ashoka, one of the most magnificent names in India's history and the world. It is well-known that at this moment of strife, conflict, and intolerance, our minds should go back towards what India stood for in the ancient days and what, I hope and believe, it has essentially stood for throughout the ages.

Since I have mentioned the name of Ashoka, I should like you to remember that the Ashoka period was essentially an international period of Indian history. It was not a narrow national period. It was a period when India's ambassadors went abroad to far off countries, not in the way of an empire and imperialism, but, as ambassadors of peace, culture, and goodwill. Therefore, this flag that I have the honour to present to you is not, I hope and trust, a flag of an empire, a flag of imperialism, a flag of domination over anybody, but, a flag of freedom, not only for ourselves but to all people, who may see it, and wherever it may go, and I hope it will go far, not only where Indians dwell as our ambassadors and ministers, but across the far seas where it may be carried by Indian ships. (Pandit Nehru's dream came true when the Indian National-flag went round the world on board the *Trishna* in 1982). It will bring a message of freedom and of comradeship, a message that India wants to be friends with every country of the world, and that India wants to help any people who seek freedom."[1]

---

1. *Varanika* Congress Centenary Issue, p. 127.

Describing the design and dimensions of the flag, Pandit Nehru said: "The National-flag of India shall be the horizontal tricolour of deep saffron (kesari), white and dark green in equal proportions. In the centre of the white band, there shall be a wheel in navy blue to represent the charkha. The design of the wheel shall be that of the wheel, which appears, on the abacus of the Sarnath Lion Capital of Ashoka." The inclusion of the chakra, in place of the charkha, was suggested by S.D. Kalelkar. He visualised in the wheel the Kisan Movement, Kranti (revolution) and the spirit of Buddhist Dharma-chakra.

Pandit Jawaharlal Nehru concluded by saying: "So sir, now I present to you not only the resolution but the flag itself. There are two of these National-flags before you, one is on silk-khadi, the one I am holding, and the other, on the other side, is of cotton-khadi. I beg to move this resolution."

It was a memorable speech. The proceedings of the assembly excelled the expectations of everyone. Hindus, Muslims, Sikhs, Christians, Parsis, and all others vied with one another in acclaiming the flag.

Mr President: *I have got notice of three amendments to this Resolution.*

Mr H.V. Kamath (from Central Province and Berar): *Mr President, Sir, my amendment reads as follows:*
That the following new para be inserted in the motion: That inside the chakra, in the centre of the white band, the Swastika, the ancient Indian symbol of Satyam, Shivam, Sundaram, be inscribed. When I sent in the amendment, I had not seen the design of the flag. There were at that time two or three considerations uppermost in my mind. I thought that this flag, being the flag of our new Indian Republic, of Bharatavarsha, should adequately symbolise our ancient culture ... But, Sir, I

have now seen the flag and I find that it is somewhat hard to fit the Swastika into this chakra. It would look cumbersome because of the design of the chakra...Mr President, Sir, after having seen the design of this flag, I do see that it is difficult to fit the Swastika in, much as I would like to see it fitted in. It would make it rather clumsy and cumbersome. In these circumstances, I do not press this amendment and beg leave of the House to withdraw it.

Mr President: *Mr Tajamul Hussain.*

Honourable Members: *He is not present.*

Mr President: *Dr Deshmukh*

Dr P.S. Deshmukh (Central Province and Berar: General): *Mr President, Sir, after such an impressive and emotional speech by Pandit Nehru one hesitates to say or add anything that may be interpreted or considered to take away from its effect ... I have some very strong grounds on which my amendment was based ... My idea was essentially based on the retention of the tricolour absolutely intact with the charkha retained as it is. The charkha, which is the emblem of ahimsa and the common toiling man, is associated so inseparably with the acquisition of our political freedom ... But, in view of the fact that the House would rather stick to the flag that has been proposed, I do not wish to move the amendment.*

Mr President: *Now we shall discuss the resolution.*

Seth Govind Das (C.P. and Berar: General): *Mr President I have come here to support the resolution moved by Pandit Jawaharlal Nehru. I consider this day a landmark in the history of India. Today, Independent India is displaying her National-flag. I support this resolution with all my heart.*

Mr V.I. Muniswami Pillai (Madras: General): *Sir, I appear before you today to support the Resolution so ably moved by our great National leader, Pandit Jawaharlal Nehru. Sir, I particularly welcome the introduction of the wheel in the centre ... I also welcome the introduction of the Sarnath Lion capital of Ashoka. Ashoka, coming as he did after the great Buddhist order, has given us the great Panchaseelam, above all, sympathy for humanity.*

The Harijan classes and all those communities who are in the lowest rung of the ladder of society, feel that the Constitution, which is on the anvil of this supreme body, is going to bring solace to millions of the submerged classes. The principle of Buddha who exhibited practically his great sympathy for suffering human beings, I am sure, Sir, will be practically carried out after accepting this great flag.

With these words, I support the Resolution.

Chaudhri Khalizuzzaman (United Provinces: Muslim): *Mr President, I support the resolution moved by Pandit Nehru.* (Cheers). *I think that from today everyone, who regards himself as a citizen of India, be he a Muslim, Hindu or Christian, will as a citizen make all sacrifices to uphold and maintain the honour of the flag which is accepted and passed as the flag of India.* (Cheers). *With these words I support the motion.*

Sir S. Radhakrishnan (United Provinces: General): *Mr President, Sir, I do not wish to say very much after the very eloquent way in which Pandit Jawaharlal Nehru presented this flag and the Resolution to you. The flag links up the past and the present ... Ashoka's wheel represents to us the wheel of the Law, the wheel of the dharma. Truth can be gained only by the pursuit of the path of dharma ... The red, the orange, the bhagwa colour represent the spirit of reincarnation ... The green is there, our relation to the soil, our relation to plant life here on which all other life depends ... This flag tells us 'Be ever alert, be ever on the move, go forward, work for a free, flexible, compassionate, decent, democratic society in which Christians, Sikhs, Muslims, Hindus, Buddhists will all find a safe shelter.*

Thank you. (Loud cheers).

Mr Tajamul Husain: *We would like to hear the 'Bulbul-e Hind'.*

Mr President: *I will call upon her at the end. I am sure it will be the sweetest speech and we should, according to our old custom, end with sweets.* (Cheers).

Mr R.K. Sidhwa: *Mr President, Sir, it is not the proud privilege of only Hon'ble Pandit Nehru today, but it is the proud privilege of the whole nation to see this flag round which the people have struggled hard to win freedom has become an accomplished fact, that the National-flag, hereafter, shall be an officially recognised flag...*

Mr Frank R. Anthony: *I believe sincerely that this is really a beautiful flag in its physical aspect and also in its motives. Today, this flag is the flag of the Nation. It is not the flag of any particular community, it is the flag of all Indians. I believe that while this is a symbol of our past, it inspires us for the future. This flag flies today as the flag of the nation, and it should be the duty and privilege of every Indian not only to cherish and live under it, but if necessary, to die for it.*

Giani Gurmukh Singh Musafar (East Punjab: Sikh): *Mr President ... We have reached the position today that we can install our flag wherever we like. Now it is equally incumbent upon us to maintain the dignity of this fluttering flag...*

Mr Tajamul Husain: *I want to speak a few words. My name is not on the list but I will not exceed two or three minutes. Have I your permission?*

Mr President: *No. I have got more than twenty-five names on the list, but I had promised earlier that I will call Mrs Naidu to make the final speech. So I request her to address the House.*

Mrs Sarojini Naidu (Bihar: General): *Mr President, the House knows that I had refused over and over again this morning to speak. I thought that the speech of Jawaharlal Nehru, so epic in its quality of beauty, dignity and appropriateness, was sufficient to express the aspirations, emotions and the ideals of this House.*

Many, many times in the course of my long life, in my travels abroad, for I am a vagabond by nature and by destiny, I have suffered the most terrible moments of anguish in free countries, because India possessed no flag. A few of those moments I would like to recall.

In 1945, during the celebrations at New York after the Versailles Treaty had been signed, forty-four nations had their flags fluttering there. I looked upon the flags of all these nations and when I spoke, it was with humility that I said: 'I do not see in this great assembly of free nations the flag of India'. On another occasion, forty-two nations of the world had sent their women delegates to Berlin for an International Conference. There was a flag parade. Some of the Indian women present at the Conference tore up six of their green, white and saffron coloured saris and stitched a National-flag of India for the occasion ... While the Peace Treaty was being signed at Versailles, I had gone to an opera. There was great rejoicing everywhere and the flags of all the forty-four nations were on the platform. A famous actress, with a beautiful voice, was performing that night. The performance was interrupted in order to enable the French to wrap a flag of France around the actress as a tribute to her performance. An Indian sitting next to me sighed and said, 'when shall we have our flag'?

Winding up her speech, Mrs Naidu said:

Under this flag, there is no difference between a prince and a peasant, between the rich and the poor, between man and woman.

The climax was reached when, raising her hands, she dramatically said: "Now, I bid you all to rise and salute this flag".

To avoid any future controversies, Dr S. Radhakrishnan also made it very clear that the colours had no communal significance. He said:

Bhagwa or the saffron colour denotes renunciation or disinterestedness. Our leaders must be indifferent to material gains and dedicate themselves to their work. The white in the centre is light, the path of truth to guide our conduct. The green shows our relation to the soil, our relation to plant life here on which all other life depends. The Ashoka wheel in the centre of the white is the wheel of the law of dharma. Truth or satya, dharma or virtue ought to be the controlling principles of all those who work under this flag. Again, the wheel denotes motion. There is death in stagnation. There is life in movement. India should no more resist change, it must move and go forward. The wheel represents the dynamism of a peaceful change and hence this deviation does not revolt against the original idea of having a spinning wheel in the National-flag.

Mr President, I would ask Members to express their assent to the Resolution which has been placed before them and show their respect to the flag by getting up and standing in their places for half a minute.

The motion was adopted, the whole Assembly standing.

The Honourable Pandit Jawaharlal Nehru: *Mr President, Sir, may I respectfully suggest that these two flags which have been displayed this morning may be specially preserved and subsequently deposited in the National Museum.* (Applause).

Mr President: *I accept that suggestion.*

An Honourable Member: *I request you on behalf of the House to convey our homage to Mahatma Gandhi and tell him that we are observing this day very magnificently.*

Mr President: *I will do that with the greatest pleasure.*

The Assembly then adjourned till 10 a.m. on Wednesday, 23 July 1947, after adopting the motion on the National-flag of free India.

Significance of the Colours in Tiranga

While adopting Tiranga as the National-flag of India, Pandit Jawharlal Nehru asserted that the colours in the Flag have no communal import. He said: "some people, having misunderstood its significance, have thought of it in communal terms and believe that some part of it represents this community or that. But, I may say, when this flag was devised there was no communal significance attached to it".

There are three principal colours –saffron, white, green, and one secondary colour, the blue of the chakra. Each has its own significance.

The Saffron

The saffron has been one of the ancient colours commonly used in India. It was the colour that was widely donned by gods and goddesses of this holy land. The *pitambara* (long scarf) of Lord Krishna is well-known to all devout Hindus. The saffron is obtained with a combination of yellow and red in a certain proportion. The yellow is the colour of *Brihaspati*, the epitome of wisdom and the teacher of the gods; while red is the colour of valour, being suggestive of the God of War, Mars, who is full of action. Thus, saffron denotes both wisdom and action. It is also the colour of fire. The ego has to be burned to ashes by a true sanyasi. Hence, the Saffron colour is chosen for sanyas.

In the words of Dr Radhakrishnan: "The red, the orange and the bhagwa colours represent the spirit of renunciation. It is said: *Sarve Tyage Rajadharmesu Drishta* (All forms of renunciation are to be embodied in Rajadharma). If we are not imbued with the spirit of renunciation in these difficult days, we will again go under."

On the occasion of adopting the National-flag, Seth Govind Das said in the Constituent Assembly: "I want to tell those who say that the saffron colour represents the Hindus, that it is wrong to say so. No doubt, at one time, it was the colour of the Hindus. During the regime of the Peshwas it was the colour of the Hindus. In their fights for freedom the Rajputs used saffron dress."

Saiyid Mohammed Saadulla drew an analogy from nature and said: "The saffron represents the condition of the earth, the scorched condition caused by the torrid heat of the Indian sun .The saffron, as is well-known, is the colour of all those people who live the spiritual life not only among Hindus, but, also among Muslims. We should keep ourselves on that high plane of renunciation which has been the realm of our sadhus and saints, pirs and pandits.".

There was general agreement among scholars that saffron stood for courage and sacrifice and that it has been part of Indian culture since ancient days. Therefore, they have been advocating in the past for inclusion of this sacred colour in the flag of India. The Sanskrit Congress which met at Calcutta in 1924 advocated for saffron. In the same year Dvijendranath Tagore and C.F. Andrews suggested to Gandhiji inclusion of ochre colour in the National Congress's flag. In 1929, a Sikhs deputation met Gandhiji at Lahore and demanded the Sikh colour, a shadow of yellow to be included in the flag.

Later, in 1931 Dr Suniti Kumar Chatterjee, the late national professor in Humanities in India, wrote in his letter in reply to the questionnaire sent to him by Dr Pittabhi Sitarammya, the convenor of the Flag Committee of 1931: "It seems that the ideas of renunciation and harmlessness (*Vairagya* and *Ahimsa*) form the key note of Indian life, whether Hindu or Muhammedan or Christian. This is the ideal, which would send the king in his old age to the forest hermitage in Hindu India, the same ideal of renunciation made Prince Siddhartha, the Buddha that was to don the saffron garb of the ascetics. The Geru or Gairika, the red ochre or saffron colour worn by the Indian Sanyasi brings to our mind most forcibly the picture of this great ideal of Detachment and Harmlessness. This saffron colour is also the colour of discipline in the life of *Brahmacharins*. A modification of this saffron colour is the yellowish brown, the *Kasaya* or *Kashaya* of Buddhism." With these ideas Dr Suniti Kumar pleaded with the Flag Committee of 1931, the inclusion of saffron in the National Congress flag, which the Committee finally included in the Flag.

At the time of adopting the Tiranga as the National-flag of the nation in 1947, Veer Savarkar sent a telegram to the Adhoc Committee on flag strongly pleading inclusion of saffron in the National-flag of India.

The adhoc Committee on Flag, taking into consideration all these ideas and opinions, decided to include saffron in the flag of Independent India.

The White

The white colour of the centre band in India's National-flag, according to Dr Radhakrishnan, represents the white of the sun's rays. White denotes the path of light. It is necessary for us to dissipate the clouds of darkness and control our conduct by the ideal of light, the light of truth, of transparent simplicity which is illustrated by the colour white. We cannot attain purity, we cannot gain our goal of truth unless we walk in the path of virtue.

Saiyid Mohammed Saadulla explained that white, both among the Hindus and the Muslims, is the emblem of purity. The presence of the white portion in this flag should remind every one who takes it up that we must be pure, not only in words, but, also in deeds. Purity should be the motto of our life.

The white, according to H.J. Khandekar, denotes "peace and tranquility" and indicates "unity amongst all the communities in this country". For this reason "this flag represents every religion and every language in this country".

White is the universal symbol of purity, chastity, temperance and virginity. It denotes holiness, spirituality and perfection. Being the fullness of all colours, white signifies the perfection of God. "The white colour is symbolical of purity and truth, and the traditional colour in which Saraswati is represented as the Goddess of Learning and Truth" explained professor Radhakumud Mookerje.

The Green

The green is symbolical of vegetation and agriculture on which depend the vast majority of the Indian people. It indicates that India through the ages has been a rural and not an urban civilisation whose roots were grown in Asrams and hermitages of the forests which were the abode of seers and saints who pursued the philosophy of simple living and high thinking.

In the words of Dr Suniti Kumar, green, the colour of vegetation, is the colour of life and growth, therefore, we can very well have the symbol of life in our National-Emblem. Green is also the colour of hope and we largely live in hope.

The green in our National-flag reminded Seth Govind Das of the First War of Independence. At that time, the colour of the revolt flag was green. Muslims attach great significance to it, green being the colour of the flag of Fatima, the daughter of the great Prophet. Green is also associated with Buddha. The green of the Buddha is the emblem of prosperity and happiness. Dr S Radhakrishnan thus explained the significance of green in our National-flag. "The green is there to show our relation to the soil, and to the plant life here on which all other life depends."

The Blue

The blue of the Ashoka Chakra in the flag of India is also very significant. The blue signifies the boundless sky above and the fathomless sea below. The twenty-four spokes of the chakra are suggestive of movement and continual progress of the country.

Blue is the colour of Lord Vishnu's complexion. Krishna and Rama, too, were bluish in their complexion which implies inner energy. When the heat of fire is augmented it turns from yellow to red and from red to blue, before turning white. The lotus flower associated with Siva is blue. Sita, the wife of Rama, and Rukmini, the wife of Krishna, both hold a blue lotus in their left hand.

In conclusion, it can be summed up that the designers of India's National-flag selected its colours and design after detailed deliberations and considerations, keeping the cultural heritage of India and its future aspirations in mind.

Why the Ashoka Chakra?

The National-flag of India has a wheel in the centre of its white band. The design of the wheel is that of the Ashoka Chakra as it appears on the pillar at Sarnath. The chakra substituted the charkha on the Congress flag when Tiranga as the National-flag of Independent India was adopted. Dr S.K. Chatterjee pleaded the substitution of the charkha with a chakra in 1931. Charkha, according to him, represented our desire for the simple life and the will to combat poverty with the wholesome remedy of our cottage industries. But charkha was cumbersome on our flag and its substitution by a chakra meant eternity, time and progress.

The *Sudarshan Chakra* of Lord Vishnu is the cosmic disc which comprehends all that is animate and inanimate in this cosmos. The wheel and its variants appear on early Indian coins. The wheel appears in a pictographic legend on a stamp seal found at Mohenjo-Daro. The wheel is seen even on the Harappan pottery. Thus, the wheel, as a solar symbol, has been used since ancient times in India.

However, at the time of selecting a wheel or chakra for the National-flag of India, the members of the Flag Committee chose the Ashoka Chakra as it appears on the Ashoka Pillar at Sarnath for the reason that amongst all the charkas that came to their mind the Sarnath Chakra was the most beautiful to look at and every part of it symbolised the culture of India. Pandit Nehru while describing the chakra remarked: "It is beautiful and artistic."

Some people, however, tried to create an impression that Gandhiji was peeved at the disappearance of the charkha from the National-flag of India. In fact, Gandhiji published an article 'Thoughtful Suggestion' by S.D. Kalelkar in the *Harijan* of 6 July 1947, paving the way for the Constituent Assembly to adopt the simple wheel, as symbolic of the charkha, making it easier to draw symmetrically in design without creating confusion with the obverse and reverse sides of the flag. Pandit Nehru countered all criticism on this point in his press statement dated 31 August 1947. He said: "In the resolution of the Constituent Assembly it was stated clearly that the wheel in the center represented the charkha. This symbolic representation retains in its entirety the conception behind the charkha and is in fact, a continuation of that idea in a somewhat more feasible and artistic form, more suited to the Flag".

Preparations of First Independence Day Celebrations

With the adoption of the National-flag on July 22nd, 1947, preparations to celebrate the first Independence Day of the new domain of India were in full swing. A Celebration

Hearty Welcome to the New Flag

Tiranga made the headlines in the national dailies on July 23, 1947.

Committee was formed under the aegis of Mr. B.S. Puri, OBE, ICE, the then Chief Engineer of CPWD. The Committee further formed 5 Sub-committees so as to timely manage the mega event within the limited span of time available to authorities.

The Celebration Committee held its first meeting in the North Block Secretariat on July 24th followed by meetings on July 28th, 30th and and 31st and August on 5th and 11th. During these meetings a number of desisions were taken in connection with the celebrations of the first Independence Day. The foremost decision was that Delhi would be illuminated on the occasion with as much floodlights as could be possible. The Council Chamber, Constituent Assembly Hall, both the Blocks of the Central Secretariat, Red Fort, Qutub Minar, Delhi Gate, Ajmeri Gate and Kashmiri Gate were to be decked to give a festive look to the city.

The Sub-committee on the National-flag proposed that 2 lac mini paper flags to be printed on the occasion for free distribution in public as a goodwill gesture. It was estimated that 70 large size khadi and silk flags would be required for various Central Government buildings in the capital for the flag hoisting ceremony on "15th August". The arrangements were made to manufacture these flags as also to prepare samples of the National-flag to be despatched to different provincial Governments all over the country and also to Embassies and High Commissions abroad so that they could timely manufacture National-flags for the flag hoisting ceremony on the first Independence Day.

Another significant decision taken by the Flag-committee was that on most Central Government buildings in the country the Union Jack hauled down after sunset on August 14th would not be hoisted on those buildings at sunrise on

"15th August" In addition, arrangements were made at the civil shop in the North Block Secretariat (a canteen now exists there) to make available the National-flags after August 7th. Only two, one large and one small flag could be purchased for residential purpose by Government employees against their identity cards. All these restrictions were laid down because the stock available was in scarcity. All Government office buildings in Old and New Delhi were to be decorated with flags by the CPWD. The Secretariat of the Constituent Assembly received numerous requests from all quarters for samples of the flag's approved design. The Secretariat, therefore, published an authorised design for them to facilitate the manufacture of the National-flag at their end.

It was also decided that 1 lac Independence Medals in copper be struck at the Bombay Mint for distribution to all the Government and convent schools' students in Delhi. The medals that were struck had the likeness of Tiranga on the obverse and "Jai Hind" on the reverse with the date as "15th August 1947". Besides being gifted as souvenirs to Delhi's school students, the medals were also given to members of the Diplomatic Corps. The Mint Master, Bombay, Major Deane was awarded a letter of appreciation for executing the job with promptitude.

It is interesting to note that conforming to an ages old tradition followed on such blissful days, the Government of India decided to release certain prisoners and commute death sentence to life imprisonment on the historic day.

The Director of Health Deptt, Delhi Col. Fraser was granted a sum of Rs. 1500/-(those days it was a big amount) to spend on special feeding of indoor patients of the Delhi hospitals on "15th August, 1947". The Delhi provincial Celebrations Committee made arrangements for feeding of the poor and orphans on the occasion. The Delhi Municipal Committee separately made arrangement for 5000 packets of sweets for distribution to students of unaided schools.

As a goodwill gesture, *The Hindustan Times* distributed free to its readers a paper flag souvenir along with its issue of July 28, 1947 to acquaint people with the approved design of the National-flag.

The paper flag souvenir of Tiranga, that The Hindustan Times *distributed free to its readers on July 28, 1947.*

Interestingly, the issue of the August 10, 1947 of *The Hindustan Times* carried an advertisement which read:

NATIONAL FLAG

For two and a half annas

If you have any difficulty in
getting *khadi*–cotton
or a silk flag of free
India, please book your
order with us:

**FREE INDIA FLAG
MANUFACTURING CO.,
KATRA NEEL, DELHI.**

15

Specifications for the National-flag of India

 On July 22, 1947, as an Honourable Member of the adhoc committee on the flag, Pandit Jawaharlal Nehru presented to the Constituent Assembly two flags, specially designed and manufactured for adoption as the National-flag of India. Presenting the flags, he moved the following Resolution:

Resolved that the National-flag of India shall be horizontal tricolour of deep saffron (kesari), white and dark green in equal proportions. In the centre of the white band, there shall be a wheel in navy blue to represent the charkha. The design of the wheel shall be that of the wheel which appears on the abacus of the Sarnath Lion Capital of Ashoka.

The diameter of the wheel shall be approximate to the width of the white band.

The ratio of the width to the length of the flag shall ordinarily be 2:3 (two breadths by three breadths).

Indian Standard

SPECIFICATION FOR
THE NATIONAL FLAG OF INDIA
(COTTON KHADI)

U.D.C.

929·9 (54):677·21·064]   (083/75) (54)

National Flag Sectional Committee, TDC 8

Chairman

Mr. Basant Ram   Delhi Cloth and General Mills Co. Ltd., Delhi

Members

Mr. M. Krishnamurthy   Ministry of Defence, New Delhi
Mr. Dwarka Nath Lall   All-India Spinners' Association, Wardha
Mr. G. H. Lobsien   New Egerton Woollen Mills, Dhariwal
Dr. D. M. Nabar   Council of Scientific & Industrial Research, New Delhi
Dr. N. L. Narayan   Government of Rajasthan, Jaipur
Mr. A. V. Raman   Ministry of Home Affairs, New Delhi
Mr. Vishetra Narain Sharma   Shri Gandhi Ashram, Bhawsa
Mr. Ramdhir Singh   Directorate General of Industries and Supplies, New Delhi

Dr. Lal C. Verman (*Ex-officio*)   Director, Indian Standards Institution, Delhi

Staff

The Late Mr. C. P. Hasmati   Formerly Assistant Director (Textiles), ISI, Delhi
Mr. Manohar Kishore   Assistant Director (Textiles), ISI, Delhi
Mr. T. Balakrishnan   Technical Assistant, ISI, Delhi

Price Rs 2

INDIAN STANDARDS INSTITUTION
19 UNIVERSITY ROAD, CIVIL LINES
DELHI 8

*The cover page of the first Specification for
the National-flag of India, 1951.*

The motion was adopted by the august Assembly. However, at the time of its presentation, the Resolution did not purport to furnish full details regarding the quality of cloth and other particulars required for mass production of flags. Hence, the necessity was later felt for preparation of self-contained specifications for the National-flag for its manufacture in the country.

In 1951, at the request of the Ministry of Home Affairs and the Army Headquarters, the Indian Standards Institution (now the Bureau of Indian Standards) brought out the specifications on the National-flag for the first time. These specifications were revised in 1964, with a view to completely change the dimensions to the metric system. On August 17, 1968, the specifications were revised a second time. These specifications cover all the essential requirements of the National-flag for its manufacture.

While the initial specifications were being developed by the then ISI, the Government of India expressed a desire that the cloth for the manufacture of the flag for use by the Government should be handspun and hand-woven khadi. It may be noted here that Gandhiji in his article on the National-flag, published in *Young India* (April 13, 1921), had suggested that the flag must be made of *'khaddar'*, for it is through coarse cloth alone that we could make India independent of foreign markets for her cloth. Even Dr Suniti Kumar Chatterjee, in his article on the National-flag that appeared in the *Modern Review*, June 1931, had suggested that 'the cloth for the National-flag should on all cases be handspun and hand-woven, whether cotton or silk.'

Accordingly, it was decided that the cloth, be it cotton, woollen or silk, would be hand-woven and the yarn used for making the cloth, too, would be handspun. Interestingly, it was decided that even the sewing thread of the three colours, namely India-saffron, white and India-green, for stitching the flag would also be khadi. The sewing threads of the three colours were to be well-spun, evenly twisted and free from knots, short lengths and other defects.

The Indian Standard Institute describes the design and constructional details of the National-flag of India thus:

> The flag shall be rectangular in shape and ratio of the length to the width shall be 3:2. The flag shall be a tricolour panel made up of three rectangular panels or sub-panels of equal widths.
>
> The colours of the top panels shall be India-saffron (kesari), and that of the bottom panel shall be India-green, the middle panel shall be white bearing at its centre the design of Ashoka Chakra in navy blue colour.
>
> The Ashoka Chakra shall have twenty-four spokes equally spaced and shall preferably be screen printed or otherwise printed or stenciled or suitably embroidered with navy blue colour. In all the cases, the chakra shall be completely visible on both sides of the flag in the centre of the white panel.

Of the two flags that Pandit Jawaharlal Nehru presented to the Constituent Assembly at the time of moving the Resolution on the National-flag, the one of khadi was handed over to the Indian Standards Institution (ISI) for conformity of design, colour, etc. Once necessary action was taken by the ISI, the flag was sealed and kept in the custody of the Chief Inspector, Chief Inspectorate of Textiles and Clothing, Kanpur.

Design of the Ashoka Chakra

The spectrophotometer value of all the colours described by the ISI as India-saffron, India-green and white, was measured and determined in conformity with the colours of the sealed sample held at Kanpur. This was done by the Technical Development Establishment Laboratory (Stores) in Kanpur, using the illuminant 'C' as specified by the International Commission on Illumination, 1931.

The precise terms and details about the colours of the flag have been defined in the Indian colour standard for the National-flag.

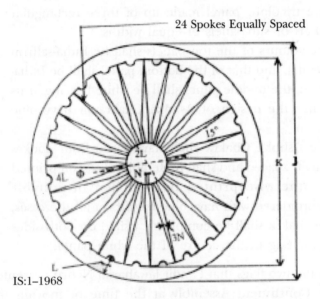

24 Spokes Equally Spaced

IS:1–1968

Design of the Ashoka Chakra as to be depicted on the Tiranga.

Colour	Trichromatic Values			Brightness %
	X	Y	Z	
(a) India-saffron	0.538	0.360	0.102	21.5
(b) India-green	0.288	0.395	0.317	8.9
(c) White	0.313	0.319	0.368	72.6

Although, no embargo is levied on the manufacture of the National-flag by private agencies, it is extremely desirable to maintain the honour and dignity of the flag. Therefore, all flags manufactured must conform to the specifications laid down by the ISI.[1]

All flags have to be marked on the sleeve with the following details before they are marketed:

(a) Flag size no.

(b) Length x width in millimeters,

(c) Manufacturers name or trademark,

(d) Year of manufacture, and

(e) Any other information required by the buyer.

The flags may also be marked with the ISI certification mark.

In 1951, when the specifications for the National-flag were initially developed, there were only five standard sizes of the flag. However, at the time of revising these specifications in 1968, the flag had seven standard sizes. As on date, there are nine standard sizes of the National-flag, the last two sizes added to the list include the sizes for VVIP aircraft and table-flags meant for use during State protocols. Interestingly, flags of all the sizes are to be manufactured from one layer of bunting except the flags to be used on VVIP motor-cars and aircraft, which are to be manufactured from two layers of bunting. This is because the flag flaps vigorously as the car or aircraft moves. Similarly, the table-flags, too, are to be made of two layers of silk bunting for reasons of magnanimity.

---

1. The details about the colours of the Flag have been taken from the Indian Standard Specification for the National-Flag of India. (Cotton khadi) 1968, published by the Indian Standards Institution, Manak Bhawan, New Delhi.

16

Amended Flag Code-India, 2002

It is one of the fundamental duties of every citizen to respect the National-flag. To accord due respect to this solemn symbol of the nation, one ought to know the codes related to the National-flag, as well as the courtesies and ceremonies connected with it. With a view to familiarising ourselves and for general guidance, the amended Flag Code-India is enumerated as under:

The Indian National-flag represents the hopes and aspirations of the people of India. It is the symbol of our national pride. Over the last five decades, several people, including the members of the armed forces, have ungrudgingly laid down their lives to keep the tricolour flying in its full glory.

There is universal affection and respect for, and loyalty to, the National-flag. Yet, a perceptible lack of awareness is often noticed, not only amongst people, but, also in the organisations/agencies of the Government in regard to laws, practices and conventions that apply to the display of the National-flag. Apart from non-statutory instructions issued by the Government from time to time, the display of the National-flag is governed by the provisions of the Emblems and Names (Prevention of Insults to National Honour Act, 1971, No. 69 of 1971). The Flag Code of India, 2002, is an attempt to bring together all such laws, conventions, practices and instructions for the guidance and benefit of all concerned.

For the sake of convenience, the Flag Code of India, 2002, has been divided into three parts. Part I of the Code contains the general description of the National-flag. Part II of the Code is devoted to the display of the National-flag by members of the public, private organisations, educational institutions, etc. Part III of the Code relates to display of the National-flag by Central and State governments and their organisations and agencies.

The Flag Code of India, 2002, took effect from January 26, 2002 and supersedes the 'Flag Code-India' as it existed.

PART I

GENERAL

1.1 The National-flag shall be a tri-colour panel made up of three rectangular panels or sub-panels of equal widths. The colour of the top panel shall be India-saffron (kesari) and that of the bottom panel shall be India-green. The middle panel shall be white, bearing at its centre the design of Ashoka Chakra in navy blue colour with twenty-four equally spaced spokes. The Ashoka Chakra shall preferably be screen printed or otherwise printed or stenciled or suitably embroidered and shall be completely visible on both sides of the flag in the centre of the white panel.

1.2 The National-flag of India shall be made of handspun and hand-woven wool/cotton/silk khadi bunting.

1.3 The National-flag shall be rectangular in shape. The ratio of the length to the height (width) of the flag shall be 3:2.

1.4 The standard sizes of the National-flag shall be as follows:

Flag Size No.	Dimensions in ft. & inches	in mm	Generally Used On
1	21' × 14'	6300 × 4200	On a very lofty and hefty flagmast
2	12' × 8'	3600 × 2400	Red Fort, Delhi; Rashtrapati Bhawan; Gun carriages
3	9' × 6'	2700 × 1800	Parliament House and other medium sized public buildings
4	6' × 4'	1800 × 1200	Small sized public buildings and during State and military funerals
5	4.5' × 3'	1350 × 900	Smaller sized public buildings
6	3' × 2'	900 × 600	In rooms on cross bars and walls
7	18" × 12"	450 × 300	VVIP aircraft and President's train
8	9" × 6"	225 × 150	VVIP motor cars
9	6" × 4"	150 × 100	As table-flags

1.5 An appropriate size should be chosen for display. The flags of 450 × 300 mm size are intended for VVIP flights, 225 × 150 mm size for motor-cars and 150 × 100 mm size for table flags.

PART II

HOISTING/DISPLAY/USE OF NATIONAL-FLAG BY MEMBERS OF PUBLIC, PRIVATE ORGANISATIONS, EDUCATIONAL INSTITUTIONS, ETC.

SECTION 1

2.1 There shall be no restriction on the display of the National-flag by members of the general public, private organisations, educational institutions, etc., except to the extent provided in the Emblems and Names (Prevention of Improper use) Act, 1950* and The Prevention of Insults to National Honour Act, 1971**.

* The Emblems and Names (Prevention of Improper Use) Act, 1950.

Section 2:   In this Act, unless the context otherwise requires:-
(a) "emblem" means any emblem, seal, flag, insignia, coat-of-arms or pictorial representation specified in the Schedule.

Section 3:   Notwithstanding anything contained in any law for the time being in force, no person shall, except in such cases and under such conditions as may be prescribed by the Central Government, use, or continue to use, for the purpose of any trade, business, calling or profession, or in the title of any patent, or in any trade mark of design, any name or emblem specified in the Schedule or any colourable imitation thereof without the previous permission of the Central Government or of such officer of Government as may be authorised in this behalf by the Central Government.

NOTE: The Indian National-flag has been specified as an Emblem in the Schedule to the Act and the Prevention of Insults to National Honour Act, 1971** and any other law enacted on the subject. Keeping in view the provisions of the afore-mentioned Acts–

(i) The flag shall not be used for commercial purposes in violation of the Emblem and Names (Prevention of Improper Use) Act, 1950;

(ii) The flag shall not be dipped in salute to any person or thing;

(iii) The flag shall not be flown at half-mast except on occasions on which the flag is flown at half-mast on public buildings in accordance with the instructions issued by the Government;

(iv) The flag shall not be used as a drapery in any form whatsoever, including private funerals;

(v) The flag shall not be used as a portion of costume or uniform of any description nor shall it be embroidered or printed upon cushions, handkerchiefs, napkins or any dress material;

** The Prevention of Insults to National Honour Act, 1971.

Section 2: Whoever in any public place or in any other place within public view burns, mutilates, defaces, defiles, disfigures, destroys, tramples upon or otherwise brings into contempt (whether by words, either spoken or written, or by acts) the Indian National-flag or any part thereof, shall be punished with imprisonment for a term which may extend to three years, or with a fine, or both.

Explanation 1: Comments expressing disapprobation or criticism of the Indian National-flag or of any measures of the Government with a view to obtain ... Or an alteration of the Indian National-flag by lawful means do not constitute an offence under this section.

Explanation 2: The expression 'Indian National-flag' includes any picture, painting, drawing or photograph, or other visible representation of the Indian National-flag, or of any part or parts thereof, made of any

substance or represented on any substance.
Explanation 3: The expression 'public place' means any place intended for use by, or accessible to the public and includes any public conveyance.

(vi) Lettering of any kind shall not be put upon the flag;

(vii) The flag shall not be used as a receptacle for receiving, delivering, holding or carrying anything; Provided that there shall be no objection to keeping flower petals inside the flag before it is unfurled as part of celebrations on special occasions and on National Days like the Republic Day and the Independence Day;

(viii) When used on occasions like unveiling of a statue, the flag shall be displayed distinctly and separately and it shall not be used as a covering for the statue or monument;

(ix) The flag shall not be used to cover a speaker's desk nor shall it be draped over a speaker's platform;

(x) The flag shall not be intentionally allowed to touch the ground or the floor or trail in water.

(xi) The flag shall not be draped over the hood, top, sides or back of a vehicle, train, boat or an aircraft;

(xii) The flag shall not be used as a covering for a building; and

(xiii) The flag shall not be intentionally displayed with the 'saffron' down.

The Flag Code of India 2002 was amended on May 8, 2003. Following the amendment, certain non–statutory instructions contained in Part II of Section 1 (2.1) of the Flag Code of India 2002, were included as part of the Prevention of Insults to National Honour Act 1971, with a view to prevent insult to the National-flag. With this amendment, the so far non-statutory instructions of the above Section have assumed legal sanctity being part of the Act, and as such are punishable under the Prevention of Insults to the National Honour Act 1971. The amended Act is reproduced as under:

THE PREVENTION OF INSULTS TO NATIONAL HONOUR ACT, 1971

No. 69 of 1971   (23rd December, 1971)

(AMENDED BY THE PREVENTION OF INSULTS TO NATIONAL HONOUR (AMENDMENT) ACT, 2003)

No. 31 of 2003   (8th May, 2003)

AN ACT TO PREVENT INSULTS TO NATIONAL HONOUR

Be it enacted by Parliament in the Twenty-second year of the Republic of India as follows:

1. SHORT TITLE AND EXTENT

   (1) This Act may be called the Prevention of Insults of National Honour Act, 1971.

   (2) It extends to the whole of India.

2. INSULT TO INDIAN NATIONAL FLAG AND CONSTITUTION OF INDIA

Whoever in any public place or in any other place within public view burns, mutilates, defaces, defiles, disfigures, destroys, tramples upon or *otherwise shows disrespect to or brings into contempt (whether by words, either spoken or written, or by acts) the Indian National Flag or the Constitution of India or any part thereof, shall be punished with imprisonment for a term which may extend to three years, or with fine, or with both.

Explanation 1.   Comments expressing disapprobation or criticism of the Constitution or of the Indian National Flag or of any measures of the Government with a view to obtain an amendment of the Constitution of India or an alteration of the Indian National Flag by lawful means do not constitute an offence under this section.

Explanation 2:   The expression, "Indian National Flag" includes any picture, painting, drawing or photograph, or other visible representation of the Indian National Flag, or of any part of parts thereof, made of any substance or represented on any substance.

Explanation 3:   The expression "public place" means any place intended for use by, or accessible to, the public and includes any public conveyance.

*Explanation 4:   The disrespect to the Indian National flag means and includes—

(a)   a gross affront or indignity offered to the Indian National Flag; or

(b)   dipping the Indian National Flag in salute to any person or thing; or

(c)   flying the Indian National Flag at half-mast except on occasions on which the Flag is flown at half-mast on public buildings in accordance with the instructions issued by the Government; or

(d)   using the Indian National Flag as a drapery in any form whatsoever except in state funerals or armed forces or other para-military forces funerals; or

(e)   using the Indian National Flag as a portion of costume or uniform of any description or embroidering or printing it on cushions, handkerchiefs, napkins or any dress material; or

(f)   putting any kind of inscription upon the Indian National Flag; or

(g) Using the Indian National Flag as a receptacle for receiving, delivering or carrying anything except flower petals before the Indian National Flag is unfurled as part of celebrations on special occasions including the Republic day or the Independence Day; or

(h) using the Indian National Flag as covering for a statue or a monument or a speaker's desk or a speaker's platform; or

(i) allowing the Indian National Flag to touch the ground or the floor or trail in water Intentionally; or

(j) draping the Indian National Flag over the hood, top, and sides or back or on a vehicle, train, boat or an aircraft or any other similar object; or

(k) using the Indian National Flag as a covering for a building; or

(l) intentionally displaying the Indian National Flag with the "saffron" down.

3. PREVENTION OF SINGING OF NATIONAL ANTHEM

Whoever intentionally prevents the singing of the Indian National Anthem or causes disturbances to any assembly engaged in such singing shall be punished with imprisonment for a term, which may extend to three years, or with fine, or with both.

*3A MINIMUM PENALTY ON SECOND OR SUBSEQUENT OFFENCE

Whoever having already been convicted of an offence under section 2 or section 3 is again convicted of any such offence shall be punishable for the second and for every subsequent offence, with imprisonment for a term, which shall not be less than one year.

NOTE: *Inserted vide The Prevention of Insults to National Honour (Amendment) Act, 2003 (No. 31 of 2003 dated 8.5.2003)

2.2 A member of the public, private organisation or an educational institution may hoist/display the National-flag on all days and occasions, ceremonial or otherwise, consistent with the dignity and honour of the National-flag.

(i) Whenever the National-flag is displayed, it should occupy the position of honour and should be distinctly placed;

(ii) A damaged or dishevelled flag should not be displayed;

(iii) The flag should not be flown from a single masthead simultaneously with any other flag or flags;

(iv) The flag should not be flown on any vehicle except in accordance with the provisions contained in Section IX of Part III of this Code;

(v) When the flag is displayed on a speaker's platform, it should be flown on the speaker's right as he faces the audience or flat against the wall, above and behind the speaker;

(vi) When the flag is displayed flat and horizontal on a wall, the saffron band should be upper most and when displayed vertically, the saffron band shall be on the right with reference to the flag (i.e. left to the person facing the flag);

(vii) To the extent possible, the flag should conform to the specifications prescribed in Part I of this Code.

(viii) No other flag or bunting should be placed higher than or above or side by side with the National-flag; nor should any object including flowers or garlands or emblem be placed on or above the flagmast from which the flag is flown;

(ix) The flag should not be used as a festoon, rosette or bunting or in any other manner for decoration;

(x) The flag made of paper may be waved by the public on occasions of important national, cultural and sports events. However, such paper flags should not be discarded or thrown on the ground after the event. As far as possible, it should be disposed off in private, consistent with the dignity of the flag;

(xi) Where the flag is displayed in the open, it should, as far as possible be flown from sunrise to sunset, irrespective of weather conditions;

(xii) The flag should not be displayed or fastened in any manner as may damage it; and

(xiii) When the flag is in a damaged or soiled condition, it shall be destroyed as a whole in private, preferably by burning or by any other method consistent with the dignity of the flag.

SECTION II

2.3 The National-flag may be hoisted in educational institutions (schools, colleges, sports camps, scout camps, etc.) to inspire respect for the flag. A model set of instructions for guidance is given below:

(i) The School will assemble in open square formation with pupils forming the three sides and the flag-staff at the centre of the fourth side. The Headmaster, the pupil leader and the person unfurling the flag (if other than the Headmaster) will stand three paces behind the flag-staff.

(ii) The pupils will line-up according to classes and in squads of ten (or other number according to strength). These squads will be arranged one behind the other. The pupil leader of the class will stand to the right of the first row of his class and the form master will stand three paces behind the last row of his class, towards the middle. The classes will be arranged along the square in the order of seniority with the senior most class at the right end.

(iii) The distance between each row should be at least one pace (thirty inches); and the space between Form and Form should be the same.

(iv) When each Form or Class is ready, the Class leader will step forward and salute the selected school pupil leader. As soon as all the Forms are ready, the school pupil leader will step up to the Headmaster and salute him. The Headmaster will return the salute. Then, the flag will be unfurled. The School pupil leader may assist.

(v) The School pupil leader in charge of the parade (or assembly) will call the parade to attention, just before the unfurling, and he will call them to salute when the flag flies out. The parade will keep to the salute for a brief interval, and then on the command 'order', the parade will come to the attention position.

(vi) The flag salutation will be followed by the National Anthem. The parade will be kept to attention during this part of the function.

(vii) On all occasions when the pledge is taken, the pledge will follow the National Anthem. When taking the pledge the Assembly will stand to attention and the headmaster will administer the pledge ceremoniously and the Assembly will repeat it after him.

(viii) In pledging allegiance to the National-flag, the practice to be adopted in schools is as follows:-
Standing with folded hands, all repeat together the following pledge:
"I pledge allegiance to the National-flag and to the Sovereign Socialist Secular Democratic Republic for which it stands".

PART-III

HOISTING/DISPLAY OF THE NATIONAL FLAG BY THE CENTRAL AND STATE GOVERNMENTS AND THEIR ORGANISATIONS AND AGENCIES

SECTION I

DEFENCE INSTALLATIONS/HEADS OF MISSIONS/ POSTS

3.1 The provisions of this Part shall not apply to Defence installations that have their own rules for display of the National-flag.

3.2 The National-flag may also be flown on the Headquarters and the residences of the Heads of Missions/Posts abroad in the countries where it is customary for diplomatic and consular representatives to fly their National-flags at their headquarters and their official residences.

SECTION II

OFFICIAL DISPLAY

3.3 Subject to the provisions contained in Section I above, it shall be mandatory for all Governments and their organisations/agencies to follow the provisions contained in this Part.

3.4 On all occasions for official display, only the flag conforming to specifications laid down by the Bureau of Indian Standards and bearing their standard mark shall be used. On other occasions also, it is desirable that only such flags of appropriate size are flown.

SECTION III

CORRECT DISPLAY

3.5 Wherever the flag is flown, it should occupy the position of honour and be distinctly placed.

3.6 Where the practice is to fly the flag on any public building, it shall be flown on that building on all days including Sundays and holidays and, except as provided in this Code, it shall be flown from sunrise to sunset irrespective of weather conditions. The flag may be flown on such a building at night also but this should be only on very special occasions.

3.7 The flag shall always be hoisted briskly and lowered slowly and ceremoniously. When the hoisting and the lowering of the flag is accompanied by appropriate bugle calls, the hoisting and lowering should be in synchronisation with the bugle calls.

3.8 When the flag is displayed from a staff projecting horizontally or at an angle from a windowsill, balcony, or front of a building, the saffron band shall be at the farther end of the staff.

3.9 When the flag is displayed flat and horizontal on a wall, the saffron band shall be upper most and when displayed vertically, the saffron band shall be to the right with reference to the flag, i.e. it may be to the left of a person facing it.

3.10 When the flag is displayed on a speaker's platform, it shall be flown on a staff on the speaker's right as he faces the audience or flat against the wall above and behind the speaker.

3.11 When used on occasions like the unveiling of a statue, the flag shall be displayed distinctly and separately.

3.12 When the flag is displayed alone on a motorcar, it shall be flown from a staff, which should be affixed firmly

The Indian cricket team with National-flag in the rearguard.
However, it is desirable that the flag bearer always be in the vanguard and not
as seen in the picture.

The National-flag is to be draped over the bier or coffin with the saffron
towards the head touching the neck and the Ashoka Chakra has to be in the
centre, on the chest of the deceased, and not as seen in the picture.

either on the middle front of the bonnet or to the front right side of the car.

3.13 When the flag is carried in a procession or a parade, it shall be either on the marching right, i.e. the flag's own right, or if there is a line of other flags, in front of the centre of the line.

SECTION IV

INCORRECT DISPLAY

3.14 A damaged or dishevelled flag shall not be displayed.

3.15 The flag shall not be dipped in salute to any person or thing.

3.16 No other flag or bunting shall be placed higher than or above or, except as hereinafter provided, side by side with the National-flag; nor shall any object including flowers or garlands or emblem be placed on or above the flagmast from which the flag is flown.

3.17 The flag shall not be used as a festoon, rosette or bunting or in any other manner for decoration.

3.18 The flag shall not be used to cover a speaker's desk nor shall it be draped over a speaker's platform.

3.19 The flag shall not be displayed with the "saffron" down.

3.20 The flag shall not be allowed to touch the ground or the floor or trail in water.

3.21 The flag shall not be displayed or fastened in any manner as may damage it.

SECTION V

MISUSE

3.22 The flag shall not be used as a drapery in any form whatsoever except in State/Military/Central Para military forces funerals hereinafter provided.

3.23 The flag shall not be draped over the hood, top, sides or back of a vehicle, train or boat.

3.24 The flag shall not be used or stored in such a manner as may damage or soil it.

3.25 When the flag is in a damaged or soiled condition, it shall not be cast aside or disrespectfully disposed off, but, shall be destroyed as a whole in private, preferably by burning or by any other method consistent with the dignity of the Flag.

3.26 The flag shall not be used as a covering for a building.

3.27 The flag shall not be used as a portion of a costume or uniform of any description. It shall not be embroidered or printed upon cushions, handkerchiefs, napkins or boxes.

3.28 Lettering of any kind shall not be put upon the flag.

"Lettering of any kind is not to be put upon the flag nor is it to be superimposed by any figure as seen in the picture."

3.29 The flag shall not be used in any form of advertisement nor shall an advertising sign be fastened to the pole from which the flag is flown.

3.30 The flag shall not be used as a receptacle for receiving, delivering, holding or carrying anything.

Provided that there shall be no objection to keeping flower petals inside the flag before it is unfurled, as part of celebrations on special occasions and on National Days like the Republic Day and the Independence Day.

SECTION VI

SALUTE

3.31 During the ceremony of hoisting or lowering the flag or when the flag is passing in a parade or in a review, all persons present should face the lag and stand at attention. Those present in uniform should render the appropriate salute. When the flag is in a moving column, persons present will stand at attention or salute as the flag passes them. A dignitary may take the salute without a head-dress.

SECTION VII

DISPLAY WITH FLAGS OF OTHER NATIONS AND OF UNITED NATIONS

3.32 When displayed in a straight line with flags of other countries, the National-flag shall be on the extreme right, i.e., if an observer were to stand in the centre of the row of the flags facing the audience, the National-flag should be to his extreme right. The position is illustrated in the diagram below:-

3.33 Flags of foreign countries shall proceed as from the National-flag in alphabetical order on the basis of English versions of the names of the countries concerned. It would be permissible in such a case to begin and also to end the row of flags with the National-flag and also to include the National-flag in the normal country-wise alphabetical order. The National-flag shall be hoisted first and lowered last.

3.34 In case flags are to be flown in an open circle, i.e., in an arc or a semi-circle, the same procedure shall be adopted as is indicated in the preceding clause of this Section. In case flags are to be flown in a closed, i.e. complete circle, the National-flag shall mark the beginning of the circle and the flags of other countries should proceed in a clockwise manner until the last flag is placed next to the National-flag. It is not necessary to use separate National-flags to mark the beginning and the end of the circle of flags. The National-flag shall also be included in its alphabetical order in such a closed circle.

3.35 When the National-flag is displayed against a wall with another flag from crossed staffs, the National-flag shall be on the right, i.e., the flag's own right, and its staff shall be in front of the staff of the other flag. The position is illustrated in the diagram below:

3.36 When the United Nation's flag is flown along with the National-flag, it can be displayed on either side of the National-flag. The general practice is to fly the National-flag on the extreme right with reference to the direction which it is facing (i.e. extreme left of an observer facing the masts flying the flags). The position is illustrated in the diagram below:-

3.37 When the National-flag is flown with flags of other countries, the flagmasts shall be of equal size. International usage forbids the display of the flag of one nation above that of another nation in time of peace.

3.38 The National-flag shall not be flown from a single

Improper display of Tiranga

When the National-flag is displayed against a wall with another flag from a crossed staff, the flag has to be on the left of the observer not to his or her right as seen in the picture. It is an improper display of the Flag.

masthead simultaneously with any other flag or flags. There shall be separate mastheads for different flags.

SECTION VIII

DISPLAY OVER PUBLIC BUILDINGS/OFFICIAL RESIDENCES

3.39 Normally the National-flag should be flown only on important public buildings such as the High Court, Secretariats, Commissioners' Offices, Collectorates, Jails and offices of the District Boards, Municipalities and Zilla Parishads and Departmental/Public Sector Undertakings.

3.40 In frontier areas, the National-flag may be flown on the border customs posts, check posts, out-posts and at other special places where flying of the flag has special significance. In addition, it may be flown on the camp-sites of border patrols.

3.41 The National-flag should be flown on the official residences of the President, Vice-President, Governors and Lieutenant Governors when they are at Headquarters and on the building in which they stay during their visits to places outside the Headquarters. The flag flown on the official residence should, however, be brought down as soon as the dignitary leaves the Headquarters and it should be re-hoisted on that building as he enters the main-gate of the building on return to the Headquarters. When the dignitary is on a visit to a place outside the Headquarters, the flag should be hoisted on the building in which he stays as he enters the main gate of that building and it should be brought down as soon as he leaves that place. However, the flag should be flown from sunrise to sunset on such official residences, irrespective of whether the dignitary is at Headquarters or not on Republic Day, Independence Day, Mahatama Gandhi's Birthday, National Week (6th to 13th April, in the memory of martyrs of Jallianwala Bagh), and any other particular day of national rejoicing as may be specified by the Government of India or, in the case of a State, on the anniversary of the formation of that State.

3.42 When the President, the Vice-President or the Prime Minister visits an institution, the National-flag may be flown by the institution as a mark of respect.

3.43 On the occasions of the visit to India by foreign dignitaries, namely, President, Vice-President, Emperor/

King or Heir Prince and the Prime Minister, the National-flag may be flown along with the flag of the foreign country concerned in accordance with the rules contained in Section VII by such private institutions as are according receptions to the visiting foreign dignitaries and on such public buildings as the foreign dignitaries intend to visit on the day of visit to the institution.

SECTION IX

DISPLAY ON MOTOR CARS

3.44 The privilege of flying the National-flag on motor cars is limited to the:

1. President;
2. Vice-President;
3. Governors and Lieutenant Governors;
4. Head of Indian Missions/Posts abroad in the countries to which they are accredited;
5. Prime Minister and other Cabinet Ministers;
6. Ministers of State and Deputy Ministers of the Union;
7. Chief Minister and other Cabinet Ministers of a State or Union Territory;
8. Ministers of State and Deputy Ministers of a State or Union Territory;
9. Speaker of the Lok Sabha;
10. Deputy Chairman of the Rajya Sabha;
11. Deputy Speaker of the Lok Sabha;
12. Chairmen of Legislative Councils in States;
13. Speakers of Legislative Assemblies in State and Union Territories;
14. Deputy Chairmen of Legislative Councils in States;

15, Deputy Speakers of Legislative Assemblies in States and Union Territories;

16. Chief Justice of India;

17. Judges of Supreme Court;

18. Chief Justice of High Courts;

19. Judges of High Courts.

3.45 The dignitaries mentioned in Clauses (5) to (7) of paragraph 3.44 may fly the National-flag on their cars, whenever they consider it necessary or advisable.

3.46 When a foreign dignitary travels in a car provided by the Government, the National-flag will be flown on the right side of the car and the flag of the foreign countries will be flown on the left side of the car.

SECTION X

DISPLAY ON TRAINS/AIRCRAFT

3.47 When the President travels by special train within the country, the National-flag should be flown from the driver's cab on the side facing the platform of the station from where the train departs. The flag should be flown only when the special train is stationary or when coming into the station where it is going to halt.

3.48 The National-flag will be flown on the aircraft carrying the President, the Vice-President or the Prime Minister on a visit to a foreign country. Alongside the National-flag, the flag of the country visited should also be flown, but, when the aircraft lands in countries enroute, the National-flags of the countries touched would be flown instead, as a gesture of courtesy and goodwill.

3.49 When the President goes on tour within India, the National-flag will be displayed on the side by which the President will embark or disembark from the aircraft.

Tiranga atop the Tiger Hill, Kargil. Jawans showing the victory sign after capturing it.

Republic Day Parade at Rajpath.

The flags of the three armed forces of India at the Amar Jawan Jyoti, India Gate. Air Force Ensign (left) Naval Ensign (centre) and Army Flag (right).

Sea cadets marching through the streets of Mumbai carrying the National-flags of their respective countries.

Former Prime Minister Atal Bihari Vajpayee with his counterpart in Iran. National-flags of both the countries are mounted on mobile flagstands.

The Lahore bus leaving Delhi. The Indian Tricolour and Pakistan's National–flag are seen on the bonnet of the bus.

A young cricket fan supports the Indian team by displaying a paper Tiranga on his cap.

Cricket star Sachin Tendulkar sporting the Tiranga on his helmet.

Lata Mangeshkar donning a tricolour bordered saree to give a patriotic flavour to the song Vande Mataram.

Vishwanathan Anand playing against a Russian chess champion.
National-flags of both the players are placed on their respective sides of the table.

Wills World Cup 1996 Trophy. An enamelled Tiranga is seen on the base of the
trophy along with the flags of other countries.

A table Tiranga amidst other flags of south-east Asian countries.

Tiranga suspended from a rope at the Indo-Pak border with Pakistan's National-flag.

Tiranga in a happy home.

A ten rupee commemorative coin depicting Tiranga — 1972.

The first postal stamp of Independent India.

Independence Day celebrations on the ramparts of the Red Fort.

SECTION XI

HALF-MASTING

3.50 In the event of the death of the following dignitaries, the National-flag shall be half-masted at the places indicated against each on the day of the death of the dignitary:

Dignitary	Place or places
President	
Vice-President	Throughout India
Prime Minister	
Speaker of the Lok Sabha	Delhi
Chief Justice of India	
Union Cabinet Minister	Delhi and State Capitals
Minister of State	
Deputy Minister of the Union	Delhi
Governor	
Lt. Governor	
Chief Minister of a State or Union	Throughout the State
Chief Minister of a Union	Territory Concerned Territory
Cabinet Minister in a State	Capital of the State Concerned

3.51 If the intimation of the death of any dignitary is received in the afternoon, the flag shall be half-masted on the following day also at the place or places indicated above, provided the funeral has not taken place before sunrise on that day.

3.52 On the day of the funeral of a dignitary mentioned above, the flag shall be half-masted at the place where the funeral takes place.

3.53 If State mourning is to be observed on the death of any dignitary, the flag shall be half-masted throughout the period of the mourning throughout India in the case of the Union dignitaries and throughout the State or Union Territory concerned in the case of a State or Union Territory dignitary.

3.54 Half-masting of the flag and, where necessary, observance of State mourning on the death of foreign dignitaries will be governed by special instructions which will be issued from the Ministry of Home Affairs in individual cases.

3.55 Notwithstanding the above provisions, in the event of a half-mast day coinciding with the Republic Day, Independence Day, Mahatama Gandhi's Birthday, National Week (6th to 13th April, in the memory of martyrs of Jallianwala Bagh), any other particular day of national rejoicing as may be specified by the Government of India or, in the case of a State, on the anniversary of formation of that State, the flags shall not be flown at half-mast except over the building where the body of the deceased is lying until such time it has been removed and that flag shall be raised to the full-mast position after the body has been removed.

3.56 If mourning were to be observed in a parade or procession where a flag is carried, tow streamers of black crepe shall be attached to the spear-head, allowing the streamers to fall naturally. The use of black crepe in such a manner shall be only by an order of the Government.

3.57 When flown at half-mast, the flag shall be hoisted to the peak for an instant, then lowered to the half-mast position, but before lowering the flag for the day, it shall be raised again to the peak.

Note: *By half-mast it is meant hauling down the flag to one half the distance between the top and the guy-line and in the absence of the guy-line, half of the staff. This custom dates back to 1912 in Spain when its Navy lowered its flag to half-mast to mourn the death of its Admiral in a sea battle.*

3.58 On occasions of State/Military/Central Para-Military Forces funerals, the flag shall be draped over the bier or coffin with the saffron towards the head of the bier or coffin. The flag shall not be lowered into the grave or burnt in the pyre.

3.59 In the event of death of either the Head of the State or Head of the Government of a foreign country, the Indian Mission accredited to that country may fly the National-flag at half-mast even if that event falls on Republic Day, Independence Day, Mahatama Gandhi's Birthday, National Week (6th to 13th April, in the memory of martyrs of Jallianwala Bagh) or any other particular day of national rejoicing as may be specified by the Government of India. In the event of death of any other dignitary of that country, the National-flag should not be flown at half-mast by the Missions except when the local practice or protocol (which should be ascertained from the Dean of the Diplomatic Corps, where necessary) require that the National-flag of a Foreign Mission in that country should also be flown at half-mast.

FLAG OATH

I,... solemnly pledge allegiance to our National-flag Tiranga and to the Sovereign Socialistic, Secular and Democratic Republic of India, for which it stands.

17

Ordinary citizens and the National-flag

 In ancient times, a flag essentially represented and belonged to a king, his kingdom and his army. However, in the modern heraldic sense, a National-flag represents an independent sovereign state duly recognised by the world community, especially by the United Nations Organisation. In contemporary times, a National-flag is not a flag of an emperor or an empire, it is a flag of the whole nation. Modern history is replete with instances when people launched civil wars against their own or alien rulers under flags they designed themselves. Thus, a National-flag in true sense is the flag of the nation, its people, its honour, its ideals and its achievements. And as such, its nationals have every right to adore, regard and to display it.

At the time of moving the resolution to adopt the National-flag of India, on July 22, 1947, Pandit Jawaharlal Nehru said:

"Therefore, this flag that I have the honour to present to you is not, I hope and trust, a flag of an empire, a flag of imperialism, a flag of domination over anybody, but a flag of freedom, not only for ourselves, but to all people, who may see it."

On the same day and on the same occasion, winding up her speech in honour of the National-flag, Mrs Sarojini Naidu said:

"Under this flag, there is no difference between a prince and a peasant, between the rich and the poor, between man and woman."

Way back in 1921, this Tiranga, whose modified form is the present National-flag of India, was conceived and designed by ordinary but brave citizens of India. It was this flag in its original form, that the citizens of India fearlessly wielded against the British and brought freedom to the nation.

Notwithstanding, the sprit of the originators, the original Flag Code-India prohibited a free use of Tiranga by ordinary citizens. A judicial battle to liberate the National-flag from the shackles of restrictions on its free use and liberal display was waged by Naveen Jindal, a young industrialist of the country. After a prolonged judicial battle, the National-flag was freed with effect from January 26, 2002, as a result of a decision of the Union Cabinet on January 15, 2002.

While most nations have more or less an identical code for their National-flags, they, however, differ as to who is entitled to use it. Another significant feature is that the flag codes in the case of the majority of countries are without any legal or federal authority, though they are usually followed.

In the U.K., according to the code for the Union Jack, it is clear as to how it is to be correctly flown, but it is not clear as to who is entitled to fly it. The old heraldic view is that the Union Jack is a royal flag and indeed a coat-of-arms in the form of a shield and ensigned by the Royal Crown and is, therefore, one of the Royal Badges. And also, when the present design was made official in 1801 it was ordered to be flown on all His Majesty's domains. Moreover, it is hoisted over government buildings, offices, and national museums and picture galleries on official days or rejoicing. With this view, it is an emblem of 'Her Majesty's Service' and should not be used by ordinary citizens.

Notwithstanding, the English do fly the Union Jack in their private gardens, hotels, etc. for they consider it as their own. There is a strong view on the subject that the British would feel aggrieved in case they are forbidden to fly their flag. Moreover, its use by ordinary citizens is a long established custom which is never likely to be interfered with by law. It was, indeed announced in the British Parliament, in the past, that because the Union Jack is the National-flag, every member of the nation is entitled to fly it on land.

The Canadians look at the question pragmatically. According to the ceremonial procedures of the Public Works Canada, the Canadians hold the view:

"We must be cognizant of the fact that although most of our ceremonial traditions reach far back in history, we must always be prepared for changes and improvements. A good example of this is the change of emphasis that has occurred in recent years since the introduction of the Canadian flag in 1965. As Canadians show an ever increasing interest in this unique national symbol, we, who are in the position of providing ceremonial support services, find more and more requests for larger and more frequent flag displays."

The National-flag of Canada may be flown by individuals and organisations at any time. It will be flown on all Federal Government owned or leased buildings, airports, on Canadian Forces bases and establishments and worn as the ensign staff by H.M.C. ships in commission and by all other vessels in the service of the Canadian government. Besides Canada, Brazil is another country which allows an unrestricted display of her National-flag by her citizens.

On June 14, 1923 (the U.S. Flag day), the National American Committee of the American Legion called a conference in Washington. Delegates from seventy-two organisations assembled and adopted a universal flag code. Although, that code lacked any federal authority, it was generally followed. When World War II started, the Congress was asked to enact a federal flag code. This was done, and on June 22, 1942, the President of the United States signed the joint resolution, known as Public Law 621.

The first section of this Public Law declares the codification of the existing rules and customs for the guidance of civilians not required to conform to the regulations issued by different official branches of the Government.

As is the universal heraldic custom, the U.S. National-flag is displayed only from sunrise to sunset on all government buildings and on stationary flagstaffs in the open. However, the flag may be displayed at night on special occasions, when it is desired to produce a patriotic effect. Unlike most cases, the U.S. National-flag should not be displayed on days when the weather is inclement. (In India, however, the National-flag is to be flown on all government buildings and premises on all days, regardless of weather conditions).

Most flag codes of the world, such as those of Australia, Indonesia, China, Germany and Italy, allow unrestricted display of their National-flag only on certain occasions, and

'I love Tiranga' – Aamir Khan.

do not permit free use of their National-flag by their citizens. It is observed that more and more people, the world over, exhibit their National-flags as stickers on their cars, as logos on their shirts and T–shirts, etc. In Malaysia, the National-flag is all over the country. Malaysians display mini flags on and inside their cars, use it as stickers anywhere they like with the legend 'Proud to be a Malaysian'. In India, too, advertisers have started a liberal use of the National-flag in publicity campaigns, especially as part of government-sponsored TV commercials. Strictly speaking, such liberal use of the National-flag for commercial use is not permissible under the Emblems and Names (Prevention and Improper Use) Act 1950. It is possible that people feel patriotic and the authorities show indifference towards such a use of the flag. In New Zealand, the National-flag can, however, be officially used with decency in advertising. The New Zealand code is explicit on this subject, though most nations of the world do not permit commercial use of their National-flag.

In India, though restriction on the free use of the National-flag has been waived with effect from January 26, 2002, it is incumbent on all citizens to pay due respect to the flag. Any offences committed to the National-flag are punishable under the Prevention of Insults to National Honour Act, 1971 and also under the Emblems and Names (Prevention and Improper Use) Act, 1950. The former Act prohibits any insult to the National-flag and enunciates "whoever in any

Young fans displaying the Tiranga on their T-shirts at a Sports Meet.

Ordinary citizens and the National-flag **243**

public place or in any other place within public view burns, mutilates, defaces, defiles disfigures, destroys, tramples upon or otherwise brings into contempt (whether by words, either spoken or written or by acts) the Indian National-flag or the Constitution of India or any part shall be punished with imprisonment for a term which may extend to three years or wiu fine or with both".

Jubilant display of their National-flag by citizens of different countries during international sports events and tournaments, including the Asiads and Olympics is a universal practice, though such a wanton use of the National-flag under most flag codes of the world is restricted. In such free display and waving of the National-flag on these occasions, the patriotic feelings in people are paramount rather than any inadvertent disrespect shown to the flag by sports lovers. Through their display of the National-flag, people make a public expression of their nationalism. Therefore, this fundamental right must not be denied to citizens. They should be encouraged to show their love for this solemn symbol of the nation by distinctly displaying it in their drawing rooms, in their study on a mast, in their gardens, etc. However, it is highly desirable that while displaying the National-flag due care ought to be taken by all to ensure that the National-flag is not subjected to any inadvertent disrespect or insult.

Display of National-flag in Sports

The National-flag of a country is being increasingly used in sports. During international cricket and football tournaments, National-flags of participating nations are hoisted on the pavilion or the main VIP area. Besides, the sports fans carry, wear, wave, fly and differently display their flags to enthuse and support their team. During the Olympics, Asiads, and other international sports meets, the National-flags have a

A Victory Banquet.

special role to play. The National-flags of participating
countries are hoisted on their arrival at the Games Village
during International Sports Meets. On the occasion of the
opening ceremony, all contingents of the participating nations
are led by a flag-bearer carrying his country's National-flag.
During the actual competitions, when a country wins a gold
medal, the National-flag of his/her nation is hoisted, and the
national-anthem of that country played to honour and pay
tribute to the achievement. During international chess
tournaments, a mini National-flag of both the participating
players is placed on the right side of the table and next to
the players to denote their nationality. During the recent
2002 World Cup held in Japan and Korea, National-flags of
the participating nations were innovatively displayed by
football fans. People painted their National-flag on their
head and face to exhibit support and love for their country.

18

Curious facts about the Tiranga

Our National-flag is fondly known as the Tiranga, the corrupted form of '*Tri-ranga*', which literally means having three colours. However, strictly speaking, Tiranga is a misnomer, since our National-flag has four and not three colours, namely the saffron, white, green and the blue. The blue colour used for the device of the flag, the chakra on the middle white band, is often omitted. The chakra in blue, with its twenty-four spokes, denotes continual progress of the country and signifies the boundless limit of progress, like the unending vastness of blue sky above and the fathomless sea below. The saffron in the flag stands for renunciation and courage, the white signifies purity and truth while the green implies plentifulness and chivalry.

In our day-to-day conversation we refer to the three colours of Tiranga as saffron, white and green. However, according to the specifications of the National-flag as laid down by the

Indian Standards Institute (now Bureau), the exact description of the three principal colours in the flag is 'India-saffron' (kesari), 'India-green' and white. This is so because both saffron and green have many shades, therefore, the Indian Standards Institute specified the exact shade of both the colours. Another reason for specifying the shades was to minimise confusion with the colours of national-flags of some of the countries that use the same colour combination in their national standards, particularly Niger, Iceland and Ivory Coast.

On July 22, 1947, at the time of moving the Resolution on the National-flag in the Constituent Assembly, Pandit Jawaharlal Nehru had presented two flags, one of cotton-khadi and the other silk-khadi. While presenting these flags, he had proposed that the flags be kept as national property in the National Museum. But, of the two flags, the one of cotton-khadi is kept sealed as the standard flag in the custody of the Chief Inspector, Chief Inspectorate of Textiles and Clothing, Kanpur. But the whereabouts of the silk-khadi flag are obscure. A likely possibility is that the silk-khadi flag might have been used during the first-ever flag hoisting ceremony of free-India on August 15, 1947, instead of the same being preserved in the National Museum.

The common belief that the Tiranga was hoisted for the first time on the ramparts of the Red Fort on August 15, 1947, is not true. The Tiranga was hoisted for the first time on Red Fort by Pandit Jawaharlal Nehru on Saturday at 8:30 a.m. on August 16, 1947. As a matter of fact, on August 15, 1947, the national leaders were busy in other important State functions.

On the day of Independence (August 15, 1947), the Tiranga was hoisted not only within the country, but, abroad too. Some of the erstwhile State rulers, too, unfurled the Tiranga in their respective States.

It is a fact that when the entire world was aware that India was a free nation, the in-charge at the lighthouse of Minicoy, in the Lakshadweep and Minicoy Islands, remained ignorant of the transfer of power from British to Indian hands for the next nine years, and kept on flying the Union Jack on the lighthouse until April 2, 1956. To rectify the mistake, the then Superintendent of the British Lighthouse Service, Mr Rees, was specially sent to India by the British Government. On April 2, 1956, when the Union Jack was lowered for the last time from the flagmast of the lighthouse and the Tiranga hoisted in its place, Mr Rees was so emotionally moved, that he could not utter a word on the occasion. Leaving the function midway, he sailed off to his ship by boat. Although, the Tiranga started flying on the lighthouse with effect from April 2, 1956, the official transfer of the lighthouse took place only on September 19, 1963. The British Parliament took seven more years to enact the Bill and obtain the Queen's approval for the same.

At the time of Independence, Goa, Daman and Diu were under the Portuguese Rule. The Indian Navy and Army liberated these territories on December 16, 1961 and hoisted the Indian tricolour there for the first time. On October 21, 1954, the French authorities handed over the administrative control of Pondicherry to the Indian Government and, thus, the Tiranga started flying over this former French colony. Likewise, on August 2, 1954, Dadra, Nagar and Haveli were liberated from the Portuguese Rule and the Tiranga hoisted for the first time on that day. However, it was only on August 11, 1961 that the territory was officially integrated into the Indian Union. Till then it was administered and ruled by the people themselves. On April 10, 1975, the Sikkim Assembly resolved that the institution of the Chogyal shall be terminated and that Sikkim should be fully integrated with India as the

22nd State of the Indian Union. In response to this resolution, a Constitutional (38th Amendment) Act was passed by the Indian Parliament and Sikkim thus became an Indian state on April 26, 1975. The Tiranga was hoisted there, for the first time, once Sikkim was integrated with India.

Since 1947, the tricolour has not only become a symbol of our independence and sovereignty, but it has set forth on a course of adventures. It has accompanied our adventure seekers everywhere whether it was a mountaineering expedition, charting of the rough seas or a voyage into space.

On May 29, 1953, the tricolour had the rare honour of being first hoisted on Mt. Everest along with the Union Jack and the Nepalese National-flag by Sherpa Tenzing and Edmund Hillary, when they became the first men to climb the peak. Later, other Indian mountaineers also carried it to the top of the world. So far, the Tiranga has gone up to Mt. Everest eight times. The Tiranga that was unfurled on the Mt. Everest in 1953 is now preserved at the museum in the Rashtrapati Bhawan, New Delhi.

In 1971, the Indian tricolour, for the first time, travelled in space on board Apollo-15. This space odyssey was repeated when it was worn by Cosmonaut Wing Commander Rakesh Sharma as a medallion on the space suit during the Indo–Soviet joint space flight in April 1984.[1]

On January 9, 1982, the first Indian Antarctica expedition took the Indian flag over Dakshin Gangotri, and was hoisted for the first time, on the South Pole on January 17, 1989 by Colonel J.K. Bajaj.

On April 21, 1996 at 0352 hrs. (IST), the first Indian and perhaps the first in Asia, Squadron Leader (now Wing

---

1. The flag that was sent into space and the space suit worn by Wing Commander Rakesh Sharma are on display in the Nehru Planetarium at New Delhi.

Commander) Sanjay Thapar, holder of many national and international records in para jumping and sky-diving, jumped from an altitude of ten thousand feet from an MI-8 helicopter and hoisted, for the first time, the Indian tricolour at the North Pole. On August 6, 1997, Squadron Leader Sanjay Thapar set a world record in sky-diving when he jumped out of a helicopter at a height of seven thousand feet and unfurled a mammoth-sized (2,226 sq.mtrs.) Tiranga at a height of five thousand feet.

On September 28, 1985, the Tiranga set out on an around the world sailing expedition on board the *Trishna*, under Colonel T.P.S. Chowdhary and successfully returned home on January 10, 1987, cruising the high seas of the world and covering over thirty thousand nautical miles in 470 days.

The hoisting of the Indian flag in the farthest corners of the world fulfilled the dream which Pandit Nehru visualised at the time of presenting the National-flag to the Constituent Assembly on July 22, 1947, when he had said: "…. And I hope it (flag) will go far, not only where Indians dwell as our ambassadors and ministers, but, across the far seas where it may be carried by Indian ships, it will take a message of freedom and comradeship, a message that India wants to be friends with every country of the world…."

It is interesting to note that as per the standard specifications, the cloth to be used for the manufacture of the National-flag has to be only handspun khadi. Even the sewing threads of the three colours, namely saffron, white and green, are also to be made of khadi. All the sewing threads should be well-spun, evenly twisted, free from knots, short lengths and other defects. Curiously, Garag, a small village in Dharwad district in North Karnataka, once known for making barbed wire, is the only place in the country where the hand-woven khadi for the National-flag is manufactured. In 1954, a centre was established there by a few freedom fighters, under the banner of Dharwad Taluk Garag Kshetriya Seva Sangh and obtained the Centre's licence to make flags. Though, the regular production started in 1972, for about the last four decades this tiny village has been supplying the cloth for the making of flags to all government institutions. Only the flags made here truly qualify for official use, being tailor-made strictly in accordance with the National-flag Act specifications. The tricolours which flutter atop the Parliament House, Rashtrapati Bhawan, Red Fort and State Assemblies and Secretariats come from Garag only.

The flag making unit was founded by the Sangh on a 'no profit, no loss' basis for keeping alive the Gandhian tradition and values. Hence, no modern machines are used and the flags are fashioned painstakingly by hand. Only khadi cloth can be used and every inch must have forty lines of hand-knitted thread. Each flag of size 50x200 mm should have a capacity for supporting forty kgs on the warp side and thirty kgs on the weft side. For the purpose of manufacture, only number thirty-six thread made from a special cotton stock called 'Jaxadhar' is used. In accordance with the specifications, a piece of khadi measuring one square foot used for the flag must weigh 205 grammes.

Each flag piece is then sent to BITRAC, a Bombay-based Central Government body affiliated to the Khadi and Village Industries Commission, where it is dyed into saffron, green and white. Finally, the Ashoka Chakra is imprinted on both sides with utmost perfection. The flags undergo a thorough quality check, before they are distributed across the country for use.

According to the Flag Code-India there are nine standard sizes of the National-flag. The first size measures twenty-one feet in length and fourteen feet in width. Surprisingly, one does not see a National-flag of such a mammoth size flying anywhere in the country, nor is it available at any outlet. Even on the massive Red Fort, and the lofty dome of the Rashtrapati Bhawan, the second standard size of the National-flag measuring 12x8 feet is flown. Probably, it might have been used on the tallest flagmast at Fort Saint George, Chennai. However, it is only a speculation. Maybe the Home Ministry has an answer to the mystery. Nothing for certain can be said on this issue.

The smallest standard size of the National-flag is only 6x4 inches, and are used as table-flags during State functions held with foreign dignitaries and delegations. The specialty of this flag is that it is made of silk and not of khadi, because of protocol.

The standard size number eight meant for VVIP cars (9x6 inches) are made of khadi, but for their manufacture double buntings are used, while the other standard sizes are made of single bunting. This is because the flag is to flap vigorously while the car is moving.

On all the public buildings only cotton-khadi flags are used. However, on Independence Day and Republic Day, the flags that are hoisted by the Prime Minister and the President, respectively, are made of silk and not of khadi. This is done in view of the solemnity of the occasions.

As per the common practice, only one National-flag is flown on any public building. There is, however, a building in the country where not one, but four National-flags are flown at a time. And this privileged building is Parliament House. The reason for doing so is the peculiar shape and size of the building. It is a huge circular structure with no central dome. Therefore, four flags one in each direction, east, west, north and south, are flown so that the National-flag can be seen from all sides. Similarly, two National-flags are flown at a time on each of the sentry towers of the North and South Blocks of the Central Secretariat, New Delhi. For the purpose, both the sentry towers have two slanting flag-masts, which have been specially fitted. This practice is a result of the British legacy when, during the British-India rule, two Union Jacks on each tower used to fly and that practice continues till today.

On August 23, 1998, Prime Minister Atal Behari Vajpayee presented a model of the Tiranga, made in eighteen carat gold and studded with diamonds and gemstones to the President of India, K.R. Narayanan, in commemoration of the completion of fifty years of India's Independence. As a mark of tribute to the nation, the Gem and Jewellery Export Promotion Council dedicated the model of the tricolour to the Office of the President on the occasion of the 51st Independence Day. The flag, nine inches in height, was designed by Ms Namita Pandaya Shankar and is on display in the museum of the Rashtrapati Bhawan.

On January 26, 1950, India became a Republic. At that time, the President of India adopted a personal standard, the President's standard. It consisted of four rectangular panels, the diagonally opposite ones being of the same colour, deep blue and crimson. The ratio of its length to its breadth was 3:2. The first blue panel depicted the Ashoka Pillar (from Sarnath), the national emblem signifying the national unity; the second crimson panel depicted an elephant (from the Ajanta frescos) advancing towards the hoist, symbolising patience and strength; the third crimson panel had a pair of scales (from Red Fort, Delhi) denoting equality and justice; and the fourth blue panel had a lotus bowl (from Sarnath) signifying plentifulness and prosperity. The Governors of all states, also, had their standards uniformly in saffron with the national emblem, the Ashoka Pillar, in its centre as its device. Below the Ashoka Pillar, the name of the state was inscribed in brown.

With the abolition of 'Privy Purses' in 1971, the former rulers of the princely states were obliged to give up their individual state flags. Even the President of India ceased to fly his personal standard, as also the Governors of all states. Instead, they adopted the National-flag. Under Article 370 of the Indian Constitution, one exception was made in the case of Jammu and Kashmir where the state flag is still allowed to fly along with the Indian tricolour. In October 1947, when the Delhi Agreement was drawn-up between the Government of India and the erstwhile Government of Jammu and Kashmir, continuance of the state flag beyond the accession of the state to the Union of India was recognised on account of historical and other reasons related to the freedom struggle in the state. In 1938, the National Conference had evolved a flag which embodied the basic programme of the organisation, which emphasised the upliftment of the weaker sections of the state population, peasants and working class, both manual and intellectual. To bring out the supreme need for the promotion of the interests of the vast masses of the cultivators, the plough was adopted to represent them in the flag. The three horizontal broad lines next to the flag-mast denoted the three regions of the state. The red background was to signify the ascendancy of the working class to a position of dignity and honour.

It is for these reasons the Jammu and Kashmir flag, as evolved by the National Conference, is allowed to fly along the Tiranga. However, as per heraldic conventions, when the two flags are flown side by side, the flagmast of the National-flag of India ought to be to the right of the state flagmast and also taller, the height difference being at least equal to the width of the National-flag. This practice, however, is not strictly observed and the two flags are seen flying on flagmasts of equal heights.

19

Display of Royal Flags by the Erstwhile Princely States

Between 1858 and 1947, British-India had about 565 major and minor princely states. The British Crown had graded them in accordance with their size and importance. Accordingly, each state was granted a status by the British system, one indication of which was the number of gun-salutes accorded to the ruler of the state. Though, the status of each state depended on various factors, however, one common practice was the use of respective state flag, royal emblem and the coat-of-arms by all princely states. Prior to the Delhi Durbar of 1912, these major and minor princely states had their traditional family flags. By and large, the Hindu states, such as Jaipur, Jaisalmer, Alwar, Gwalior, Baroda, Mysore, Travancore and Cochin, used a red or saffron field for their flags. Both the red and saffron stood for 'sakti', the power. The Muslim states, particularly Hyderabad and Junagarh, predominantly adopted a green field for their state flag, while the Sikh states of

The Royal Flag of the former State of Jodhpur.

Patiala, Nabha, Jind, Faridkot and Kapurthala had pure white flags. Amongst the Sikh states, Kapurthala was an exception, which had a blue lining along the white flag. Originally, the practice of having a coat-of-arms, as was prevalent in the west, was missing in India.

Before the Delhi Durbar, an English flag designer was specially stationed at Calcutta, the then capital of India, to re-design flags of the Indian princely states and introduce their coats-of-arms. And thus, a new generation of flags was born in 1912. All the states which participated in the Durbar re-designed their flags based on western traditions, and a coat-of-arms and a new state emblem were also adopted by most states. These were used on their ceremonial dresses, cars, furniture, etc. While westernising and re-designing the new flags, due care was taken to include traditional devices as part

*State Emblems of certain former
Indian princely states.*

Deputy Prime Minister Sardar Vallabhbhai Patel with Maharaja Hari Singh, the then ruler of the state of Jammu and Kashmir.

of the new design so as to keep the old symbols and values intact.

The Delhi Durbar was thus a turning point in the heraldic history of the princely states, when they adopted new state flags on the lines, patterns and traditions of their masters. The princely flags adopted ever since the Delhi Durbar continued till the Indian Independence and beyond.

During the division of British India, most princely states agreed to the accession to India on the appeal of the Deputy Prime Minister, Sardar Vallabhbhai Patel. At the time of accession to the Indian dominion, each state depending on its size, revenue collection and geographical location, was granted a 'Privy Purse' by the government of India. Besides an annual financial grant, the ex-rulers were officially allowed to retain their princely privileges, including the flying of the state flag on their palaces, private villas, forts and cars within and outside the state. The state emblems and flags could be seen flapping on the cars of the former rulers even after independence.

With the abolition of the 'Privy Purse' on August 15, 1971, the privilege of flying the state flag was withdrawn by the Union Government. However, instances have come to light when the families of the ex-rulers were seen using the state flag on certain occasions. The former royal flags were often used on ceremonial occasions such as marriages and birthdays and also during funerals. Legally, though the position is unambiguous, certain provincial governments have been indifferent and the state authorities have looked the other way when being informed that the erstwhile state flags were still being flown on the residences of the former rulers. There are reports about some influential ex-rulers flying the state flag over their private houses even in New Delhi, the seat of the Union Government. In certain cases, the erstwhile state flags have also been used by members of royal families standing for election to the Parliament or State Assemblies.

In view of the abolition of the 'Privy Purse' in 1971, none of these practices has the legal sanction. However, fact remains that since many of these states existed for centuries, enjoying unbridled privileges and also considering that many of the ex-royal families still stay in massive palaces, it will naturally take some more time to erase the royal memories and feel at par with the common citizen. As things stand today, a few, if not many, State flags still fly on the residences of some of the former rulers, but the flags are not used beyond the boundaries of their palaces and forts.

Appendix 1

Secret

CRIMINAL INTELLIGENCE OFFICE

History Sheet of Madame Bhikaiji Rustom K.R. Cama

Madame Cama was born about 1875, and was the daughter of Sorabji Framji Patel of Bombay. Her husband is the son of K.R. Cama, the Parsi reformer, and is a well-to-do solicitor at Bombay. Madame Cama received her early education at the Alexandra Parsi Girls' School, Bombay, and speaks several languages fluently. According to her own account, she has been in Europe since about 1902, spending about a year each in Germany, Scotland, Paris and London.

2. In August 1907, Madame Cama attended the International Socialist Congress at Stuttgart, Germany, in the company of Sardarsinghji Rewabhai Rana, the well-known Paris seditionary, and at the meeting of this body, on August 22, she made a speech, "for the dumb millions of Hindustan, who are undergoing terrible tyranny under the English Capitalists and the British Government." She said thirty-five million pounds were taken annually from India to England without return, and as a consequence, people in India died of poverty

at the rate of half a million every month. At the close of her speech she unfolded the Indian National-flag, a tricolour in green, yellow and red, with the words 'Vande Mataram' on the middle band, and bearing emblems to represent the Hindus, Muhammedans, Buddhists and Parsis. She implored them to read Comrade Hyndman's paper on the impoverishment of India, and again waving the flag before them she said she had every hope of seeing the republic of India established in her lifetime. Madame Cama and S.R. Rana attended this Congress as delegates from the Paris Indian Society, and according to the Indian Congress Organ, India, "they were not entitled to membership of the Congress, but were admitted by the courtesy of the British section, to whom Mrs Cama desires to tender her thanks."

3. The following appeared in the *Indian Sociologist* for September 1907:

> *We announce with great pleasure that at the instance of Mrs Bhikaiji Rustom K.R. Cama, with whose name our readers are familiar, some Indian ladies residing in Paris have offered a lectureship.....*

9. Madame Cama addressed other meetings and appears to have gone on tour in the United States for this purpose. There is no record of the date of her return to Europe, but, a Paris correspondent, referring to a meeting of extremists held there on September 14, 1908 to receive Lala Lajpat Rai, mentions that Madame Cama was not present as she was away in the north of France. She was back in Paris in October and attended a meeting on the 25th at the house of one Khemchand; the gathering was to meet B.C. Pal who was passing through Paris on his way to England and it was reported that Madame Cama returned specially to Paris for this purpose.

10. On November 24, 1908, Madame Cama was present at one of the usual Sunday meetings at India House, 65, Cromwell Avenue, Highgate, London. Mrs Krishna Varma presided and B. C. Pal spoke on Hindu Politics. Madame Cama also made a speech in which she advised her listeners to follow the self-sacrificing example of the Bengal murderers (whom she named, each name being greeted with loud cheers) and to be prepared for death. She also displayed a National-flag woven in silk and gold with the inscription "In memory of the Martyrs of 1908".

11. On December 19, Madame Cama attended one of a series of lectures on "Indian Nationalism" by B.C. Pal, and at the conclusion of his speech she waved two flags in the air and demanded a hearing. She made a very violent speech which was afterwards reprinted in the *Free Hindusthan*, and copies of the speech in the form of a leaflet, purporting to be signed by her, were afterwards sent in large numbers to India, posted, apparently to avoid interception, in nearly a dozen different postal districts of London.

12. The leaflet was as follows:

Bande Mataram
A message to the People of India

Countrymen, lend me your ears, I will not take up much of your time; only five minutes. I fully understand the responsibility of what I say. I have come prepared for everything. I have but one life to give, one Avatar to sacrifice. I want to speak on Methods, as I cannot keep quiet, since such tyranny is going on in our country, and so many deportations are cabled every day, and all peaceful means are denied to us.

I have neither power nor the authority to recommend this or that course to our patriotic countrymen. People who suffer in that land are the best judges of the methods to adopt. However, I speak the truth and I know when I say that the recent events in India will not affect the forward movement in the least. Are our people afraid? No! No! The new regulations are perhaps a little worse than the old ones. They may be quicker in action, but they cannot be more unjust in fact.

Some of you say that as a woman I should object to violence. Well, Sirs, I had that feeling at one time. Three years ago it was repugnant to me even to talk of violence as a subject of discussion, but, owing to the heartlessness, the hypocrisy, the rascality of the Liberals, that feeling is gone. Why should we disprove the use of violence when our enemies drive us to it. If we use force, it is because we are forced to use force. How is it that the Russian Sophy Perovoskai and her comrades are heroines and heroes in the sight of Englishmen and Englishwomen while our countrymen are considered criminals for doing exactly the same thing for the same cause. If violence is applauded in Russia, why not in India? Tyranny is tyranny, and torture is torture, wherever applied. Success justifies any action. Struggle for freedom calls for exceptional measures. Successful rebellion against the foreign rule is patriotism. What is life without Freedom? What is Existence without Principles? Friends, let us put aside all hindrances, doubts, and fears. In Mazzini's words, I appeal to you: 'Let us stop arguing with people who know our arguments by heart and do not heed them. If our people appear degraded, it is an added reason to endeavour at all risks to make them better.' Show self-respect, Indians, and set to work. The days for calling meetings and passing resolutions are now over. Do silent but solid work. A handful of foreigners, a few Englishmen, have declared war on us. Who can wonder if we millions accept the challenge and declare war on them? The price of liberty must be paid. Which nation has got it without paying for it?

Thank God that our people have learnt that it is a sin to tolerate despotism. They have learnt to combat without pause; they have learnt rather to die fearless than perish like worms. We are awakened to the sense of our power, and in the name of our ancestors and our glorious country we defy our oppressors.

The lives of four young men, who are done to death, are burnt away just like incense on the altar of the Motherland. Bande Mataram. On the altar of truth, justice and liberty, these noble lives are sacrificed. This flag of Bande Mataram which I have before you, was made for me by a noble selfless young patriot who is standing at the bar of the so-called court of justice in our country? What a mockery to talk of justice and jury! We have seen such a travesty of justice in the cases of Tilak and Pillay!

Why are they imprisoned and exiled? For what? For speaking the truth.

Why that cringing creature, John Morley, is always talking of his Western institutions and English oak? We do not want his English institutions. We want back our own country. No English oak is wanted in India. We have our own noble banyan tree and our beautiful lotus flowers. We do not want to imitate British civilisation. No, Sir, we will have our own which is higher and nobler. What is Morley's civilisation? Persecution of women! For what? For asking their human rights. What do I see all round in this country? Poverty, misery, robbery, and despotism.

Hindustanis! Our Revolution is holy. Let us send our congratulations to our countrymen and women who are struggling against the British despotism and for their liberty. May their numbers be daily increased! May their organisations become ever so formidable! May our country be emancipated speedily! My only hope in life is to see our country free and united. I beg of you young men to march on! March forward, Friends, and lead our helpless, dying, downtrodden children of our Motherland to the goal of Swaraj in its right sense. Let our motto be–We are all for "India for Indians".

13. On December 29, 1908, Madame Cama had a prominent place on the platform at the Guru Gobind Singh celebration held in the Caxton Hall by V.D. Savarkar, Lala Lajpat Rai, B.C. Pal and others with the object of underlining the loyalty of the Sikhs.

14. In January 1909, it was reported that Madame Cama was contributing money towards the funds of the Nationalists in London and, in particular, was paying for the printing of the seditious documents sent from Europe to India.

15. On February 11, 1909, B. Bhattacharji was convicted of an assault on Sir William Lee-Warner and ordered to find two sureties of £ 10 or in default to suffer one month's imprisonment. On the occasion, Madame Cama and others offered to stand surety for him, but he chose to go to prison.

16. At a meeting of the London Indian Society, held on February 20 at Essex Hall, Strand, after Haidar Raza had spoken on "The Relations between Hindus and Muhammedans in India", Madame Cama also spoke, and before commencing took from her pocket a silk flag on

which were inscribed the words Swadeshi and Bande Mataram, saying that she was in the habit of speaking under that flag, which was hung over her head on the wall.

42. In September 1912, it came out that the proofs of the Bande Matram were corrected for Madame Cama by S.R. Rana, and the copies received showed that he did it very badly.

43. In December 1912, it was reported that Madame Cama has received letters from Hem Chandra Das and Ganesh Damodar Savarkar, both prisoners in the Andamans, and had replied to them.

44. In February 1913, it was found that Madame Cama was in regular communication with S.R. Rana, D.S. Madhav Rao and Virendranath Chattopadhyaya, whom she met or consulted by letter or telephone almost daily. She had lately received, from San Francisco, a large number of copies of a pamphlet of fifteen pages called *Sidelights of India*, consisting of reprints of articles which appeared in *The Bulletin*, a newspaper published in San Francisco. The writer is a certain John. D. Barry, and there is a preface by Har Daya headed *To My Countrymen*, which concludes as follows:

Be of good cheer, dear comrades. Our cause is furthered by the wise and good men and women of all nationals. Our voice is stifled at home, but it is heard in other lands. The sympathy of all who love freedom is with you. You are not alone in your struggle. In due time you shall reap, if ye faint not.

Copies of this were sent out to India along with copies of a most seditious four-page leaflet headed *Yugantar Circular*. This appears to have been prepared by Har Dayal and printed in Europe. It is known that Madame Cama had in her possession 1,500 copies of the *Yugantar Circular* for distribution.

45. In March 1913, Madame Cama is known to have sent 124 francs to the printer of Bande Mataram in Rotterdam to pay for the issues for February and March. She continued to correspond with V.D. Savarkar in the Andamans, M.P. Tirumal Acharya in New York and other leading agitators, and she is known to send money regularly to Narayan Damodar Savarkar.

46. The character of Madame Cama's campaign can be best ascertained by a perusal of the extracts from the Bande Mataram, which is published by her under her own name, printed in the Appendix.

Appendix 2

Text of the Article on the National-flag written by Mahatma Gandhi in *Young India*, April 13, 1921. Mr Gandhi was jailed for six years for writing this article on March 18, 1922.

A flag is a necessity for all nations. Millions have died for it. It is, no doubt, a kind of idolatry which it would be a sin to destroy. For a flag represents an ideal. The unfurling of the Union Jack evokes in the English breast sentiments whose strength it is difficult to measure. The Stars and Stripes mean a world to the Americans. The Star and the Crescent will call forth the best bravery in Islam.

It will be necessary for us Indians, Hindus, Muhammedans, Christians, Jews, Parsis, and all others to whom India is their home, to recognise a common flag to live and to die for.

Mr P. Venkayya of the National College, Masulipatnam, has for some years placed before the public a suggestive booklet describing the flags of the other nations and offering designs for an Indian National-flag. But, whilst I have always admired the persistent zeal with which Mr Venkayya has prosecuted the cause of a National-flag at every session of the Congress for the past four years, he was never able to enthuse me; and in his designs I saw nothing to stir the nation to its depths. It was reserved for a Punjabi to make a suggestion that at once arrested attention. It was Lala Hansraj of Jullundur who, in discussing the possibilities of the spinning wheel, suggested that it should find a place on our swaraj flag. I could not help admiring the originality of the suggestion. At Bezwada I asked Mr Venkayya to give me a design containing a spinning wheel on a red (Hindu colour) and green (Muslim colour) background. His enthusiastic spirit enabled me to possess a flag in three hours. It was just a little late for presentation to the All-India Congress Committee. I am glad it was so. On maturer consideration, I saw that the background should represent the other religions also. Hindu-Muslim unity is not an exclusive term; it is an inclusive term, symbolic of the unity of all faiths domiciled in India. If Hindus and Muslims can tolerate each other, they are together bound to tolerate all other faiths. The unity is not a menace to the other faiths represented in India or to the world. So I suggest that the background should be white and green and red. The white portion is intended to represent all other faiths. The weakest numerically occupy the first place, the Islamic colour comes next, the Hindu colour red comes last, the idea being that the strongest should act as a shield to the weakest. The white colour, moreover, represents purity and peace. Our National-flag must mean that or nothing. And to represent the equality of the least of us with the best, an equal part is assigned to all the three colours in the design.

But India as a nation can live and die only for the spinning wheel. Every woman will tell the curious that with the disappearance of the spinning wheel, vanished India's happiness and prosperity. The womanhood and the masses of India have been awakened as never before at the call of the spinning wheel. The masses recognise in it the giver of life. The women regard it as the protector of their chastity. Every widow I have met has recognised in the wheel a dear forgotten friend. Its restoration alone can fill the millions of hungry mouths. No industrial development scheme can solve the problem of the growing poverty of the peasantry of India covering a vast surface 1,900 miles long and 1,500 broad. India is not a small island, it is big continent which cannot be converted like England into an industrial country. And we must resolutely set our face against any scheme of exploitation of the world. Our only hope must centre upon utilising the wasted hours of the nation, for adding to the wealth of the country, by converting cotton into cloth in our cottages. The spinning wheel is, therefore, as much a necessity of Indian life as air and water.

Moreover, the Muslims swear by it just as much as the Hindus. As a matter of fact, the former are taking to it more readily than the Hindus. For the Muslim woman is *purdahnashin*[1] and she can now add a few paisas to the poor resources that her husband brings to the family. The spinning wheel, therefore, is the most natural, as it is the most important, common factor of national life. Through it we inform the whole world that we are determined, so far as our good and clothing are concerned, to be totally independent of the rest of it. Those who believe with me will make haste to introduce the spinning wheel in their home and possess a National-flag of the design suggested by me.

It follows that the flag must be made of khaddar, for it is through coarse cloth alone that we can make India

---

1. *Young India*, 13-4-1921 One who observes purdah.

independent of foreign markets for her cloth. I would advise all religious organisations, if they agree with my argument, to weave into their religious flags, as for instance the Khilafat, a miniature National-flag in the upper left hand corner. The regulation size of the flag should contain the drawing of a full sized spinning wheel.

Appendix 3

Jhansi Ki Rani Laxmibai's flag

It was a triangular flag made of pure silk, woven with gold thread weighing 2.5 kgs and studded with precious stones, jewels and *navaratanas* having a figure in its centre of Lord Hanuman resting a mountain on his left palm. The flag was kept in the silver-room of  the Rajputana Rifles Regimental Centre, Delhi Cantt.

In 1977, the flag mysteriously disappeared from there. Eleven years later, the C.B.I. took over the investigation and filed a case on December 6, 1988, under Section 380 IPC, 126 B, 25 and Section 3 of the Antiquity and Art Treasures Act 1972. But, the investigation in India as well as abroad bore no fruit and the C.B.I. moved an application on May 13, 1994 to close the case.

The Chief Metropolitan Magistrate, J.P. Sharma, however, rejected the application. Under the circumstances, the fate of the flag is unknown.

Appendix 4

कवि शिरोमणि पं॰ माखनलाल चतुर्वेदी का अपने भाई को पत्र

नागपुर

१६.२.२३

प्यारे भाई,

मैं यहाँ आ पहुँचा, आशा है आप वहाँ कुशल से हैं। अब मेरे वहाँ पहुँचने की परिस्थितियों का पता आप पा चुके होंगे। जयलाल जी, महात्मा भगवानदीनजी तथा नीलकंठरावजी, देशमुख, नागपुर के तथा प्रदेश के तीनों नेता जेल में हैं। मैं जिस दिन, जिस समय पहुँचा उसी समय कोई तीस मिनट बाद ही गिरफ्तार हो गए। मैंने यहाँ का भार अपने निर्बल हाथों में डरते–डरते ले लिया। बहुत संभव है पत्र अधिक न लिख पाऊँ। यह तो और भी अधिक संभव है कि शीघ्र ही बंद कर दिया जाऊँ। गिरफ्तारियों का क्रम इस प्रकार है—

583   पिछले—

6   ता॰ १७ को

4	जयलालजी, भगवानदीनजी, देशमुख साहब और आबिद अली
275	ता॰ 18॰ म॰ गांधी दिन को अपने–अपने डेरों में सोते हुए गिरफ्तार
15	सत्याग्रही 275 की गिरफ्तारी के बाद ता॰ 17 को
8	यहाँ के जुलूस के समय

---

891   जोड़ ता॰ 17 को

ता॰ 17 की रात को मैंने कार्य हाथ में लिया। सरकार को अभी भयंकर बागी सूत्रधार का पता नही है आप भी स्पष्ट रुप से न दीजिए। अस्पष्ट शब्दों में चाहे जो लिखिए। सहायता कीजिए। रामराव पत्रकार को मध्यप्रदेश भर के लिए आप अपना प्रेस रिर्पोटर बनाइए।

आज नागपुर में भयंकर सख्ती है। जिन्होंने जुर्माने नहीं दिये, देहातों में उनके घर की चीज़ें नीलाम की जा रही हैं। उन्हें तकलीफ दी जा रही है। गाय–बैल, खटिया पलंग, जो मिलता है, नीलाम किया जा रहा है। सत्याग्रही स्वयं–सेवक रेलों में टिकट नहीं पाते। 50-50, 60-60 मील की पैदल यात्रा करके स्वयं–सेवक आ रहें है। मार्ग में वे रोके जा रहे हैं और तकलीफ दी जा रही हैं। तार जाने नहीं दिए जाते। चिट्ठियाँ खोली जाती हैं। सफेद टोपी और झंडे वाले पकड़े जाते हैं। नगर में खूब उत्साह है। पकड़ लिए जितने

से भी दस गुने बलिदान होने आगे बढ़ते हैं। रात को सभा हुई। मैं सभापति था। जवाहरलालजी, टण्डन जी और मैं, तीनों बोले। उपस्थिति 15000 थी।

सभापति ने (मैंने) व्याख्यान में घरों पर झंडा लगाने को कहा। **आज नागपुर में झंडे ही झंडे दिख रहे हैं।**

आपका

माखनलाल चतुर्वेदी

पं झाबरलाल शर्मा – अभिनंदन ग्रंथ पृष्ठ–७२

Appendix 5

Statement of Jawaharlal Nehru, Purushottamdas Tandon, V.G. Joshi, George Joseph and Arjunlal Sethi on June 18, 1923 to boost the morale of satyagrahis

"People of Nagpur,

You have seen what the Government has done. You have been patiently and steadfastly, during the last six weeks in the face of all India, keeping up the battle of flag. You have been offering a steady stream of sacrifice. Your patience and stubbornness will have triumphed over the patience of the Government. The district authorities, exasperated at the slow breaking down of their will, have hit out and gathered in one single swoop the men that had assembled from all parts of India to consecrate the memory of June 18 in the service of the flag. The patience of the Government has vanished, but not its determination to drag the honour of the National-flag in the dust. The battle will go on to its appointed end. On you have come the main burden of it, but we assure you that all India watches you sympathetically and admiringly. The hundreds that were arrested this morning are only a first contribution. We are confident that you will keep the good fight, but should your strong arms tire, others will stretch forth brave hands to sustain the flag'.

Appendix 6

Procedure for *dhvaja-vandana*

All *swayamsewaks* and public stand facing the dhvaja
The *dhvaja-rakshak* blows a whistle to caution all present.
- All come to attention at the caution *saavdhan.*

The Dhvaja vandana *Vande Mataram* is then sung aloud by all.
- The flag is hoisted by the President. The dhvaja-rakshak and the President both stand facing each other.
- At the order *salaami aam do*, all greet the flag by looking at it with folded hands.
- At the order *jaise the*, all present resume the attention position. The President and the dhvaja-rakshak now stand facing the audience.

Next, the Dhvaja-vandana *'Jhanda Uncha Rahe Hamara'* is sung.
- At the order *aasan ho*, all stand at ease.

The President then addresses the audience.
- *Saavdhan*

Jaya-Jaya-Kaar 'Azad Hind Zindabad'. Kaumi Naara: Vande-e-Mataram
- At the order *'Barkhaast'*, all disperse.

N.B.: The dhvaja-vandana was devised by some volunteers of the Belgaum Seva Dal and was conducted for the first time during the Belgaum Congress in 1924.

ध्वज-वंदना

श्री श्यामलाल 'पार्षद'

विजयी विश्व तिरंगा प्यारा।
झंडा ऊँचा रहे हमारा।।

सदा शक्ति बरसाने वाला। प्रेम सुधा सरसाने वाला।
वीरों को हर्षाने वाला। मातृभूमि का तन मन सारा।।
झंडा........ ।।

स्वतंत्रता के भीषण रण में।
लखकर जोश बढ़े क्षण में।।
काँपे शत्रु देखकर मन में।
मिट जाए भय संकट सारा।।

झंडा........ ।।

इस झंडे के नीचे निर्भय ले स्वराज्य यह अविचल निश्चय।
बोलो भारत माता की जय। स्वतंत्रता है ध्येय हमारा।।

आओ प्यारे वीरों आओ।
देश धर्म पर बलि जाओ।।
एक साथ सब मिलकर गाओ।
प्यारा भारत देश हमारा।।

झंडा........।।
इसकी शान न जाने पाए। चाहे जान भले ही जाए।
विश्व विजय करके दिखलावें। तब होवे प्रण पूर्ण हमारा।।
झंडा........।।

विजयी विश्व तिरंगा प्यारा।
झंडा ऊँचा रहे हमारा।।

नवीन तुमने क्या काम किया है।
घर-घर को तुमने ही तिरंगा धाम किया है।।
जिन्दल तुम्हारी जिन्दादिली याद रहेगी।
वनवासी तिरंगे को, राजा राम किया है।।
- राजेश चेतन

उपरोक्त पंक्तियाँ उच्च्तम न्यायालय द्वारा तिरंगा फहराने को 'मूल अधिकार' मानने पर नवीन जिन्दल को बधाई रूप में भेजा गया एक सन्देश।

Shyamlal Gupta Parshad was born on September 16, 1893 and died on August 10, 1977. He used to write patriotic songs since childhood. In 1924, he was inspired to pen a flag-song. In his maiden attempt he composed a song which was much too literary and difficult to sing. The opening stanza of the song was:

राष्ट्रगान की दिव्य ज्योति
राष्ट्रीय पताका नमो-नमो।।
भारत जननी के गौरव की
अविचल शाका नमो-नमो।।

Since the wording of this song was rather cumbersome, he was induced by the well-known journalist, Ganesh Shankar Vidyarthi to write another flag-song and that is how विजयी विश्व तिरंगा प्यारा was born. The song soon caught the imagination of the people and it became part of all functions. The song was first published in 1925 in *Pratap*, a weekly of Kanpur. The Government of India awarded a sum of Rupees two thousand to the author after Independence for the song.

Appendix 8

Text of the article written by Dr Suniti Kumar Chatterjee, in *Modern Review*, June 1931. In fact, the article was a reply to the letter, addressed to a select group of people, by Dr B. Pattabhi Sitaramayya, the Convener of the Flag Committee, 1931.

At the last session of the Congress it was decided to go into the question of the National-flag. It was a good thing that this decision was finally arrived at. A flag stands as a symbol of something; and a National-fag is the symbol of our national ideals and aspirations, of our hopes and achievements as a people. It is a beacon of light showing people the path to sacrifice, often to the supreme sacrifice: 'they are hanging men upon the common, for the wearing of the green'. Consequently, it is not to be treated lightly as something which does not have any special or deep significance. The Flag Committee of the Congress fortunately realises the importance of the question, and also their responsibility in the matter. Dr Pattabhi Sitaramayya, the Convener of the Committee, has issued a questionnaire inviting opinions from different Congress and other organisations, as well as from individuals.

There is no ancient flag or banner, whether of Hindu or Muhammedan times, which we can think of for adoption as the flag of our country as a whole. Imperial or local princely houses had their standards, e.g., the garuda standard of the Imperial Guptas. But even when nearly the whole of India was united under the Mauryas in the third century B.C. and the Moguls in the seventeenth century A.D., no National-flag or crest seems to have been thought of India was never physically a nation *militante,* and so there was no need for a national symbol to rally round in opposition to other nations. Besides, the political unity of India that we are now conscious of is an entirely new thing. But underlying this new sense of political unity is the unseen foundation of a sense of geographical and cultural unity which is as old as our history, and which transcends all diversities and oppositions of race, language, and creed.

If we set about trying to find a National-flag for India, what should be, in the first instance, the right attitude to take up? If we aim at having a united Indian nation, or a federation of Indian nationalities, we must not, as the most solemn article of our political creed, countenance anything that will help to perpetuate cleavages in the community. We must not think in terms of different communities, whatever be their language or religion or geographical situation. We cannot, therefore, think of quartering our National-flag to perpetuate a sense of communal distinctness among our people. Any explanation of the colours in our National-flag as symbolising Hindus, Mussalmans, Christians and other communities should be regarded as pernicious and anti-national.

The colours in a National-flag for a country like India, which has been the most remarkable meeting-ground of people, should thus represent ideas and aspirations which are of universal significance and which have not merely accidental connection with any section's past, a past which is sought to be employed for communal or national chauvinism. If any particular community finds a secret pleasure in thinking of a certain colour or symbol which has been adopted in the National-flag as being specially connected with its own little or big world within the bigger world of India, either spiritually or historically, it does not matter, so long as that is not forced upon the national interpretation and so long as other communities also find it appropriate, from a national supra-communal stand point.

Let us now see how far our National-flag and crest, like many national anthems, either had an accidental beginning at the psychological moment, or a deliberate promulgation. The official British flag for India (the Union Jack with a star with an English motto 'Heaven's Light Our Guide') belonging to the latter category and having no reference to our history and traditions or to anything universal could have no appeal for the Indian body politic; and hence the need for a truly Indian flag was felt by our leaders. There were many tentative attempts at flag making: a green field with five white lotuses in a row there, a row here, a white lotus in a red field there, an outline map of India on a blue background at some place. More than twenty years ago, the late Sister Nivedita suggested in an article in the *Modern Review* a design for the National-flag in which the thunderbolt and the lotus were included, to symbolise the spiritual aspirations of India. Green and red were probably first hoisted as the national colours for India by Mrs Annie Besant and Mr Wadia in the year 1917. Green then stood for life and hope, and red for blood and sacrifice. In 1921-22, the white was added to the red and green, and with the political atmosphere being surcharged with the spirit of Khilafatism and communal compartmentalism, the communal interpretation of the colours came into being, green was made to represent the Muhammedans, red the Hindus, and the neutral white all the lesser communities.

Objections were put forward to these colours from time to time, but, a general loyalty to Mahatmaji and to the Congress and the intensity of the political struggle did not allow any serious opinion to crystallise. Sanskrit scholars, at the All India Sanskrit Conference held in Calcutta in 1924, mildly talked of including saffron or ochre colour and the *gada* mace of Lord Vishnu as Hindu symbols in the flag. On the eve of the Belgaum session of the Congress in 1924 a letter was sent from Rabindranath's institution at Shantiniketan, signed, among others, by the late Dvijendranath Tagore and C.F. Andrews, requesting Mahatmaji to consider the advisability of including the *gairika* (*geru*, or red ochre colour) in the National-flag. It typified the spirit of renunciation, and was a colour which symbolised an ideal common to the Hindu *yogi* and *sannyasi* as well as to the Muslim Faqir and Darwesh. (In this connection, see the *Modern Review* of November 1930). Recently, the Sikhs brought the question to a head by making a firm demand that the Sikh colour, which is equally the *geru* or saffron, should have a place in the National-flag.

Let us see what objections can be urged against the present red, white and green National-flag.

In the first instance these three colours, and these three only, already figure in the flags of at least four different countries, Persia, Italy, Bulgaria and Mexico. The dispositions of the colours are different, but Bulgaria has an identical arrangement with the present Indian flag. We do not know what these three colours symbolise for the people of these countries. But why not let India have something distinctive, something which one can relate to? Moreover, the communal symbolism suggested for the colours in our flag can be objected to; and objection can also be made for both the red and the white even on communal grounds.

We should (at least in the authoritative Congress explanation of the device) expunge all communal connotations, and further substitute some new colour scheme consisting of thee or more colours (*cf.* China, which has five horizontal bars of red, yellow, blue, white and black). We can retain three, falling in line with most countries: our tricolour will then be described, in our democratic language, as the *Hindustan-ka Tiranga Jhanda.* Or, if we have four colours, we shall then call our flag the *chaturanga,* which by itself, like the French tricolour, will suffice to indicate the Indian National-flag. Four is a number we are fond of in India. It is the basis of computation in our monetary system, in our weights and measures, and in our game of chess (*chaturanga,* i.e., the four wings of the army, Perisianised and Arabicised into *shatranj*), a great gift of India to the world. So four colours would be quite distinctive of India if included in the National-flag.

What should these colours be? How many of them? What would they represent? Once a symbol becomes popular, it should not be disturbed, for two reasons. If there is no objection, then there is no point in trying to improve upon it. Also, we must not disturb the state of things which have crystallised as something very necessary in our national life and consciousness. For the last ten years the present National-flag is being used throughout the length and breadth of this country. And these last ten years have witnessed, under the shadow of this banner, a wonderful transformation of our Indian people. We should not consequently bring in any violent or revolutionary change in our National-flag: we should, if some change is thought necessary, bring in the minimum amount of alteration required under the circumstances.

I wish to reiterate, once again, that a communal explanation or allocation of colours, like communal electorates, should be taboo. We should keep away from this poison as much as possible. We can easily revert to the original explanation of these colours as symbols of ideas, the explanation of which is also universal. I think green and red should both be retained. Green, the colour of vegetation, is the colour of life and growth, and this symbolism is current among all the nations of the earth. As a people, above all we want to live, and we can very well have the symbol of Life in our national emblem. Green is also the colour of hope, and we live largely in hope. As we want to live, we want to strive, we want to fulfill a purpose in our existence. It is a quest, it is a kind of ardour which would rise superior to all oppositions, material, moral and spiritual, in our realisation of the Ideal. Life is indeed passion, taking the neutral sense of the word, the passion which throbs in our breast and which tingles in the life blood in us. Red is the colour of this quality in our life, call it passion or suffering, call it exultation or triumph, call it sacrifice that is necessary for both. Red, the colour of blood, is the most appropriate colour for this passion, this *raga*, and this sacrifice, which the blood crushed out of the victim's existence enables us to visualise most forcefully. Green and red, therefore, both are appropriate; they are the symbols of life which is a perpetual striving and sacrifice; not petty symbols of a community or a minority, eagerly jostling with others for a place in the sun.

What should the third colour be, if we elect to retain three colours? Should the white, too, be retained? I think here practical considerations in the first instance should make us pause before we can finally accept the white. White is a good colour as it is a universal symbol of purity. But, it is likewise a colour which we associated in India with mourning. But weightier than this is the fact that white already occurs with red and green in the flags of four other countries, as mentioned before. And everywhere white does not connote purity. In the French tricolour, white is retained as the monarchist colour, the colour of the Bourbon house. This practical consideration should make us think of some other better (or at least equally suitable) colour. And it will be an additional point in favour of that colour if we can connect it in a special manner with our country.

It seems that the ideas of renunciation and harmlessness, of vairagya and ahimsa, forms the keynote of Indian life, whether Hindu or Muhammedan or Christian. This is the ideal which would send the king in his old age to the forest hermitage in Hindu India: this same ideal of renunciation made Prince Siddhartha, the Buddha that was to be, don the saffron garb of the ascetic; and behind the magnificence of the Mogul court it was this ideal, again, which dominated Akbar, whose great principle in life was *sulh-e-kull* or 'peace with all', and the austere Aurangzeb whose single-minded devotion to the straight path enjoined by the faith in which he was born, soared up in the firmament of his career with the unbroken flight of a tall mosque minaret. An Indian is never so greatly in love with life and its possessions as to think highly of a 'death in harness' in his old age: life has far deeper and more mysterious meaning for him than piling up the goods of the world, or going on building something and yet starving his soul. He would rather be a mendicant in the shrine of his own faith and pious contemplation, guiding and helping his followers and yet feeling detached from them. That is why the faith in the unseen world and preparation for it which Islam teaches with such insistence found a congenial soil in India, more than perhaps in any other land where Islam penetrated. The ideal of harmlessness is also present in the mystic and the deeper expression of Islam that is Sufism. And the Indian always associated with this spirit of detachment and of ahimsa the reddish or orange-brown colour of the garments worn by the wanderer. The geru or gairika, the red ochre or saffron colour worn by the Indian sannyasi brings to our mind most forcibly the picture of this great ideal of detachment and harmlessness. This saffron colour also is the colour of discipline in life, physically or morally and spiritually, for it is the colour enjoyed upon the *brahmacharin*. A modification of this saffron colour is the yellowish brown, the *kasava* or *kashaya*, of Buddhism, where it is the great symbol of the Buddhist brotherhood with its insistence on ahimsa. This is the colour of the earth, it is a kind of *khaki*, for the red ochre is a pigment which is a gift of Mother Earth. This red-brown tint of the earth has also been accepted by Islam in India, for Muhammedan faqirs with robes dyed in geru are as much the wanderers over the highways of India as are their brothers in the quest, the Hindu sadhus. It does not require much imagination or sense of the fitness of things to feel that in India's National-flag her great message of *brahmacharya*, ahimsa and vairagya should be symbolised by a colour which has been associated by her people with these ideals from time immemorial.

Red, green and ochre or saffron would thus be a distinctive colour scheme for India. The cloth for the National-flag should in all cases be hand-spun and hand-woven, whether cotton or silk.

There would then be less chance of confusing our national colours with other nations such as Persia, Italy, Mexico and Bulgaria. The disposition of these colours should be vertical rather than horizontal, preferably with red next to the staff, ochre or saffron at the outer edge, and green in the middle. A vertical arrangement is suggested because the oblong vertical blocks give an idea of robustness and strength which the supine horizontal blocks, one lying above another, fail to do. Any one would be convinced of that by contemplating the pictures of the flags of the different nations side by side.

The idea of having four colours may also be considered. In that case, the retention of the neutral White with addition of the saffron may be advocated. We shall have a representation of the ideal of purity as well. Here again, the white might figure after the red for better effect.

The colours as representing ideals or sentiments of universal appeal and yet with a special Indian touch in the ochre or saffron can be symbols of manifold power and significance, and can have more meanings and more kinds of appeal to communities or individuals within the state. If the Mussalman thinks of the great brotherhood of Islam when he contemplates the green in this flag, and if he finds pleasure in thinking that his creed with its insistence upon the unity of Godhead is represented with its traditional colour symbol in his National-flag, other communities will also rejoice with him and appreciate his special affection for the ideals of the democratic faith of Islam. If the Christian sees in the red the blood of his Lord, which, by His supreme act of sacrifice, helps to make men cleaner and whiter, we shall be equally happy that such a noble ideal should also be thought to have a place in our national emblem. And if the Hindu, whether Sanàtani or Brahmo or Arya Samaji, or Buddhist or Jain or Sikh, reveres the National-flag with greater awe as containing the symbol of vairagya and ahimsa, every true Mussalman and Christian will be equally glad for it. And if four colours are decided upon, and the white is retained, those who love the ideal of purity which is present through all faiths, and sometimes transcends them, will have as citizens of India an equal cause for rejoicing. Thus, the Hindus of Bali, in Indonesia, please themselves by regarding the red, white and blue banner of Holland as representing respectively Brahma, Siva and Vishnu; and the Dutch, too feel pleased at this Balinese interpretation.

Should we have any device on the flag, red, green and ochre, or red, white, green and ochre? Most countries have a device, in addition to the national colours; e.g., Ireland has the shamrock and the harp; Mexico, the cactus plant with an eagle carrying a snake; England the rose; the Soviet Union the hammer and sickle, etc. The charkha or spinning wheel has been in use with our National-flag, being painted in blue on its body. It represents India's desire for the simple life, and her will to combat poverty with the wholesome remedy of her cottage industries. But the khaddar cloth itself as the product of the charkha amply indicates this ideal. The spinning wheel as a device on a flag is cumbersome. We do not want to have a sword or a thunderbolt, or some plant or animal figure that will not be acceptable to all. But simplifying the charkha, we might have a simple wheel.

A simple wheel is the most eloquent of symbols. It represents eternity; it represents time; it stands for progress, it figures the universe. We can put any great idea or meaning to it, and it will not be vulgar. In Persian, the word for wheel, charkha, signifies also the celestial globe, the sphere of the heavens, as well as circular motion and fortune. The ancient Indian use of this symbol is as varied as it is profound. We can have symbol of eternity as something mystic behind existence as an embellishment of our National-flag. Besides, this symbol can further be employed in a most appropriate manner to indicate one great fact in our national life in a United States of India, our federalism which in principle has been accepted for the future constitution of our country. The wheel can be made to represent our India as a Federal Union: and we can then take the spokes to stand for the constituent members of the Federation, the various provinces and states. The American National-flag has a similar device in its flag of stars and stripes, the forty-eight white stars in the blue field indicate the forty-eight members of the Federation of the United States of America. But it is not necessary to make the number of the Members of the Federation and the spokes of the wheel agree. We need not press the comparison too far. The idea of the individual spokes forming the wheel should be enough, and we can have a wheel of the minimum number of spokes, three, or better four, for the flag: for we should remember the question of making the flag, and so avoid complications. If the wheel idea is thought worthy of consideration, a three or four spoked wheel in yellow or black-either of the colours will go best with the red and green, can be suggested, to find a place in the central field of the flag.

It has been suggested by some that it will be appropriate to have a spread-out Lotus, in white, with four or eight petals in place of the wheel. The lotus will be certainly poetic, and no one can take exception to this great symbol of India. But would it not be a little too weak, when compared with the wheel then, a simple wheel with four spokes will be easier to affix on the flag than the more elaborate lotus: we shall have to consider the practical side of the question too, the National-flag will have to be made in hundreds and thousands. But the lotus will be quite welcome as a beautiful symbol from nature, and the idea of Federation is exquisitely indicated by its petals. It will be quite striking when in a suitably simple and conventional form.

The above suggestions are offered for what they are worth. The present writer has discussed the matter with some of the best intellects of the country, in Bengal and outside Bengal; and the idea of vertical bands of red, green and ochre or saffron, with the three or four spoked wheel (or the four or eight petalled white lotus) in the central field, seemed to satisfy most people. It is now presented before the public, and before the Flag Committee appointed by the Indian National Congress: and it is done with the fervent wish and prayer that out of the endeavours of the Committee and with the co-operation and approval of the people of National-flag and a crest be finally evolved for India which will be in perfect accordance with her great and composite culture, her noblest ideals and achievements, and her high destiny in the future.

Note: First published, *Modern Review*, June 1931.

Appendix 9

National-Anthem of India

Guru Rabindranath Tagore's song *Jana-Gana-Mana* was adopted as the National-anthem on January 24, 1950 by the Constituent Assembly. The original song has five stanzas. However, only the first stanza has been adopted as the National-anthem.

According to an old German tape, the first ever recording of the song was done in 1941 and was played as the National-anthem by Netaji in Germany. It was Netaji's version of the '*Jana-gana-mana*', that was adopted as the country's National-anthem. It was first played on August 15, 1947, even before it was adopted as India's

Text of the National-anthem of India

Jana-gana-mana-adhinayaka, jaya he
  Bharata-bhagya-vidhata
Punjab-Sindh-Gujarat-Maratha
  Dravida-Utkala-Banga
Vindhya-Himachala-Yamuna-Ganga
  Uchchala-Jaladhi-taranga.
Tava shubha name jage,
  Tava shubha aashish mange.
Gaye tava jaya gaatha,
Jana-gana-mangala-dayak jaya hey
  Bharata-bhagya-vidhata.
  Jaya hey, jaya hey, jaya hey,
  Jaya jaya jaya, jaya hey!

National-anthem, at the Headquarters of the United Nations when India joined the UNO as a free nation.

Jana-Gana-Mana

Jana-gana-mana was first published in January 1912 in the issue of *Tattvabodhni Patrika* (edited by Tagore) under the title *'Bharat Vidhata'*. However, it had already been sung on the second day of the Calcutta session of the Indian National Congress on December 27, 1911. Later, Gurudev Rabindranath published it in his magazine. Tagore translated the song into English and titled it 'The Morning Song of India'. It was Subhash Chandra Bose's Indian Legion abroad which rendered it into Hindustani. Subhash adopted it as his Government's National-anthem and the Azad Hind-Fauj called it *'Jaya-Hey.'*

Vande Mataram

Bankim Chandra Chattopadhyay's novel *Anand Math* was published in 1882 and the song *Vande Mataram* first appeared in this novel. It was however, written much earlier, probably in the 1870s. The song was conceived by the poet while once travelling in a train. It was sung on a political occasion for the first time during the 12th session of the Indian National Congress (INC) held at Calcutta in 1896. Interestingly, the song was tuned and set to music by Rabindranath Tagore, who also sang it on the occasion.

During the Bengal-partition movement, the song became such a rallying point that people defied even an official order banning the singing of the song at public places. Later, the first two words of the song *Vande Mataram* became the rallying call in the whole country during the nationalist movement.

Text of Vande Mataram

Vande Mataram!
Sujalam, suphalam, malayaja shitalam,
Shasyashyamalam, Mataram!

Vande Mataram!

Shubhrajyothsna pulakithayaminim,
Phullakusumita drumadala shobhinim,
Suhasinim sumadhura bhashinim,
Sukhadam varadam, Mataram!

Vande Mataram!

English translation in prose of Vande Mataram as rendered by Sri Aurobindo:

I bow to thee, Mother,
richly-watered, richly-fruited,
cool with the winds of the south,
dark with the crops of the harvests,

The Mother!

Her nights rejoicing in the glory of the moonlight,
her lands clothed beautifully with her trees in
flowering bloom,
sweet of laughter, sweet of speech,

The Mother, giver of boons, giver of bliss.

Flag Terms Defined

Applique: A mode of flag manufacture in which one or more pieces of cloth are stitched on the field to form the design.

Banner: Originally a rectangular flag, hanging from a crossbar or suspended between two poles; made with great care and displaying the emblem of a king or an army, etc. Because the meaning of the word was changed over the years, it is preferable to use a more specific term: royal banner, trumpet-banner, etc. Currently, banners refer even to flags of commercial houses, political organizations and institutions.

Bannerette: A small flag such as a pipe-banner or trumpet-banner.

Battle Honour: A mark added to a colour of a unit to show its distinguished military service. It may take the form of an inscription on the flag itself or on the staff or a metal clip added to a streamer itself.

Bend on a Flag: Act of fastening a flag to halyard in order to hoist it.

Break a flag: To unfurl a flag that has been rolled and tied in such a way that a sharp tug on the halyard will cause it to open up. In fact, on August 15, the Prime Minister of India breaks the flag at the Red Fort, and it unfurls.

Bunting: Strong, loosely woven material used for making flags, originally of wool, but nowadays of other fibres such as polyester; by extension, bunting material used as decoration or, figuratively, flags collectively.

Burgee: A small distinguishing flag usually triangular or swallow-tailed used on yachts and cars of senior armed forces personnel and police officers as a distinguishing mark.

Canton: Often the area in the upper hoist corner of a flag or a rectangular field filling that area.

Colours: The term colours originally applied to British infantry flags. The plural 'colours' is often used, even for a single flag, because the name derives from the colours composing the field of the flag, as well as the British and American practice of issuing two flags simultaneously to the same unit. During medieval times in Europe, troops of various knights and warriors used to rally under flags of different hues for purpose of distinction. Over the years, such flags gained the collective name 'colours'. The colours of distinguished troops, knights, warriors, etc. had decorative devices on them. By the end of the nineteenth century the practice of carrying colours and standards to the battlefield was discontinued.

Courtesy Flag: The flag of a country being visited by a ship from a different nation, as flown by that vessel to show courtesy to the country visited. It is a modern custom followed by all navies of the world.

Dhvaja: A dhvaja is an ancient Indian flag rectangular in shape bearing a motif or an emblem on it.

Dipping a flag: Means lowering a flag briefly and then instantly raising it again at sea while sailing past a ship, particularly a warship. It is an old custom to honour, greet and salute an important person or a ship at sea.

Ensign: A generic term for flag, especially associated with naval flags of nationality (civil ensign, naval reserve ensign, etc.) and by extension in British usage with distinguishing flags of Government services on land. In the seventeenth and eighteenth centuries ensign was the normal term for colour and for colour-bearer.

Finial: The ornamental top of a flagstaff.

Flag Bearer: One who carries the Flag. During Olympics, Asiads, Commonwealth Games meets. The Flag bearer leads his contingent with his countries National-flags.

Flag Belt: A leather device worn around the waist and neck which holds the bottom end of a staff to assist a marching standard-bearer.

Flag Cancel: A printed invalidation for postage stamps, resembling a flag.

Flag Day: A day for the affirmation of patriotic values expressed in and through display of the National-flag. In India, December 7 is observed as the Flag-day when funds are raised by donations through sale of mini paper flags.

Flag House: The distinguishing flag of a commercial firm, flown especially at sea; sometimes used in reference to the personal flag of the owner of a yacht or home.

Flag Man: One who signals with or carries a flag.

Flag March: The march of armed forces through the streets of a tension torn town or city to show their presence.

Flag Officer: A naval officer entitled to display a rank flag such as Rear Admiral, Vice-Admiral or Admiral.

Flag Truce: To display a white flag as a signal to cease fighting.

Flagmast: The staff or pole on which a flag is hoisted or displayed. The terms flagpole and flagstaff also mean the same.

Flag-off: To inaugurate an event, but, more commonly to start a race.

Flagship: The ship bearing the flag of the senior most officer of a fleet.

Fly: The end of the flag which is farthest from the flagstaff and flies in the air. It is further categorised as upper-fly and lower-fly.

Gaff: A spar from which a flag is hoisted, jutting from the mizzenmast of a ship or from a staff on land.

Guidon: A small military flag, forked and rounded at its free end, serving as a guide to troops, a distinguishing flag. They are chiefly used by cavalry, but ranked below the standard. The word guidon is of Italian origin.

Hoist: That part of a flag nearest the staff; also a group of signal flags to be flown together, also a synonym for width. Hoist is further categorised as upper hoist and lower hoist.

Horsetail: A decoration for military flags, especially in China where it is usually red, made of real or simulated horsetail.

Jack: A small flag flown under certain circumstances at the prow of a vessel, usually of a warship.

Lance Flag: A small flag, usually triangular or swallow-tailed, formerly displayed at the end of a lance by soldiers, particularly of the cavalry.

National-flag: A flag representing an independent state, especially a nation-state, but by extension the flag of formerly independent states and of non-independent national groups.

Parley Flag: A plain white flag displayed during war to request negotiations. Flag-truce and parley-flag mean the same.

Pataka: A pataka is an ancient small Indian flag, triangular in shape having no emblem on it.

Pennant/ Pendant: A long tapering flag especially flown at the masthead of a naval vessel in commission. At the time of de-commissioning a ship it is removed with naval customs and honours. From its etymology ('hanging'), it appears that pennants originally always hung from a cross-bar, and may continue to do so; others are attached in the usual fashion to a vertical staff or are mounted against a flag surface such as a wall. Pennants are extensively used at sea, where they apparently originated, for signalling, for decoration, and as rank flags. Today, they are also used on land, especially as souvenir flags, award flags, and flags of business, fraternal, sports, and other associations.

Pine-staff: A pole with a decorative head to which a ceremonial flag is attached for carrying.

Pip-banner: A bannerette worn on bagpipes to decorate them.

Position of Honour: The place given to the highest ranking flag in a group of flags.

Prayer Flag: A small flag, often used in groups and decorated with inscriptions, intended to express a prayer as it flies; characteristic of Buddhists in the Himalayan region.

Sleeve: A tube of material along the hoist of a flag through which the staff is inserted, used especially for a parade flag or colour.

Standard: A distinctive personal flag of a king, knight or any other distinguished person. In olden days, it used to be very large, meant mostly to be stationary and was seldom carried to the battlefield. In course of time, the term became applicable to cavalry flags.

Striking the flag: Lowering one's flag as a sign of surrender in a war is known as striking the flag.

Swallow tailed: Having a large triangular section cut from the fly end, a characteristic of pennants and war ensigns of Northern Europe. War ensigns sometimes have a third tail between the other two; such a flag may be referred to as swallow-tailed with a tongue.

Table Flag: A small flag, mounted on a cross or single straight bar whose staff and stand make it suitable for display on a desk or podium. Such flags are usually used during the international and bi-national talks, etc. to identify nationality. These flags are made of double bunting.

Tricolour: A flag whose field is divided horizontally, vertically or diagonally into three different plain colours. About forty-nine countries in the contemporary world use tricolour flags as their National-flag.

Trumpet-banner: A bannerette used to decorate a ceremonial trumpet.

Vexillary: The one who carries a flag.

Vexillologist: A flag historian.

Vexillology: The study of the history, types and uses of flags.

Vexillosphilist: One who collects flags.

War Ensign: The National-flag flown on armed vessels; also called naval ensign.

War Flag: The National-flag flown over camps and other military establishments on land, often in conjunction with the state flag; not to be confused with a colour.

Yardam: A spar slung horizontally across a flagpole.

Thoughts on Tiranga

"A flag is a necessity for all nations, Millions have died for it. It is no doubt a kind of idolatry which it would be a sin to destroy. For, a flag represents an ideal. The unfurling of the Union Jack in the English breast evokes sentiments whose strength it is difficult to measure. The Stars and Stripes means a world to the Americans. The Star and the Crescent will call forth the best bravery in Islam. It will be necessary for us Indians — Hindus, Muslims, Christians, Jews, Parsis and all others to whom India is their home to recognise a common flag to life and to die for."

M K Gandhi

"I remember, and many in this House will remember, how we looked up to this flag not only with pride and enthusiasm but with tingling in our veins and also how when we were sometimes down and out, the sight of this flag gave us courage to go on. Then, many who are not present here today, many of our comrades who have passed, held on to this flag, some amongst them even unto death, and handed it over as they sank, to others to hold it aloft."

Jawaharlal Nehru

"Whether or not we live but this flag must remain, the country must exist. I am sure our flag will certainly outlive us for many ages to come."

Lal Bahadur Shastri

"The flag under which we are standing is not just a piece of cloth. This is a symbol of the sacrifices made in our struggle for freedom, later on the sacrifices by our brave soldiers on our borders in various wars and now of those who with their hard labour are engaged in the struggle for India's progress and also of our promising youth. Our flag and our National Anthem are no ordinary things. They unite the country and bind it together and that is why I want to say that the glory of the flag must be protected even at the cost of life."

Indira Gandhi

"The tricolour is a symbol of our freedom, of our self-respect, and of sacrifices and martyrdoms. People belonging to the older generations would certainly remember the time when young boys and girls would form themselves into small groups, take the flag in their hands, and go around villages and city streets singing, Vijayi vishwa tiranga pyara, jhanda uncha rahe hamara."

Atal Behari Vajpayee

"I must have been twenty-seven or twenty-eight when a Japanese officer came to visit us in the Azad Hind Fauz in Burma. He told us about a Japanese soldier who was wounded in battle and did not want to fall into enemy hands, so he cut up his stomach and stuffed it with the Japanese flag and then died. Such was the reverence the Japanese had for their flag and this anecdote really mad a big impression on all of us."

Capt. Lakshmi, an officer of INA

"*A*s a sportsman, to see the flag being hoisted or the National Anthem being played in the hour of your triumph is a feeling beyond compare. The flag hoisting at that moment is not something that has happened by itself or as a matter of present routine but solely because of your hard work."

Maj. Rajyavardhan Singh Rathore,
Olympic Silver Medalist

"*T*he National-flag is an emblem of our fight for freedom and an assertion of our sovereignty. It is our common property not a status symbol for V.I.P.s. We have every right to fly it where and when we like."

Khushwant Singh, Writer

"*T*he Indian tricolour is a beautiful flag. I have had many close associations with it in my 75-year career by performing on India's Independence Day and Republic Day in various parts of the world. I don't think it is appropriate that the National-flag is fashioned into a bikini or a t-shirt as is common in some countries."

Pandit Ravi Shankar, Sitar Maestro

"*T*he flag is not the property of the Government or the Parliament. It belongs to the nation and the nation is made up of crores and crores of people, most of whom are patriotic and want to express their patriotism. If they want to put up the flag at their homes or wear it on their clothes to express pride in their nation, then it should be welcomed so long as they are not cheapening or denigrating it."

Dev Anand, Actor/Director

"*I*am not sure if the idea of painting your face in the flag colours is a way to honour your country. Suppose you have your face painted like that and some one comes and slaps you. What does it mean? You have brought dishonour to the whole country?"

Kirpal Singh, Artist

"*O*ur National-flag is the most powerful brand that we as a nation have — which clearly stands head and shoulders above all other brands."

Azim Premji, Chairman, Wipro Group

"*F*or years, everyday, I made so many blouses, skirts, salwar-sets, shirts. They were all used and soon forgotten by the wearer and by me. But every flag I am making now I will remember all my life, since these are going to be saluted by big people and our soldiers, and looked at with respect by millions of people.

Annapurna, A Flag-maker

"*I*don't think what my son did was anything special. He took the pledge to honour the flag and did his duty to fight for the country to the best of his abilities. There were others who also fought but came back alive. But in no way did they have less respect for the flag. I think everyone has to honour the flag, not only the army people who take the pledge. We must all do our duty whole-heartedly regardless of our profession."

Mrs. Hema Aziz, Mother of Kargil Hero, Late Capt. Haneefuddin 11th Rajputana Rifles, VRC

"*W*hat is patriotism? The flag waving that one sees these days is only at cricket matches. I don't think cheering for your country at a cricket match is patriotism. It is looking at your country objectively and trying to improve conditions."

Aparna Sen, Film maker

"When two separated lovers look at the moon, it helps them to emotionally unite the two, regardless of the distance between them. Likewise, our spirit of patriotism and love for the motherland lie hidden in our hearts but, when we sight the National-flag, our underlying love for it instantly surfaces. Thus, the Tiranga inspires and arouses in us our love for the country."

Javed Akhtar, Lyricist